Healey:
The Handsome Brute

CHRIS HARVEY

St. Martin's Press
New York

Printed in Great Britain
Library of Congress Catalog Card
Number: 78-458
First published in the United States
of America in 1978

Library of Congress Cataloging in
Publication Data

Harvey, Chris, 1941–
    Healey: the handsome brute
Includes index
I. Austin-Healey automobile.   I. Title.
TL215.A92H37   629.22'22   78-458
ISBN 0-312-36518-7

Acknowledgements

IT SEEMED quite straightforward. Write a book on the Big Healey, one of the longest-living sports cars of the classical post-war period. I knew so many people who had owned one. I even had one myself. But this book would never have got off the ground so quickly, nor with so little pain, if it had not been for Carolyn Waters. With her husband, Jack, she introduced me to the Healey people who matter today and showed me what a wonderful spirit exists in the Midlands Centre of the Austin-Healey Club, whose members, led by Keith Boyer, were all so helpful. Derrick Ross even provided his car for the cover; Fred Draper, who must be the only man to have spent every working day with the Big Healey since it was conceived, gave me priceless information; Geoff Price told me the things only a service manager knows and introduced me to designer Barrie Bilbie, the unsung hero who was involved in 'everything under the skin' and allowed me to reproduce a wonderful set of prototype pictures. Then there were the racing people. John Chatham (whose hospitality I will never forget), Joe Cox, John Horne, Nick Pride and everybody in the South West, including John Smith; Ted Worswick in Lancashire and Thelma, Paul and Syd Segal in London, who told me all sorts of intimate things about Big Healeys that you would never learn elsewhere. I really thought I was getting to grips with the subject until I talked to Dave Kennard and Dave Jeffery in London, who imparted a vast store of wisdom, with Derek Buck, who actually let me drive his 100. Along with the Waters' Mark III, which I also had the privilege of driving, it must be one of the best cars on the road. And along with Dave and Derek, Chris Harding was of great help in the Thames Valley area, whose members I must thank for giving me such a warm welcome. Special mention must go to their newsletter editor, Nigel Unsworth, who, with Joyce and Gordon Pearce of the New Forest Centre, helped me to piece together a semblance of a history of a constantly developing club. Nigel and Joyce were of tremendous help with foreign affairs, too.

Nobody could have helped me more than Kevin Faughnan, Dave Ramstad and Keith Rischell in California. Their assistance was absolutely invaluable and I cannot thank them enough or ever tell them how much enthusiasm they gave me for my task. With the Americans who helped me with the Jaguar and MG books before this, they left me with a heartfelt desire to visit them all. Dave Birchall shrugged off jet lag from constantly crossing the Atlantic to tell me about the Canadian Healeys; and Jim McConville, Alan Jones, Pat Quinn, Mark Donaldson, Gavin Gullery and Harvey Hingston gave me great help in Australia and New Zealand, another two countries I am determined to visit one day.

I must also thank Michael Bowler, Roger Bell, Clive Richardson, Paul Davies, Mel Nichols and Ian Fraser for allowing me to swoop on the files of *Thoroughbred and Classic Cars*, *Motor*, *Motor Sport*, *Cars and Car Conversions* and *Car* for information I could not have obtained elsewhere. I think the pictures in this book are wonderful (I can say that because they are not my work), and again I am deeply indebted to Warren Allport of *Autocar*; Jim Lee of *Motor*; British Leyland's photographic departments at Cowley and Longbridge (with special thanks to Cyril Comely); and the ever-helpful Ian Elliott of British Leyland Technical Press public relations. Last, but not least, I must thank my collaborators, Paul and June Skilleter, Tim Holder and Oxford Illustrated Press; and my wife, Margaret, and family, for surviving yet another book.

Colour Plates

I

Tribute to the Big Healey

IT TAKES a rugged car to blaze a rugged trail. And there was none more rugged than the Big Healey, the first 100 mph car that the man in the street could afford. No wonder the organizers erected crush barriers to keep the crowds off the Healey 100 when it was unveiled at London's Motor Show in 1952; this pale blue car was the only one in existence. As thousands of enthusiasts fought for a glimpse of Donald Healey's latest masterpiece, his son, Geoffrey, who had helped engineer the sensational new car, was on his way back to their factory in Warwick to have a new badge made. Donald Healey had been talking to Britain's biggest car maker, Leonard Lord, of the British Motor Corporation, and the new badge was going to read Austin-Healey. By the time the show was over the revolutionary Healey 100 had become the Austin-Healey 100 and Lord had lopped £100 off its already incredibly low basic price of £850.

The Healey 100, hidden behind a pot of plants because its creators were ashamed of its nose, had needed no sales talk. The Americans ordered $7 million worth as soon as they saw the prototype, and the Healey Motor Company had planned to make only five a week in their converted aircraft hangar in Warwick. Lord's deal was to produce the Healey at his vast works in Longbridge at the rate of 200 a week and market it everywhere through his Austin sales network. He also liked it the way it was, just like the customers. The benefits were royalties for Healey and profits for BMC from the embarrassing number of engines made redundant by the failure of Lord's Austin Atlantic car. Although the deal had been publicised as having been made overnight, it had been in the air for quite some time.

Plans for an entirely new Healey sports car had begun in 1951 when Donald Healey returned from a tour of the United States confident that he had the right formula for a car which would appeal to both home and overseas markets. He said: 'I wanted to produce a very fast everyday road car with genuine sporting characteristics, capable of 100 mph, which would also be exceptionally cheap to buy and easy and economical to maintain.'

This was the dynamic new concept. Nobody had made a car capable of such speed at such a price, and which looked so good. To keep the price down, Healey chose well-known components from Austin, one of the companies which made up the new BMC. The components included the Atlantic's engine and gearbox, which

were rugged units to say the least. The Atlantic engine had its origins in a Jeep engine that had found its way into London taxis and tipper trucks. The suspension was basically Austin, too, and just as tough as the powerplant. But the body however was pure Healey, and was one of the sensational features of the new car. The sleek two-seater, with sporting, but comfortable, cockpit by current standards and a fair-sized boot (a previously-neglected export winner), presented an entirely new look in sports car design. The body owed nothing to Continental or traditional English styling; it was the work of a genius, Gerry Coker. As the car progressed, to a six-cylinder engine and eventually more sophisticated fittings, it kept its body. Fifteen years later the last Austin-Healey 3000 looked almost exactly like the Healey 100 and felt like it! It must have been one of the toughest sports cars ever made, surviving countless miles of such epics as the Liège-Rome-Liège Rally. You had to be brave to get the best out of a Big Healey. You were fighting a living beast that could be as docile as a kitten in traffic, and as wild as a tiger in the mountains. One of its greatest exponents, Pat Moss, said: 'If you do not catch it after a couple of snakes it is a case

Facing page, top: Last of the Big Healeys: Donald Healey chauffeurs Carolyn Waters in her Mark III at National Healey Day.

Facing page, bottom: The Big Healey that started it all: the 1952 show car.

Above: 'Its wild appeal sold more than 70,000 in America and gave Americans Kentucky Fried Feet, such was the heat generated by its mighty engine'.

of Goodbye and Good Luck.' Its wild appeal sold more than 70,000 in America and gave the Americans Kentucky Fried Feet, such was the heat generated by its mighty engine. The back was slung so low that countless exhaust pipes were wiped off as spinning wheels bit the tarmac or gravel. But it was a handsome brute and you could forgive it anything. 'You could tear the whole exhaust system off just by driving over a crushproof Marlborough box, but when you got out to salvage the pieces and let your glance fall over the seductive curve of the fenders you knew the car was worth all the grief,' said *Car and Driver*.

The Big Healey was the car that sold more in California than anywhere else. It was the car that doubled in value as soon as it was killed by Federal regulations. Everybody knew they would never see anything like it again. It was the car designed in the year of the bug deflector. It was the car that ignored fashion right to the end. It was the car built like the Golden Gates bridge but not painted like it. You had to do that yourself at regular intervals. It was a car to get involved in. No two Big Healeys felt the same. They all had a character of their very own. To drive one is pure nostalgia. To drive it fast is an achievement. To break it is well near impossible.

II

The Four-Cylinder Supercars

THE FOUR-CYLINDER Healey 100 was an extraordinarily successful compromise between the traditional sports car relying on cross members and engine to hold together the deep side members which, in turn, kept the axes apart, and the integrally-constructed modern saloon, which is, in effect, a rigid box with a wheel near each corner. With the Healey 100 there is a chassis frame made up of two three-inch square steel tubes only seventeen inches apart, with a fabricated cross member of three-inch by two-inch square tubes at the front, a further rectangular cross-member at the back and a cruciform structure in the middle.

Outriggers are added to this simple structure to support the back springs and a pair of cross-braced channel section hoops make up the scuttle. The front outriggers are joined to the scuttle by angle-section inner sills running parallel to the main chassis members, and joined to them by the floor section. The front of the chassis is further stiffened by two hefty rectangular members running diagonally from the top of the scuttle to the front cross member. Then the outer body skin is welded on, further strengthening the already rigid structure. In a car weighing only 18 cwt dry this combination of an old-style chassis and modern rigid body was enough to give the four-cylinder cars extremely good roadholding.

The roadholding was helped by the positioning of the engine as far back as possible without putting too much weight over the rear wheels. As it was, the slight rearward weight bias helped reduce wheelspin once satisfactory ratios had been developed to cope with the massive torque of the basically standard Austin saloon car engine. The chief design problem was building a car light enough to perform well when it had extremely heavy mechanical components (engine, transmission and rear axle), meant for a much bigger car. Like the unique combination of chassis and unitary construction, the Healey 100 was an extraordinarily good compromise in this respect.

The man responsible for the styling was Gerry Coker, although he was never really satisfied with the nose and Donald Healey removed the trendy fins which he had been considering at the back. Not only was the body good-looking, but it was aerodynamically sound, mainly because of its ultra-low build. There was a penalty here, though, that took an amazing thirteen years to clear up, from the project starting in the spring of 1951 to the introduction of the modified Mark III in 1964. Healey had to hang the exhaust system under the car, which, because of its low ground clearance, meant that countless exhaust pipes were wiped off as the rear suspension settled.

Although the suspension was basically from an Austin saloon, a great deal of development went into getting it right. Eventually, on the 100, a Panhard rod was located very low down in the frame to locate the rear axle on its half-elliptic leaf springs. The front suspension, by coil and wishbone, was less of a problem although a lot of time was devoted to getting the geometry right. The results were heartening because, despite having to use a standard Burman steering box rather than the preferred rack and pinion, it became one of the car's best features. Every 100 felt just right when new, with wonderfully accurate steering.

A lot of experiments were made before the Healeys decided to use Armstrong double-acting lever-type hydraulic shock absorbers all round. Those at the front

Big. Healey number one: note the height of the headlamps before they were raised to conform with the British road regulations.

formed part of the suspension. No trouble was experienced with the drum brakes, which were Girling hydraulic, with two leading shoes at the front, providing a total of 145 square inches of frictional area in 11 inch drums. Even then, Donald Healey was considering using the new-fangled disc brakes, but complained that they would cost more than the rest of the vehicle.

Price was of paramount importance when designing the 100. It had to sell below the magic $3,000 in America to carve out a market between the cheap MG T Series and the more expensive Jaguar XK. To this end the 2,660 cc Austin A90 engine and clutch were used virtually unmodified. The engine had a bore of 87.3 mm with a stroke of 111.1 mm reflecting its parentage in the pre-war Austin 16, designed in the days when the British taxation laws discriminated against short-stroke engines. The relatively small bore and long stroke limited effective revs but had an advantage

Fully-modified prototype 100 showing the new headlamp position.

The 100, windscreen folded flat, ready for action. Note the forty-eight spoke wire wheels.

in providing truly phenomenal torque of 150 lb/ft at an almost lorry-like speed of 2,000 rpm. Maximum power with Healey's exhaust system was 90 bhp at 4,000 rpm on a compression ratio of 7.5:1. This compression ratio was to seem low in subsequent years with the introduction of high-octane petrol, but was an advantage in export fields where good quality petrol was not always available. Now the pendulum has gone full swing and it is again an advantage in the days of lead-free petrol. Prototype 100s used the four-speed Austin A70 gearbox with a floor-change adaptor in place of the saloon's steering column linkage. But the first gear was found to be much too low with anything other than an over-high rear axle ratio, so the gate was modified to blank off that gear. Mischievous owners who filed away the gate to give themselves back the first gear found out what a waste of time it was when they burned out their rear tyres.

Three speeds was rather a limitation on a sports car, even with the massive torque of the venerable engine, so an overdrive was added. At first this was a Laycock unit working on the top two speeds, with a centrifugal switch to prevent its engagement below 40 mph. Later the control was manual. Whichever way, the result was effectively a five-speed gearbox which worked well in conjunction with a 4.125:1 lightweight spiral bevel rear axle taken from an Austin A40, in place of the 3.66 axle needed with the four-speed prototype 100. Initially the 100 was fitted with an overdrive giving 32.4 per cent reduction in engine speed, which was later changed to a 28.6 per cent when it was found that the engine was capable of pulling it at maximum revs of 4,800 rpm. The actual changeover was in mid-1953 after overdrive unit number WN1292/1.

The first twenty or so production 100 cars were made at Warwick from parts supplied by Austin with alloy bodies like that of the Tickford prototype. These bodies were built at Jensen Motors in West Bromwich a few miles from the Warwick and Longbridge works. The cars were built between October 1952 and February 1953 as work progressed on a proper two-abreast production line in an extension to Austin's works at Kelvin Way, Longbridge. Industrial trouble delayed the change-over and production did not start until May 1953, when the first export cars were shipped to America. The first twenty had been sent to selected distributors with three retained for demonstration and road test purposes. These three—called 'special test cars' in a masterpiece of understatement—were rather faster than normal, having been prepared also for the Le Mans race of that year. The first production cars also had alloy bodies and continued with these until July 1953, by which time complaints had started to filter back from the United States that the wings, doors, bonnets and bootlids were too lightly constructed. What's more, country garages didn't have a clue about welding aluminium. So, with no further ado, Austin's gave the Big Healey steel wings, doors, bonnet and boot lit, it being reasoned that there wasn't much to damage on the shroud and they didn't want the performance to suffer too much from extra weight. It was at that time that they built a corrosion problem into the car.

Most of the panels were supplied by Boulton Paul, and assembled on the chassis, from Thompsons of Wolverhampton, by Jensen. The unit was then painted, trimmed and transported to Longbridge. Throughout the life of the Big Healey there were complaints about the quality of the painting—or lack of it. Body units often had to be repainted at the assembly stage and rust reared its ugly head at a relatively early stage on the outer panels. Built-in rust traps helped, of course.

The actual changeover point to steel-and-alloy bodies is unchronicled, but people closely associated with the early production remember it as being after the first two or three hundred cars had been produced. By July 1953 production had built up to around 120 cars per week, with the new model being designated BN1. All these cars were fitted with Dunlop forty-eight-spoke wire wheels, Donald Healey being of the opinion that they would be a good selling point. For the record, the wheelbase was 7 ft 6 in, front track 4 ft 1 in, rear track 4 ft 2 in, length 12 ft 7 in, width 5 ft ½ in, height with the skimpy hood erect, 4 ft 1½ in, and turning circle, 30 ft. The hood and sidescreens looked as they were: an afterthought. They had to be small because nobody had been able to design a larger hood which would stay on at the speeds of which the car was capable. In fact, you hardly needed a hood on a Healey 100, for such was the enforced design of the windscreen, a nearly-flat piece of glass, that at any speed at all the rain went straight over the heads of the occupants and did not whip round their necks. It was only in a traffic jam that you were likely to get wet and there were not so many of those in 1953.

In the same way the noisy exhaust did not worry people so much as it only sounded bad from inside the car when the hood was up. The same applied to the excess heat produced by the engine. Much of it escaped when the hood was off. Colonial complaints about the lack of ground clearance at the back were quite serious, though, and with the limitations of a chassis that went under the rear axle, the only answer seemed to be to modify the rear springs. There was a problem with axle wind-up, too. So the springs were changed twice as the Healeys struggled with what seemed insurmountable problems. Unfortunately the exact points at which the cars changed from seven-leaf springs with five-inch camber, to seven leaves with $5\frac{3}{4}$ in camber, to eight leaves with $3\frac{3}{4}$ in camber has not been recorded: it is believed to have been at LHD drive chassis number 152233 and RHD number 152420 for the first change; suffice it to say that the last ones, fitted only in 1955, were the best. Early modifications to production cars, in the summer of 1953 included a revised throttle linkage (after Bert Hadley broke his in the Mille Miglia road race and Donald Healey realized that the ball joints were working the wrong way and the whole thing was inaccessible); and a gearbox breather after clutch slip caused by frothing gearbox oil reaching the clutch plates ruined the chances of two of the works cars in that race.

The 100 from the rear. Note the swage line starting on the front wing flash, continuing through the door and ending on the rear wheel arch.

The stark interior of the 100 prototype which varied little from that of
the production cars other than in
details such as the overdrive switch
on the steering wheel.

Below: The 100M in full regalia, complete with louvred bonnet and strap.

Late in the production run, at chassis number 221535, the rather weak, but delightfully light, alloy-nosed spiral bevel axle was replaced with a tougher, but heavier, hypoid unit. They kept the same ratio, 4.125:1, but handling suffered a little.

From the time the 100 appeared it was obvious that the car's standard production engine would stand a reasonable amount of tuning and that this would allow private owners to increase the performance for racing, picking up valuable publicity for the concern on the way. The Warwick factory therefore started marketing a conversion based on what had been found to be successful on the 1953 Le Mans entries. Parts manager Fred Draper supervised the dispatch of these Le Mans kits which consisted of $1\frac{3}{4}$ in SU carburetters and manifolds, a carburetter cold air box (to improve breathing at high underbonnet temperatures) high-lift camshaft, steel-faced cylinder head gasket, distributor with special advance curve, modified valve guides and sundry fittings (including a bonnet strap if desired). Additional items which could be purchased to improve the performance of the 100 included aero screens (bearing an A-H logo), a fifteen-gallon or twenty-five gallon petrol tank (to give a better range than the standard twelve-gallon tank), Alfin brake drums (for better cooling), negative camber rear springs (to be standard equipment on later BN1s), a $\frac{5}{8}$ in front anti-roll bar (in place of the standard $\frac{1}{2}$ in bar), a close-ratio 22 per cent overdrive, waterproof plug covers, race 'silencer', special speedometer, 3.66:1 crown wheel and pinion, uprated front shock absorbers (to be fitted to production cars from LHD chassis 153855 and RHD 153857) and double valve springs (later to become standard). Louvred bonnets as fitted to the Le Mans cars were popular wear with these conversions, although they were also fitted to standard cars after they left Longbridge.

These modified cars soon became known as the 100M and started a great mystery. To this day nobody really knows exactly what constitutes an authentic early 100M, such was the sparcity of records kept by the factory. Many of the 1,200 or so cars believed to have been converted had all the equipment listed above; some had only part of it; others had even more, depending upon which race they had been prepared for. Meanwhile production of the BN1 continued unabated until June 1955, with 10,688 being built with chassis numbers from 138031 to 228046.

The Healey works had not been standing still as the 100 was churned out at Longbridge. The continued to develop their prototypes even further, with an original 100M, registered NOJ 392, gradually turning into a 100S! The S stood for Sebring and the car was strictly for racing, although it could be driven on the road with great alacrity. The first step as development started in 1954 was to increase the engine's power output beyond that of the Le Mans kit, which was worth an extra 20 bhp over the standard unit's 90 bhp, with 144 lb ft of torque at 2,000 rpm.

The great gas-flow expert, Harry Weslake was called in to design a four-port aluminium-alloy head using the basic valve gear, which increased power to 132 bhp at 4,700 rpm with 168 lb ft of torque at 2,500 rpm in a unit built with nitride-hardened crankshaft, tri-metal bearings and extra-strong connecting rods. In fact, the engine was almost completely redesigned, with the distributor and drive moved from the right-hand side to the left and solid skirt pistons. A new dual exhaust system to take advantage of the non-siamesed ports emitted from the right-hand side of the car.

The compression ratio went up to 8.3:1 and a high-lift camshaft was fitted. To increase reliability on the race track, a finned cylindrical oil cooler was placed across the front of the car, incorporating a full-flow filter.

The 100S was fitted with a lightened steel flywheel weighing about 9 lb less than the standard 29 lb unit, a racing style single-plate clutch instead of the 9 in Borg and Beck unit, and a Healey version of a new four-speed gearbox being fitted to Austin production vehicles. This had a short remote control gearlever and syncromesh on the top three ratios. The extra power and light weight of the alloy-bodied car allowed a rear axle ratio of 2.92 to be used with 2.69, 3.66, and 4.125 options. The springs were modified to cater for the different power output, weight and operating conditions and double-acting Armstrong RXP shock absorbers fitted on reinforced mountings. Overdrive was not fitted.

With all this extra power the brakes needed development. There was only one way to go—to the four-wheel discs used so successfully by the Le Mans-winning Jaguars. No servo was necessary. In appearance the 100S was almost exactly like the 100, except for a one-piece Perspex windscreen much lower than standard, a massive churn-size outside petrol filler cap in place of the standard filler inside the boot, and an oval grille, the eventual result of Coker's constant attempts to produce a front which satisfied both himself and wind forces. Practically the only thing changed on the fifty-five such cars built between August 1954 and July 1955 was a strengthening of the rocker gear, which also found its way onto the Longbridge BN1s. Healeys made up their own woodrim and alloy-spoke steering wheel, which unfortunately did not follow the same path as the stronger rocker gear, the standard car retaining a rather horrible plastic wheel. The BN1s also kept their forty-eight-spoke wire

The prototype 100S, driven by Lance Macklin in the 1954 Sebring Twelve-Hour race.

wheels, spokes a'pinging, whereas the 100S had stronger 5.50 × 15 racing wires. It was also superior so far as cockpit ventilation was concerned with large diameter internal air trunks from the nose and slotted lightweight bucket seats. Needless to say, all excessive weight in the form of bumpers and unnecessary lights were deleted.

By June 1955 it had become obvious that the standard 100's three-speed gearbox was not man enough for the job. The layshaft, mainshaft and pinions wore rapidly under hard driving and it seemed only logical to change to the new four-speed unit being used on the big Austin saloons and successfully adapted for the 100S. Thus the BN2 was born, flowing off the production lines at Longbridge for a year from August 1955, once the summer holidays were over and BN1 production had ceased. The 28.6 per cent overdrive was retained, the front brakes were reduced in width by $\frac{1}{8}$ in to improve balance and the front coil springs increased for the same reason. BN2 numbering started at 228047 and continued until 233455 with no major changes.

Meanwhile the demand for 100M kits continued at such a rate that Healeys started converting new cars at Warwick. These were fitted with virtually all of the kit, plus high compression pistons to improve performance now that better quality petrol was more readily available. Sadly, no records were kept of chassis numbers and not all factory 100Ms were the same—the exact specification varied according to the customer's pocket and desires. No 100M manual or supplement to the existing 100 workshop manual was ever produced and the only tuning instructions issued by the factory were inadequate in that they did not cover all the options.

No doubt the Healey factory was too busy. As BN2s poured out of Longbridge and 100Ms filtered out of Warwick, they were hard at work on the BN3, a six-cylinder version of the production car. It used the standard BN2 body, a 100S gearbox, and the engine of the new Austin A105 Westminster saloon; it was the only forerunner of a new Big Healey to come.

III

The Mighty Six-Cylinders

IN SEPTEMBER 1956, the new BN4 Austin-Healey 100-Six was introduced, using the six-cylinder BMC C-type 2,639 cc engine from the new Austin Westminster. It featured updated styling, accommodation and fittings. The new engine produced 102 bhp at 4,600 rpm, and was no great improvement on the earlier four-cylinder unit, particularly as the new car was two inches longer and heavier as a result. The advantage lay in the Six's flexibility and smoothness, which made it a generally more restful and an easier car to drive. The BN2's gearbox was mated to the new engine, still with overdrive—as an option now—on third and top, and other changes included enlarging the cockpit (at the expense of some boot space), to include two very occasional rear seats for legless adults, stunted children and to please the American market. The swage line along the side was continued down the front wheel arch. Spring rates were changed to cope with the altered weight distribution, and the 100's original folding screen was scrapped in favour of a fixed affair now that glass with a greater curvature was available. The hood and sidescreens were much improved; not before time.

Styling changes included the disappearance of the last vestige of the original Healey diamond radiator grille. It was replaced by an oval grille, like that of the racing 100S model. The new-fangled rear reflectors required by law in England were faired into the tail panels rather than stuck on top of the bumper, an external fuel filler was fitted and the bonnet line was lowered with a ventilation scoop to clear the high spots of the engine. The styling, or swage, line was continued to the rear of the back wheel arch. Disc wheels were standardised in face of mounting criticism over the spoke-snapping habits of the forty-eight-spoke wires, although wires were still offered as an option for those willing to take the risk for the sake of appearance. Most people took the risk despite the extra weight of the two plus two.

The six-cylinder engine, built like the four-cylinder at the old Morris works, Courthouse Green, at Coventry, produced 12 bhp more than its predecessor. Its stroke of 88.9 mm was a considerable reduction on the 111.1 mm of the four-cylinder, reflecting the new freedom allowed by the passing of the horsepower tax. The bore remained the same, 79.4 mm, the capacity being kept in the same area by the two extra cylinders. This new unit differed from all previous BMC engines in having its camshaft on the right of the block instead of the left, a change made necessary by

Above: Earls Court 1956 and the 100-Six showing its new frontal treatment and swage line clearly. In the background, on the right, the Westminster saloon from which it derived many of its mechanical components.

Right: Last of the line: the Mark III convertible of 1967.

the Weslake-designed cylinder head. The size and number of the ports left no room for the pushrods and guides on the induction side of the head. That's why they were moved to the other side.

The four-bearing counterbalanced crankshaft had a torsional vibration damper mounted on its nose. The camshaft was driven by a Duplex chain, the drive incorporating a Reynolds tensioner with a wedge-shaped rubber head on a hollow plunger, kept in contact with the chain by a coil spring inside the plunger. The camshaft had separate skew drives for the distributor and Hobourn Eaton oil pump.

Power output with separate pancake air cleaners rather than the bulky Westminster air cleaner, and the raucous Healey exhaust, was 17 bhp up on the saloon engine at 4,600 rpm; the increase in power was partly due to the fact that the Westminster used Zenith carburetters until the introduction of the A105. The faster-revving six-cylinder engine was slightly down on torque at 142 lb ft, produced at slightly higher revs: 2,400. The compression ratio was virtually the same as that of the 100M, 8.25:1.

The chassis was modified only in detail, apart from the rear outriggers being moved back two inches to give more room in the cockpit, partly occupied by the longer six-cylinder engine, which was also mounted further forward. Alterations centred chiefly on the diagonal struts between the front side members and the scuttle, the enlarged box section now forming a neat housing for the brake and clutch reservoirs and allowing the fitting of pendant pedals. The steering box was changed to a ratio of 14:1 to cope with the extra weight and the ratio was decreased further to 15:1 after chassis number BN 68959.

The radiator was placed further forward, in front of, instead of behind the first cross member. The problem of accommodating it below the downswept part of the bonnet was solved by extending the bonnet and incorporating the air intake, which besides adding local height to clear the radiator filler cap, improved the underbonnet air flow. Taking in cool air on top of the bonnet made the cold air box used on the 100M unnecessary. The new, larger, bonnet was also hinged at the back rather than the front for improved rigidity, although it still tended to shimmy about. Two safety catches were provided at the front in place of the one used earlier to make sure that the bonnet did not spring open, now that the wind could whip under it.

In general shape, the new body was very similar to the old, although the new grille was not set so far behind the headlamps. The doors were two inches wider, with handles, and a lock on the driver's side on export models. On these left-hand drive cars, the passenger's door was secured from the inside, although this form of locking was not really effective because of the easily-opened sidescreens. These were a vast improvement over the old claustrophobic screens, bearing a much closer resemblance to proper windows.

The front seats were still separate with a padded propeller shaft tunnel as an arm rest, and two tiny semi-circular seats over the rear compartment which used to house twin six-volt batteries. Now part of that compartment was padded as the joint backrest for the kiddy seats and the battery moved into the boot for better weight distribution. Relocating the spare wheel on the boot floor, instead of over the rear axle, helped this attempt to balance the weight of the new engine and radiator (heavy when full of water) further forward in the chassis. The new place for the spare wheel gave room for the two occasional seats and helped make the battery a single twelve-volt, much more accessible. As ever, there was a penalty, and in this case it was a dramatically reduced boot space, although in the good old British tradition of compromise a luggage rack was offered as an optional extra. Some owners promptly mounted their spare wheels on the boot lid, to the detriment of the car's appearance and aerodynamics. However, the new hood certainly improved these aspects.

Weather protection had received a great deal of thought. The new fixed screen eliminated one source of possible leakage from wind and rain, and the rigid framed sidescreens another. The frames, made from extruded aluminium, were very neatly made and formed a good seal with the leathercloth hood. This mated ingeniously with the top bar of the windscreen frame, lapping over it throughout its length, being locked down by two overcentre clamps. There was a large rear window of flexible plastic and the hood was attached at the back by a series of quick-action fasteners. It stowed away neatly out of sight behind the rear seat, but needed a great deal of strength and patience to erect.

However, once it was up it was a great improvement over that of the 100. Other changes included a telescopic steering column as an option which did nothing to increase arm room, quite the reverse, in fact, and leathercloth dashboard covering to match the hide seats. As before, the overdrive switch was fitted on the instrument panel. The standard Westminster axle ratio of 3.91:1 was used on non-overdrive models, 4.125:1 being retained on overdrive cars. The upper edge of the scuttle, which now shook with the extra weight of the new screen and stiffer front springs, was also covered in leathercloth on a sponge rubber backing—much safer than the aluminium strip it replaced. A more elaborate heating and ventilation system was installed—at extra cost—which included demisting ducts and a booster for fresh air. Sadly, it was still not enough to keep the cockpit cool.

The fuel filler was mounted externally on the right taking advantage of the same channel used for the battery wiring, both being sited sensibly as far away from the right-hand exhaust system as possible. Despite a movement abroad towards amber indicators, combined rear lamps, brake lights and indicators were fitted behind the same red glass. The BN4 was much more of a touring car than the BN2 and was a good deal heavier as a result; it weighed 22 cwt, which more than absorbed the extra power.

Production of the BN4 started, again after the summer holidays, in August 1956 and *Motor Sport* visited Longbridge to watch 100-Sixes being produced in May 1957. After a sumptuous lunch they gave one of the all-too-rare, and fascinating, descriptions of the cars being made. 'The comparatively new Austin-Healey 100-Six sports car is assembled in the same shop as the brightly-coloured Nash-Metropolitans,' said *Motor Sport*. 'The bodies arrive from the Jensen factory at West Bromwich in batches of four on transporters and are lifted by hoist to be stored until required. They are delivered with the chassis frame welded in place. After being lowered on to wheeled trolleys they join the single chain conveyor line, where they have the engine, suspension units and back axles fitted at ground level. The Austin A105 engines are made at Coventry . . . each is electrically motored-in and ten per

Left: Taking your girl friend home to mum and dad is a serious business in Britain, and needed a smart car (a Mark II convertible, for instance).

Below: Last of the sidescreen specials: the Mark II of 1961.

20

Right: Suddenly the Big Healey became sophisticated with wind-up windows in 1962.

Below: The convertible's detachable rear window worked wonders for ventilation.

cent of these power units undergo a bench-test of about an hour's duration, during which a power check is made.

'The Austin-Healey assembly line is quite a short one, because the bodies are supplied complete with seats, etc. After the power unit and suspension units have been assembled the cars go up a ramp for under-chassis pipework, greasing, brake bleeding, etc, to be completed from a pit, after which they come back to floor level for the fitting of gearbox-tunnel cover, carpets (which are then rolled up and stowed in the boot until needed for final fitting) and a slave seat for the use of the test driver. Every wheel is statically balanced on a Weaver balancing machine. Dunlop supply all the wheels, which are painted by Austin, and the Road Speed tyres which arrive at the assembly line on overhead conveyors.

'A skilled electrician who has been with Austin for some thirty-five years checks all electrical wiring on the car before the completed Austin-Healey is supplied with petrol, oil and water and taken to a bay where the engine is run slowly while carburetter adjustments are made, after which it leaves for a brief road test. If the car is found to be generally satisfactory it is taken by a girl driver round the shop to another bay, any further adjustments required are carried out and the carpets and seats are fitted, any blemishes both exterior and under the bonnet are attended to, spanner marks removed from pipe unions, under bonnet flaws rectified by hand painting and the fan shield painted red, etc. Each Austin-Healey then goes to the rectification bay, in a corner of the vast assembly hall, and a very careful inspection is carried out.

'There is an air of leisure about the assembly of these popular sports cars. The production line is hand-fed throughout, some of the operations are carried out with normal spanners by calm operatives, the final inspection is very thorough and altogether, in this shop, where, before the war, Austin bodies were feverishly produced, there is the impression that the Austin-Healey is to some extent a hand-produced product. In fact, if bodies and other components do not fall into short supply, Mr Wagstaff, who is in charge, can feed Austin-Healeys off the line at the rate of more than forty a day. That, in a five-day, $42\frac{1}{2}$-hour week, represents over 200 sports cars which are selling well in dollar markets. Indeed, 95 per cent of production is of left-hand-drive cars. Since Austin-Healey production began, 59 per cent have been exported to America, earning $\$13\frac{1}{2}$ million up to January this year and just under another million dollars from Canada. Moreover, US exports have increased from 56 per cent of four-cylinder Austin-Healey production to 63 per cent of the new six-cylinder model.'

That happy scene was to go on only for a few more months at Longbridge before BMC sports car production was centralised at Abingdon, the home of their deadly rivals, MG, in the autumn of that year. In fact, the MG men welcomed the Big Healey with open arms as employment prospects soared. Abingdon became more like Longbridge, an assembly plant rather than a place where everything was made, although the rally side of the Big Healey competition programme was carried out there. Prototype work and race models stayed at Warwick. Major components were redirected to Abingdon from their outside suppliers and engines were re-routed from Coventry.

Right: Interior of the Mark II convertible. Note the late-type gearlever.

Below: Interior of the Mark III; much more refined.

Left: Exposed: the rear seats of the Mark III.

Below: Sidelight detail of the 1966 Mark III.

Bottom: Concealed: the rear seats become a luggage platform.

Soon after the six-port cylinder head was introduced. It used separate alloy inlet manifold, twin $1\frac{3}{4}$ in SU carburetters and a modified distributor. The compression ratio was increased to 8.5:1 and the power went up to 117 bhp at 5,000 rpm with maximum torque of 149 lb ft at 3,000 rpm, which immediately made the BN6 as good, if not better, performing as the old BN2. At about this time the first factory hardtops became available, being made by Jensens. These were a great advance over the rather boxy hardtops made for Big Healeys only by independent suppliers notable among which were the fabric-covered efforts by Universal Laminations. A clue to the scarcity of hood frames today was given by a report in *Motor Rally* in 1958 of their time with an early BN6: 'We were fortunate enough to have the use of a hardtop model, on which this very desirable extra could be fitted or removed much more quickly than the normal soft hood, and thus when a fine day promised it took no longer to prepare for open-air motoring than to get the car out of the garage and close the old-fashioned garage doors. To make full use of this facility, of course, it is necessary to be based at one place—not always possible on a rally or even a long-distance touring holiday—but in both the latter cases it would normally seem logical to run the car in closed form; this certainly proved to be far more relaxing and practical, although it was necessary to completely remove the side windows in order to obtain adequate ventilation; opening the sliding rear halves of these windows was not sufficient.' So, sadly for the enthusiasts to come, many hoods and frames were abandoned in their garages. . . .

By June 1958 it was evident that there was still a considerable demand for the old two-seater Healey and the factory began turning out 100-Sixes with only two seats and the old style of luggage configuration, giving a larger boot. These were called BN6s. It had been thought that buyers would use the rear seats for their excess luggage but there were a good many who preferred to lock it away while the car was open, despite the ability to cover it with the standard tonneau and support. The two-seat configuration was also better for the major rally onslaught that was just starting. About one fifth of the 14,436 100-Sixes made between August 1956 and June 1959 were two-seaters. These figures split up into 10,286 BN4s and 14,150 BN6s, with the vast majority going to America, particularly California. Most 100-Sixes were of the de luxe variety with overdrive, wire wheels and Dunlop Road Speed tyres, the standard non-overdrive models being fitted with tubeless tyres unless specially requested. About fifty BN6s were fitted with Dunlop disc brakes all round at Warwick. Heaters and radios, like the hardtops, were extras.

In the summer of 1959 the Big Healey really grew up with a bored-out 2,912 cc engine to take advantage of the three-litre international competition class. With a higher compression ratio of 9.03:1 and 83.36 mm bore, the new engine gave 124 bhp at 4,600 rpm and even more torque, 175 lb ft at 3,000 rpm. Naturally the car went quicker—it was almost exactly the same bodily as the 100-Six, being christened the 3000 in recognition of its bigger engine. Two-seater versions were designated BN7 and four-seaters BT7. Outwardly, the only change was a flash on the grille and a 3000 badge, but inwardly some significant changes had been made to cope with the extra power. The front brakes were changed for $11\frac{1}{4}$ in twin-pot caliper Girling discs in keeping with the rally cars and the clutch diameter was increased to ten inches.

Left: Luggage boot detail of the convertible, including the tool roll and battery cut-off switch in the right hand corner.

Below: Portrait of the triple SU production engine.

Actually the rally cars used Dunlop disc brakes, but the firm's patents were later taken over by Girling. The gear clusters were made stronger with curious new ratios making overdrive third roughly the same as direct top, with new axle ratios of 3.9:1 on the overdrive model and 3.545 on the standard version. Later the gearbox was changed yet again, after engine number 10897 on the overdrive model and number 11342 on the standard version. The gears were modified to increase their rigidity. In earlier versions of this modification the laygear was fitted with plain bushes, but this was later replaced by a layshaft assembly with needle roller bearings. Towards the end of 3000 production, at chassis numbers BN7 10329 and BT7 10303, the coil springs were uprated for better road holding. These were the only major changes in the 2,825 BN7s and 10,825 BT7s made between July 1959 and April 1961. Throughout the production life of the Big Healey, four and six-cylinder models, most exported to the United States were fitted with wire wheels, which were standardised on export models in the early 1960s.

The 3000 was a significant car in many ways in Austin history in that after eight years of taking whatever components were available it became the technological leader with the three-litre engine being adopted later for the saloon cars along with the disc front brakes, although these were made by Lockheed for the saloons.

Just as the use of disc brakes on the works 100-Six competition cars had heralded their standardisation, so the use of the triple carburetter layout during the 1960 season prompted the announcement of the 3000 Mark II in May 1961. The original 3000 was then frequently called the Mark I to distinguish it from this later model, as people had started to call the 100, the 100/4. The three $1\frac{1}{2}$ in SU carburetters had a new inlet manifold, of course, and with modified valve springs and a redesigned camshaft the power rose to 131 bhp at 4,750 rpm. Maximum torque was down slightly at 165 lb ft at 3,000 rpm and a brake servo was offered as an option for the first time. Outwardly, the triple carburetter version of the Mark II, of which 355 BN7s and 5,095 BT7s were built between April 1961 and March 1962, had a new radiator grille with vertical bars replacing the horizontal slats of the earlier 3000s. This was part of an Austin restyling exercise in 1961 in which the saloon cars received similar treatment. The new triple carburetters gave most of their power only at the top end of the range, and although they improved fuel consumption when properly tuned, the synchronisation was beyond the average mechanic and the 3000 reverted to twin carburetters in April 1962. It also acquired a new gearbox casing with the selector mechanism on top of the box which had the dual effect of providing $\frac{3}{4}$ in more foot room because of a narrower tunnel. This tunnel was made from fibreglass and helped reduce noise. It also made the first significant improvement in cockpit cooling. Like the other modifications, it was rally-inspired. Stiffer front springs and modified damper settings improved roadholding.

The loss of one carburetter—the twin set-up used $1\frac{3}{4}$ in SUs—cost only 2 bhp with the same torque figures. This was ably compensated by improved aerodynamics as the result of the first major styling changes in ten years.

This new car, designated BJ7 and promptly dubbed the Mark IIA by enthusiasts, was called the 3000 Convertible. It had four seats as standard, the two-seater being discontinued. But the rear seats were given more legroom and a wrapround

Latter day Mark III engine showing
its twin SU carburetters.

windscreen improved the aerodynamics so much that the car went even faster despite its loss of 2bhp. Wind-up windows with quarter lights were fitted, which improved ventilation at the expense of elbow room, but generally made the car altogether more luxurious. Sadly, the scuttle shook even more with the still stiffer front springs and even heavier windscreen. A new-style hood with detachable rear windows for better ventilation was fitted permanently to the car, which proved to be much easier to use, particularly by a driver without the aid of a passenger. The hardtop had to be discontinued as its fitting involved the removal of the hood, a labourious three-hour job that often damaged the fabric. Later the Healey Motor Company marketed and fitted around 200 hardtops which replaced the folding hood and frame. The clutch was changed to a nine-inch diaphragm unit after engine number 4898 of the 6,113 BJ7s produced between April 1962 and February 1964. Sixty-spoke wire wheels at last replaced the fragile forty-eight spokers in 1963.

    In March 1964 the most luxurious and the quickest Healey of them all was introduced, apart from the racing 100S model which was far from plush. The new Mark III—or BJ8—looked just like its predecessor from the outside—in fact the factory used the same picture on the cover of catalogues for both cars; but the inside was different. The power output was increased yet further without loss of torque to 150 bhp by using a new higher lift camshaft and twin two-inch SU carburetters on revised manifolds. The noise level had been reduced because of looming West German regulations by an entirely new exhaust system using four separate straight through silencers on the twin pipes. The two main silencers ran alongside the left hand seat, under the floor, and the two secondary silencers lay under the boot floor

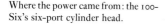

Where the power came from: the 100-Six's six-port cylinder head.

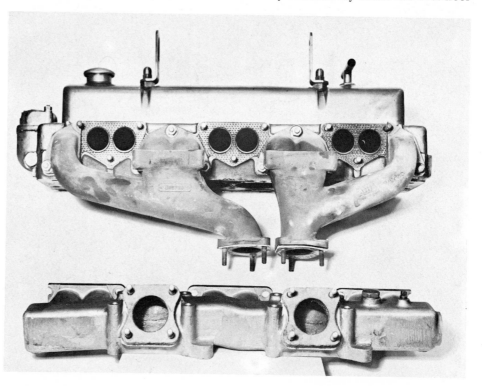

Left: Where the stopping power came from: the 3000's new disc front brakes.

Below: First of the three litres: the 3000 of 1959.

with the pipes crossing over parallel with the bumper to exit at the right hand side. They were sufficiently far back not to affect battery cooling, but too low for comfort. Although they reduced the noise level, these silencers also helped increase the power, by eliminating back pressure.

The brake servo was standardised and the gearbox improved yet again with yet another set of much stronger ratios, a strengthened layshaft and caged needle roller bearings. Alternative rear axle ratios of 4.3 and 4.875 were listed for sporty types, although the 4.3 ratio was seldom seen.

The interior was completely redesigned with a console sweeping down from the centre of the polished veneer facia along the transmission line between the bucket seats. A lockable glove box was added to the passenger's side. The backs of the rear seats were changed so that they could be folded down to form an extra luggage platform and Ambla vinyl upholstery helped keep down the price increase to £50, with leather being made an option. New reflectors conformed to changing regulations.

Nine out of ten of the cars were designated for export and it took only the production of a week to realise that the new exhaust system was impractical. So after eleven years of complaints, BMC at last did something about it. The chassis was cranked down an inch at the point where the rear axle was mounted to allow different springs to be fitted. These were of six-leaf construction and a good deal softer to give more axle movement in a raised rear end. To prevent these softer springs from winding up on acceleration, especially now 150 bhp was on tap, the axle was positively located by twin radius arms. The dampers were uprated and the ride was much improved, the handling became steadier and more predictable and the ground clearance problem was greatly improved, all in one go. To this day Healey enthusiasts are still asking why it was not done sooner.

These modifications were introduced in March 1964 at the same time as larger front and rear side lights to comply with new American regulations and a lower centre armrest to give more room for the gearchanging elbow were also introduced. Later that year the hub splines were re-inforced to cope with the extra torque and the new, 'stickier' radial tyres. The Big Healey continued virtually unchanged, except for the introduction of separate indicators in 1965, until the end of its run in March 1968, with 17,313 of the phase two Mark IIIs built and 390 of the unfortunate phase ones. No doubt the British enthusiasts would have called the phase two the Mark IIIA had they realized such a fundamental change had been made. As it was, nearly all the bottom scrapers went for export. Previously, conflicting evidence has been presented as to when the last Big Healey was made. Now Clive Richardson, deputy editor of *Motor Sport* who worked at Abingdon in the late 1960s, has been able to clear up the mystery point. He saw the last Big Healey, a British Racing Green car destined for America, leave the production lines in the first week of December 1967, and remembers one more, a white right-hand drive model being made from spare parts by the firm's show shop early in 1968. Since then there have been at least two more brand new Big Healeys assembled from spares by British garage owner John Chatham in 1971 and 1975. Chatham still has an unused chassis hanging in his roof, so who knows, perhaps there is one more Big Healey to come.

IV

Contemporary Road Testers' Reports

ROAD TESTERS have, almost without exception, liked the Big Healey. From the first road test by John Bolster of *Autosport*, to the last, by Michael Bowler, of *Thoroughbred and Classic Cars*, they have enjoyed themselves. Their reports make valuable reading as they tell what it was like to be unleashed in the car when it was new, although it must be remembered that their opinions might not be quite the same today. As the immortal Bolster said in *Autosport* in 1975 when summing up his twenty-five years as technical editor, which involved driving most of their test cars: 'Through the years, I have steadily raised my sights as cars have become better. If I were to go back and test the cars of the early 1950s again, I'm afraid I would be very rude indeed. Its fun for collectors to restore them to their original condition and they should be preserved as a little bit of history, but please don't expect them to steer or stop like modern machinery, or you are going to have a very bad accident. Between the vintage period and the modern epoch, the designers of motor cars had to learn an entirely new technique so perhaps it is not surprising that they dreamed up some rather deplorable carriages and made some dreadful mistakes. Let us not forget, too, that some of these cars might have behaved quite acceptably if modern tyres had been available.'

The Big Healey is certainly improved by fitting radial ply tyres, but it was far ahead of all but the most expensive rivals in 1952. It was the first of the modern sports cars, cheap and fast with reasonable handling. The four main magazines that tested the Healey 100 were agreed on that. They failed to agree on its maximum speed, however, and, indeed on its weight. For *Autosport*, Bolster had a wonderful time with the prototype KWD947 in October 1952. Service manager Geoff Price remembers it as having been fitted with a second-hand Austin A90 engine which might have helped performance, being rather loose, or been something of a handicap, being somewhat worn. At any rate, it performed very well for Bolster after he collected it from Donald and Geoffrey Healey at Ostend. For the actual test, on the famous Jabekke autoroute 'the editor and two stop watches occupied the passenger's seat,' said Bolster. The editor was none other than the illustrious Gregor Grant. 'We decided to time the maximum speed over the measured mile that is used for record attempts, and, of course, took the mean of runs in both directions. An average of 106 mph was achieved (with windscreen retracted, no sidescreen and two-up) with which we were more than pleased. Since the road was not closed at the time, heavy traffic, and even a herd of cows, rendered our task a difficult one. As a result quite a mileage was put in at over 100 mph, without any sign of stress.

'With such an advantageous power/weight ratio, first speed is purely an emergency gear. Even for the standing-start acceleration figures, second was used for the getaway, but no time was lost thereby, as the results prove. Rearward weight distribution, and a light axle, give exceptional freedom from wheelspin.' Bolster went on to comment on the car's good handling—'the rear end never breaks away unexpectedly'—and remarkable freedom from rattles and bangs, even when hammered over the notorious Belgian pavé. He also said that the car weighed only 16⅓ cwt, presumably unladen and at least 2 cwt lighter than recorded by any other journal. It is quite possible, though, that the prototype's alloy Tickford body weighed considerably less than the later Austin-built bodies and well-worn engine compensated for that in performance figures.

Sensational as Bolster's 106 mph test might have been, it would seem that he might have been quite badly baulked on that Belgium run. When *The Autocar* tested one of the first Austin-Healeys—a 'special test model'—in September 1953, they returned almost identical acceleration figures of 0–60 in 10.3 secs and the standing quarter mile in 17.5 secs, but extracted an average speed of 111 mph with no less than 119 mph in one direction. *The Motor* tested the same car, NOJ392, which had been raced at Le Mans three months earlier, at about the same time—and on the Jabekke road could extract only 107 mph with 11.2 secs for the 0–60 and 18.5 for the standing quarter mile. There seems no doubt that this car, and Bolster's prototype were a good deal quicker than production Healeys to come. *The Autocar* and *The Motor* were unanimous in their praise for NOJ392. 'It is roomy, comfortable to ride in, and its general road behaviour and handling qualities are of a very high order,' said *The Autocar*. There was a 'surprising amount of room inside. The general layout is so well arranged that in spite of the low overall height the driver is in no way cramped. The steering wheel is nicely placed in relation to the pedals . . . and the overdrive switch is fitted on a steering wheel spoke although on present production models this is placed on the facia.

'In the interests of performance there is a limit to the weight that can be added in the form of sound-insulating material, and in consequence some noise can be heard from the engine compartment, while a certain amount of heat is also noticed in the cockpit, particularly with the hood and sidescreens in position. Otherwise, apart from a certain amount of transmission noise from the indirect gears, the car is quite quiet, although if it is driven very fast with hood and sidescreens in position some noise is caused by wind pressure deflecting the Perspex sidescreens.' Evidently *The Autocar* were forgiving when it came to prototypes.

The Motor test concentrated more on the car's performance. They pointed out that NOJ392's overdrive could be used on all three forward gears rather than just the top two—but overdrive first was not much use as the 35 mph overdrive cutting-in speed corresponded with maximum revs in direct first gear. 'Commonsense maximum speeds in the gears were 35, 60 and 90 mph direct, 42, 70 and 106 overdrive.' *The Motor* considered the overall fuel consumption of 22.5 mpg with automatic

overdrive engagement quite remarkable.

'Certainly it is a sports car, in the best meaning of the phrase; the only adverse qualities from the point of view of everyday motoring are a moderately strident exhaust note, the rather light construction of the bodywork and doors, and a lack of heat insulation between engine compartment and cockpit. At present, the two-bladed fan seems on the small side and the passage of hot air to escape from under the bonnet inadequate, so that in town driving at least, there is a tendency for both the engine and the space around the passenger's legs to get too warm.

'Additional elbow room is provided by large recesses in the doors, but one restriction on the car tested was the inability to make any kind of signal with the hood and sidescreens up.

'These things apart, the car can quite well earn its keep for the man who needs no more than two places—two very generous places, one might add, for the internal width is 50 in—and a corresponding space for luggage. It will "potter" if need be, to such an extent that accelerating from 10 mph in top gear during the test was a pleasanter process than on many family cars, both large and small. The usual rib-chilling slipstream that goes with the older type of open car in cool weather is avoided by seats placed so low within the body that the door tops are almost at shoulder

Road test car off duty: Bert Hadley presses on in the Mille Miglia of 1953.

Road test car on duty: one of the 'special test cars' poses for a portrait in *The Autocar*'s car park.

height. The hood is frankly rather a handful for one person to put up unaided, but once it is in position and the moulded Perspex sidescreens pegged into the doors, the interior is very snug and should keep out any degree of foul weather . . .'

The Motor went on to commend the general roadworthiness of the car, even on Belgian pavé, and the astonishingly precise steering. 'It has a liveliness and delicacy of touch which can be bettered by few cars on the road. There is a nicely-judged modicum of understeer, and all that is necessary is to turn the wheel and hold it there. Pressed to the absolute limit, the car shows a sharp rear-end breakaway, the sturdy rear axle showing a slight tendency to hop on bumps.' *The Motor* also liked the 'neo-vintage' quality of steering and cornering power, although, unlike *The Autocar* and *Autosport*, they managed to make the front brakes judder under repeated heavy use. Perhaps NOJ392 was beginning to suffer a bit from all its racing and testing. *The Motor* would have liked an ammeter, but wound up by saying the Healey 100 was a 'most delightful car.'

Road and Track could not lay hands on an Austin-Healey 100 to test until 1954, but then they immediately jumped feet first into the controversy over its top speed. 'The biggest misconception,' they said 'concerning the Austin-Healey is its true top speed, *in full touring trim!* (their italics). In much (very much) modified form it has achieved 142.63 mph on the Bonneville Salt Flats. That was with 135 bhp and a certain amount of body fairing. In slightly modified form, developing just over 100 bhp, the Le Mans model attained 119.12 mph on the famous circuit, in competition.'

Road and Track then listed comparative road test figures with 'two British magazines' estimating the true maximum speed of a production Austin-Healey at between 101.5 mph and 103 mph with windshield erect, top and sidescreens in position. *Road and Track*'s chart read:

Magazine	*Road and Track*	'A'	'B'
Average	102.3	103	101.5
Best run	106	108	107.72*
Gear ratio	3.12	3.12	2.78
Test weight	2470	2500	2464

with windshield and top folded down

'A' was *The Autocar*, of course, and 'B' *The Motor*. *Road and Track*'s 102 mph must have been on the conservative side, though, as their figures were taken in bad weather. It was not recorded whether they used a steel or an alloy-bodied car. Later evidence suggests it might have been an alloy-bodied car. Like magazines A and B, *Road and Track* were thrilled with the car. 'To put it quite frankly, the Austin-Healey is one of the very few cars which we have driven at this speed without adding a few grey hairs,' they said. 'It holds a straight line without the slightest difficulty and always felt safe.

'Our testers were unanimous in rating the 100 as the best all-round handling car encountered this year. The ride is at least as good as any sports car we've tested in the past year, cornering is very flat and controllable, there is a small amount of understeer, a good feel of the road with no kick-back. The only fault we could find in this department was a slight backlash in the steering, which certainly did not seem to hurt the controllability. This particular test car had 10,000 miles on the odometer and the steering gear had never been adjusted in that time.'

That particular car seemed to have had a hard 10,000 miles. Its clutch was so fierce it made acceleration figures difficult to obtain, its overdrive was beginning to slip, and the rear springs wound up. Nevertheless, *Road and Track* managed 0-60 in 11.7 secs and a standing quarter mile in 18 secs, despite other deficiences which included an engine that 'smoked noticeably and showed, at times, an extreme reluctance to stop.' However, Healeys have always been tough cars, and the engine temperature never went over 80 degrees F (that was in California) and 'although the transmission tunnel does get warm, the ash-tray does not get uncomfortably hot,' said the witty men from Newport Beach. It is significant that they did not complain about cockpit heat to the extent of their colleagues in Britain, who had the advantage of cooler weather and not sitting over the exhaust pipe in the case of the driver. This was probably because it was so cool in Britain that most motoring was done with either the hood up and sidescreens or in a heavy topcoat, whereas the Americans rarely erected the hood in sunny California, and so some of the engine heat escaped that way.

The Healey family took a lot of notice of road test reports, although they did nothing about the ventilation problem. 'Later models have a more conventional type of side curtain with signalling flaps,' said *Road and Track*. First the gearbox, then the back springs, then the sidescreens. The Healey family obviously read their road tests. Less charitable observers would have said they lacked a development engineer. But it must have taken quite a bit of muscle to get many changes past Leonard Lord in the middle of a highly successful production run. Perhaps the printed evidence of the road tests helped convince him changes were needed.

Fourteen months later, *Road and Track* tested an Austin-Healey 100S, and immediately felt the difference. It was the car which had raced at Pebble Beach that year, and the only change to specification since then was the substitution of a 'standard 100S' axle ratio of 2.92:1 instead of 3.66. The experienced Bill Pringle gave a hand with the tests and 'he had no trouble at all in making good fast starts, and subsequent experience with this machine (and another nearly new one) showed that the one vice of the 90 bhp Austin Healey, rear-end bottoming, is not present in the 100S during standing starts.

'As might be expected, the 100S is a joy to drive. The Austin-Healey has always been noteworthy in the good-handling department and the 100S is equally good for the simple reason that the 100 couldn't be much improved. The ride is noticeably firmer and cornering roll is either non-existent or so small as to be non-detectable. But it is the beautiful close-ratio four-speed gearbox that really makes this machine, both in town and on the highway. We can find little or no fault with the Austin-Healey 100S. It offers a genuine competition machine in the not-too-competitive class D at a very fair price.'

In February 1956, *Motor Sport* gave performance details of their 100 stable car which had been converted to 'M' specification. It was about 10 mph faster all the way up the range, they said.

Next month, *Road and Track* tested a factory-converted 100M. 'It falls between the 90 bhp of the standard 100 model and the 132 bhp of the strictly-for-competition 100S model tested last September,' they said. 'The performance, as might be expected, also falls about midway between models, as per the following data:

Model	100	100M	100S
Top speed	102	109	119
0–60 mph	11.7	9.6	7.8
SS ¼ mile	18.1	17.4	16.1

The 100 and the 100M ran with top and sidescreens in place, and, of course, the 100S had neither. It would seem, however, that *Road and Track*'s 100M was one of the later steel-bodied cars straight from the production line, as it weighed no less than 235 lb more than their 100 test car. They said that the 100M was not such a pleasant car to drive because of its harsher ride, although, undoubtedly better for competition work than the standard 100; the gearbox on the 100M was the same as that on the 100S, plus overdrive operating on all four gears. *Road and Track* found it useful only on top gear as overdrive third on this box co-incided with direct fourth. The actual car had been taken to America by Donald Healey for the Nassau races that year and finished ninth in class D beaten by one other Austin-Healey and a flock of Ferraris. It had then been driven to California by Roy Jackson-Moore who helped with the test. You couldn't do that with a modern racing sports car.

One of the few tests on the BN2 was carried out by *The Autocar* in August 1956.

'General outlines and specifications have changed little since 1952,' said the tester, Harold Hastings, who was on his way to report the Scottish Rally. 'The engine now drives through a four-speed gearbox with overdrive on third and top giving, in effect, six speeds. The car weighs, with five gallons of fuel, approximately 18¾ cwt.

'A surprisingly large amount of gear can be stowed in the luggage locker—tow rope, the usual road test tool kit (capable of dealing with anything from a blown fuse to an axle change, but on this occasion unopened from start to finish), spare petrol can and a suitcase. The case seemed to be enormous—what do women do with all the things they take away with them? However, when the spare wheel was lifted the case lay flat on the locker floor, held firm by the fuel filler neck. We tempted the weather by folding the hood.

'On entering the driving seat it was found that there was just nowhere for the driver to put his somewhat large left foot when it was not operating the clutch pedal. In the end the foot had to stay on the pedal and, although it says in the book that this is a *bad* thing to do, the clutch did not seem to complain.'

Hastings then blasted the car to the Highlands at speeds up to an indicated 108 mph and stepped out to say: 'It had not taken a very long time to get there, and we both felt that we could have gone on for another two hundred miles or so. The fresh air had a great deal to do with it—why do we shut ourselves in closed cars?'

How refreshing it would be if we could do that now. There's hardly a new car left that can go topless to Scotland and none in which you are supposed to do 108 mph. Bolster felt quite refreshed, too, when he tested one of the first 100-Sixes in October 1956. 'Having been in at the beginning, as it were, I was delighted to take part in a most ambitious programme, just prior to the announcement of the latest six-cylinder version,' he said in *Autosport*. 'Appropriately, the party started at Ostend again where ten lucky journalists were handed a new Six apiece. Mine was a white one, and I examined it with much interest in conjunction with the printed specification. . . .'

He then went on to describe the mechanical changes and commented on the body: 'The greatest change is here. The body is now of the "occasional four" variety. This should greatly increase the sales appeal of the car, for many young couples have to forswear sports cars when their family begins to arrive. The extra seats are normally hidden by a tonneau cover, and the body then has the appearance of being a two-seater. The hood can be persuaded into a small space behind these seats, and there is room in the boot for a moderate amount of luggage. Most people agree that it is an even better looking car than its predecessor.

'Although my car had only just over 1,000 miles on the clock, it seemed fairly free. Accordingly, I got my toe well down and was soon on my way to Brussels via the Jabbeke road. I kept up a steady 103 mph for most of the way, 110 mph being indicated on one occasion. The machine was very easy to handle at such speeds, running dead straight hands-off.

'Next day a long journey into Germany was undertaken, including many miles of the most atrocious cobblestones in the industrial areas. The suspension was quite outstandingly good under these conditions, and the new Austin-Healey must be one of the most comfortable sports cars ever built . . .

'As the engine is carried well back in the frame, there is plenty of weight on the rear wheels. This allows full power to be applied on wet roads without excessive wheelspin. Since the steering is fairly light, it might be worthwhile to list an alternative drop arm for those who prefer an extra quick response under slippery conditions.

'It is in smoothness and silence that the new Austin-Healey excels its predecessor. The indirect gears are quiet, and the axle inaudible, while the flexibility is most marked. As a stunt, it is possible to start from a standstill in top gear without touching the clutch, merely by switching on the ignition and pressing the starter!

'However, such performances are not in the curriculum of the sports car driver, but the next test I carried out would make any enthusiast's mouth water. This was nothing less than three hours' uninhibited driving round the Nurburgring. The famous Ring is easily the finest circuit in the world from the driver's point of view, and I made the very fullest use of my opportunities.

'Eventually, I found it best to use third and overdrive third all round the circuit, except for the run down the undulating straight where I attained 5,500 rpm in direct top. The machine stood up perfectly to its ordeal, and no brake fade was experienced, though naturally the travel of the pedal increased somewhat towards the end. As regards handling the car behaved exceptionally well, considering that it was in touring trim. If I were racing it seriously, I would certainly specify higher tyre pressures and a harder suspension setting, at the expense of spoiling that superb ride over bumps and cobblestones. For everyday use, however, the makers have chosen the right compromise.'

For the record, Bolster's hard driven Six did 104 mph, 0–60 in 13.2 secs and 23 mpg. Like his first test car, it had left-hand-drive.

The Autocar, the American edition of *Sports Car Illustrated* and *Motor Sport* also tested the BN4 to good effect. *The Autocar* commented on the restyled front, saying it bore the unmistakeable imprint of Longbridge, and paid tribute to its exceptionally smooth and torquey engine. They thought the overdrive model would be the most popular, although they expected the non-overdrive car to reach its maximum quicker and more often. Little could be gained from using direct fourth when changing down, they said, it being quicker to switch straight from overdrive to overdrive third—virtually the same ratio. Upward overdrive changes were smooth if the throttle was kept open as recommended by the makers. Maximum speed worked out at 103 mph with a 107 mph best, much the same as the Four with screen up, but acceleration was down at 12.9 secs to 60 probably because of the extra weight —22 cwt unladen—with only an extra 12 bhp.

The Autocar found the Austin-Healey very comfortable and untiring to drive and their testers were grateful for a place to put their clutch feet. The only real drag was trying to raise the hood, a Herculean two-man operation. If the driver only attempted such a feat he would probably be soaked by the time he completed it.

Karl Ludvigsen was quick off the mark with his BN4 test. He really put the car through its paces for *SCI* before any other American magazine and reached 108 mph flat out with 0–60 in 11.6 secs and the standing quarter mile in 18.2. He welcomed the smoothness of the engine 'which digs in with a solid pull instead of a series of bangs.'

Ground clearance was still a problem, although bottoming under acceleration seemed to have been eliminated. 'The tail squats, the tyres growl briefly and you pump through shifts at thirty, fifty and seventy occompanied by a soaring moan of power and a satisfying slug in the shoulder blades,' said the happy *SCI* technical editor.

The new seating got top marks and one of *SCI*'s staff managed to cope with the hood on his own. Two together found it easy.

Handling was as good as ever although 'the 100-Six rear axle is solid and heavy and you know its there on a tight, bumpy corner. This Healey had the optional new Dunlop Road Speeds, with rounded treads. Knowing the wet-weather reputation of the older Road Speeds, we threw the car around on everything from damp concrete to drenched bricks. On the latter we could apply full bore at 20 mph in first gear without breaking loose, and there was absolutely no loss of controlability in all kinds of corners. The new Dunlops are excellent.'

SCI considered the headroom was something else. It was inadequate for anybody taller than 5 ft 10 in with the hood up and to cap it all there was a hood rail right above your head. They also found the doors awkward with the hood up despite their two extra inches. All the same, they loved the car, and wondered what was in store next year.

Motor Sport liked the car, too, and commented favourably on its low price. Editor Bill Boddy took his BN4 up to 'well over 100 mph and a standing-start quarter mile of less than 19 seconds' in August 1957. He took a little while to get used to the offset pedals, but found them comfortable. Like *SCI*, *Autocar* and *Autosport*, he commented on a stiff gearlever—but the cars were hardly run in, it seemed. 'Excellent rainproof Perspex sidescreens are provided, with sliding windows, these becoming, however, unpleasantly stiff to open in wet weather, due to the felt seals swelling. The hood provides reasonable protection in torrential rain, but requires patience to erect, or to stow behind the squab of the occasional seat . . . In the end the hood came completely adrift on the near side; after finger-pinching and skin removal we got some sense out of it after a very wet twenty minutes. This wouldn't have mattered to the young enthusiast but as the car is now a two/four seater something better should be provided—there is, of course, a hard top for £90 extra. The windscreen, commendably, is of Triplex laminated plate glass and a good, traditional, divided tonneau cover is provided.'

Good comments on the mechanical side of the car followed with an interesting variation on the overdrive game: 'The change out of overdrive is obtained by accelerating and it is thus possible to select normal drive but not engage it until required for rapid acceleration, which is an attractive feature.' Just like the pre-selector gearboxes on the old Grand Prix cars that had to have them because you need both hands on the steering wheel all the way through corners and had none left for gearchanging.

Boddy was the first journalist to highlight the car's scuttle shake, and he didn't like it one bit. 'On rough roads very vicious scuttle float and judder develop, which affects the steering column and conveys appreciable vibration to the driver's hands,' he said. 'On main roads this is not particularly evident but it is, nevertheless, something which no designer worth his salt would permit. Although it was recently stiffened, the bonnet top still skiffles a little. Apart from that the car's performance and appearance got top marks, except for a 'rather ugly' radiator grille and the fairing behind the front bumper 'which seemed to constitute unnecessary weight.'

Late in 1957, the Healey family pursued their policy, started with *Autosport*, of releasing a pre-production model for testing by a well-known journalist. In this case, the lucky man was a Dennis May, the British correspondent of *SCI*, seeing as a vast majority of sales were in America, and the prototype was in Britain. May was very enthusiastic about his first run in the Mille Miglia 100-Six. Naturally he devoted a lot of words to describing the modifications to the car placed second in its class in the Italian classic that year, which was, in fact, the BN6 prototype. Its registration number, UOC741, was to be remembered for years as the car which had survived all manner of ordeals. The only real difference in its mechanical specification, he said, was a dual exhaust system worth an extra 5 bhp and too noisy for normal road work. May did a good job in his evaluation: he noted that, seeing as the car had been built for the Mille Miglia, it probably had a very carefully-assembled engine, which was probably better than the average production unit; but, as compensation, the car had done a hard 18,000 miles by the time he went along to the test track with Geoffrey Healey and sales representative Tom Wilson-Gunn.

The faithful six-port car promptly averaged 120 mph over ten laps with a best of 121.7; reached 60 mph from rest in 8.8 secs and covered the standing quarter mile in 16.9—a considerable advance on the earlier four-porter, which had 21 bhp less, of course.

The gearbox still had overdrive on third and fourth, with third overdrive corresponding with direct fourth. 'Life would be much the same if it weren't there,' said May. After several pages of eulogising on the technical improvements under the bonnet, he turned his attention to the chassis, and in the best traditions of specialist journalism, came up with a couple of constructive criticisms. The first was an *aide memoire* to those concerned. It didn't escape our notice that the exhaust system is still too close to the ground.' We had heard that before . . . but the second criticism was brand new: 'A driver's ability to make himself cent per cent comfortable is somewhat a matter of luck, governed by his personal dimensions. If he's tall, has long legs and average arms, everything is fine. But if he's below average height, has longish arms for his build and likes an almost straight-arm driving position, he'll find that the right fore/aft seat setting makes it hard to reach the pedals. And this won't do because clean and easy gearshifts are dependent on using nearly the full clutch travel. Not even a telescopic steering column would lick his problem because he needs to get the wheel further way from him, and its already as far forward as it can go without cramping clearance between its top arc and the dash,' said May, who was a shade on the short side. He wound up his test by introducing the two-seater version of the BN6 and pointing out that its hood was a good deal easier to put up and down than that on the two plus two.

Doubtless stung by *SCI*'s scoop, *Road and Track* really went to town on their BN6 when they got their hands on it in April 1958. Their car was a production model producing 117 bhp. 'Two distinct types of sound emanate from the exhaust system,' said *Road and Track*. 'One is a rather pleasant rap similar to the sound of the

XK120M, but which at certain rpm gets to be quite annoying to the car's occupants due to the severe "cab noise". It sounds almost as though the exhaust system were welded to the body. A subsequent check revealed that the sound is not bothersome to people outside the car (especially minions of the law) as we suspected it might be.

'The other sound coming from the pipes is that of scraping metal whenever any but the most gradual of driveways is entered. It is a continual source of amazement that the designers of the Austin-Healey have apparently made no attempt to increase the ground clearance of the car in general, or at least of the appendages, such as the exhaust pipes, that could be more easily arranged.

'Getting in or out of the Healey with the top up is still a chore. Fortunately, Healey owners spend more time driving the car than they do getting in and out. Entrance and exit are made much easier when the top is lowered; however, lowering and storing the top takes the joint efforts of a score of trained circus roustabouts.

'Once one is in, the true bucket seats are fairly comfortable. The controls are well placed with the exception of the choke, which is hidden alongside the steering column and about midway between the instrument panel and the firewall. Healey engineers must feel that the choke is so seldom used that it doesn't need to be located on the panel with the other controls. They appear to be right, too, though California is not the best place to determine this.

'The driver's seat is adjustable fore and aft (the passenger's seat is not), and both fold forward to allow admittance to the jump seats from either side of the car. Both front seats are placed in such a manner that the occupants' heads are between the first and second of the three top bows. In spite of this, everyone who rode in the car managed to crack his head against the top bows at least once. Seat belts would be a distinct aid in this respect, although they are not needed for lateral support . . .'

Road and Track went on to describe how handling, control, and riding qualities were as good as ever and 'strongly recommended that a fender-mounted rear view mirror be installed because of the limited visibility with the top up. This, of course, is not a condemnation of the Austin-Healey, but would be most practical for any car with a low seating position and somewhat obscured vision inherent with roadster or convertible tops.'

Road and Track's performance figures were a good deal down on those of *SCI*, with a best run of 104.6 mph, 0–60 of 10.4 secs and standing quarter mile of 17.4 secs. However, they pointed out that they took their figures with a passenger in the car which probably added about a second to the 0–60 time and estimated the top speed at 109 mph. They also observed the rev limit of 4,800—factors which would explain some of the difference in the figures when the extra horsepower of the Mille Miglia car was taken into account. The rest would be explained by the car being a lightweight like the first road test BN1 cars.

Road and Track concluded by asking: 'Just what is keeping the Austin-Healey in its place in new-car sales?' And answering their own question: 'The combination of good looks, compact size, reliability adequate performance and reasonable price all add up. Some cars have at least two or three of these attributes to a better degree than the Healey, but none of the others has more good points all wrapped up in one attractive package. This, plus the generally excellent service and parts which are readily obtainable over most of the US, must be the answer.'

The Autocar got their BN6 up to 111 mph in May 1958 with acceleration figures of only 11.2 secs for 0–60 and 18.1 for the standing quarter mile. But their model came with all the goodies: hardtop, Road Speed tyres, heater, overdrive and wire wheels and probably weighed a lot more than the California roadster, although the hardtop was credited with improving the top speed by 2–3 mph. They found that the speedometer needle could be 'kept on the 100 mph mark for mile after mile; the overdrive top gear fuel consumption is then between 20 and 22 mpg.' *The Autocar* went on to pay the usual compliments to the car's performance and added: 'It was found that ease of steering was affected to a considerable degree by the tyre pressures and the recommended 20 lb front and 23 lb rear for normal driving made the steering feel unduly heavy at slow speeds. An increase of 3 lb on these figures gave a noticeable improvement for everyday journeys. The steering becomes rather heavy towards full lock.

'When travelling fast the 100-Six steers best if the wheel is held lightly. This is especially apparent on heavily-cambered roads abroad. A firm grip becomes tiring, and the directional stability is not improved if the driver is tensed—the Austin-Healey is much better when given its head under these conditions . . .'

'The detachable hard top has many advantages. It does not detract from the appearance of the car and does not turn the cockpit into a sound box; wind and road noise are negligible. The advantages of having available saloon car protection from the elements are many . . . the only criticism one has of the hard top as fitted to the Austin-Healey is its cost, which does appear to be rather high.' *The Autocar* testers also suffered from fumes with the £90 hard top in place, a complaint that many enthusiasts were to make over the years that followed. It was also noted that there was no room, no matter how cramped, for an adult in the back when the hard top was in place. In fact, *The Autocar* thought the rear seats were a complete waste and looked forward to the promised two-seater BN6 with extra, much-needed, luggage accommodation.

Six months later John Christy's Healey test for *SCI* took in more track than road—the competition with *Road and Track* was intense. Christy advised against using the overdrive in competition, saying, with feeling: 'You *can* break it,' and going on to enthuse over the handling: 'Austin-Healeys have always been noted for their excellent handling characteristics and the newest 100-Six is no exception. If anything, it handles better than previous models, at least one of which had a spooky tendency toward rear-end skitter on bumpy or wet roads when a shade too much throttle was given. This has definitely been eliminated in current models. That heavy frame and light body combination has much to do with the Austin-Healey handling. Make no mistake, it can and will slide but there is never the feeling that the thing is going to tip. It's a driftable car and properly controlled this driftability can be used to advantage in getting around both tight corners and fast bends. Too exuberant sliding, however, can result in incidents. That low centre of gravity (the frame runs under the back axle in classic British tradition) also provides a low roll centre, the result of which is that if the tail is allowed to poke out too far there's no getting it tucked back in. Once it starts to go there's nothing to do but hang on and

let'er rip, which it will do in a long gentle sweep. There's nothing particularly nasty about it—it's not a sudden snap or whipping. And there's little or none of that "it's going to dump" feeling. You get the idea that the car will do its level best to hold you safely upright even though you've been damn fool enough to spin it through your own ham-fisted lack of driving ability. You feel as though you ought to apologise to the car. On the record, Healeys have been haybaled, spun and looped but few have flipped.' Great words. That's just how the Americans who bought new Healeys felt.

Christy went on to explain the intracies of the current racing tyres and how the hood had improved from the 'rain rags' fitted to the four-cylinder car at the expense of fingernails. He opined that the new hardtop was one of the prettiest and most functional in existence. He reckoned the driving position problem outlined by May had been cleared up by more adjustment for the seat and headroom was still meagre with the hood, but better with the hardtop. He loved the instrument lay-out and liked the 'whoo-o-o-om' from the exhaust which he considered just right and designed in tune with a cash register. Performance figures were slightly slower than May's, plus 11 mpg for racing, 19 mpg for hard driving and 25 mpg for average driving—'below 60 mph.'

At about that time, the Donald Healey Motor Company were offering a considerable quantity of special parts to help the 100-Six go faster. Christy tested two

One of the first and most-famous 100-Six test cars, UOC741, in the Alpine Rally of 1958. It is now owned by Dave Jeffery.

Healeys next month, December, in *S C I*—one straight from the showroom and one which he had been racing, with all the optional equipment. The high performance car had contour-topped pistons, thick gasket, 9.5:1 compression, high lift cam, nitrided crank, matched and polished ports, 3.6 rear axle instead of 4.1, no overdrive, competition springs and shock absorbers, four-wheel Dunlop disc brakes and R3 racing tyres. The result was not dramatically faster in a straight line—17 secs for the 0–60, in fact, quite like May's Mille Miglia machine times, supporting the theory that the Mille Miglia car was not so standard as the Healeys reckoned.

The real difference in Christy's high-performance car showed up on a circuit which took the standard car 1 min 20 secs or so: the race model managed it a good five seconds faster, chiefly because of its handling and braking. 'Where the shut-off point for the stocker was the hundred foot marker, the prepared car could be floor-boarded right down to the fifty-foot mark before backing off and braking,' said Christy. 'The turn entering the straight is a fast right-hand bend just at the foot of a steep hill and it requires a good deal of practice before the right line and the optimum cornering speed can be found for any given car. The competition car could motor through this bend at a speed somewhere between 80 and 85 mph. The stock machine began to be distinctly uncomfortable at anything over 70, a pretty respectable speed for any production sports car and suicidal in a Detroiter. The same situation applied on the other bends and corners. While the stock Healey was quicker coming out of slow corners, the competition car maintained a higher rate of speed all the way through and would come out with as much as 10 mph edge on the normal car. Now you begin to see whence comes that five-second difference in lap times—the prepared car could go deeper into a corner and go through it faster. In a ten-lap race the difference is almost a lap.'

Nothing quite so exciting happened to the scribes of *The Motor* when they tested the BN6 in April 1959. 'High performance motoring in armchair comfort' was their headline. Closed or open, the low-built Austin-Healey (with an occasionally vulnerable silencer) had a purposeful appearance, said *The Motor*, adding: 'Without question, the great attraction of this car is its versatility. With never a trace of temperament, it will potter gently around a big city on business or social errands day after day, yet when the opportunity occurs to wind the tachometer around its scale the Austin-Healey will hurl itself forwards in most impressive fashion, reaching nearly 80 mph within a quarter-mile of starting from rest and 100 mph in less than a mile. To find a comparable combination of performance and of smooth-running comfort in any but a much larger and more expensive car would seem extremely difficult.'

The answer was on the way. In August 1959, *S C I* got their first test 3000. John Christy said it was the best Big Healey he had driven and you could feel the difference in the seat of your pants. He described the additional power (130 bhp against 117 bhp and 149 lb ft torque against 123) of the three-litre engine with its 'great gobs' of torque, and said: 'To take advantage of the added power there are a host of other minor changes, some apparent and some not so noticeable. The first and most noticeable change is a switch to Girling disc (segment type) brakes on the front wheels. The back wheels retain the 11 in by $2\frac{1}{4}$ in drums. Stopping power is, though quite smooth, of the *right now* variety. Not nearly as much pedal pressure is required as with the racing-option full disc set-up nor, for that matter, as with the earlier drums. No matter how we pounded it we could not induce fade or more than a tiny fraction of pedal loss. This tiny loss could probably be traceable to lining wear in the rear drum brakes which were kept working overtime to keep up with the discs. Stops

Pouring on the coal, doing 90 mph, in the first of the three-litres, the 3000 of 1959.

were almost as powerful as with the full Dunlop racing disc layout on the Sebring Healey.

'Another change, which will probably be noticed by those familiar with the BN-cars is found in the gearbox. Low gear has been raised to 2.93:1 as opposed to 3.076 in the earlier box. Second has been *dropped* in ratio to 2.053 as opposed to 1.913 and third has been raised to 1.309, replacing the former 1.333. The effect is a bit disconcerting at first to a BN6 driver due to the close spacing of first and second gears and the wide jump into third. We fail to see the reason for increasing this spread unless it is to produce second gear lugging ability . . .

'The overdrive unit, too, has been changed. It's less radical now with a 0.822 step-up instead of the 0.778 ratio used formerly. This has the favourable result that the engine can now peak in overdrive, formerly virtually impossible . . .'

Christy wound up by saying the handling was even better with final mild over-steer, although he couldn't just see how it had been achieved, and the top was much better. Different coil springs was the answer, but to continue his summing up 'the new Austin-Healey 3000 is a comfortable car, a fast car, and a very quick car. Above all it is an eminently safe car. Even more important, it's a good *sports* car.'

The Autocar managed to land a 3000, with hardtop, in the same month, and devoted much of their test to performance figures. 'Compared with the last road test of a six-cylinder Austin-Healey which was fitted with a 4.1:1 axle ratio—that of the 3000 is 3.9:1—there is a cut of 4.9 secs in the time from 0-100 mph. Acceleration in the gears pays more generous dividends from the 50-70 mph range and upwards; over that range in overdrive third, top and overdrive top, there are reductions of 0.7, 0.6 and 1.3 secs on the last model's times. As the engine speed rises, the times are cut further, and in the same gears between 70-90 mph, the times come down by 1.1, 1.0 and 3.2 secs. In the 80-100 mph range in top gear and overdrive top improvements of 4.1 and 3.4 secs are recorded.

'A noteworthy achievement is the gain in maximum speeds. In overdrive top there is an increase of 5 mph to 116 mph, while in normal top the speed has gone up from 100 mph recorded by the 100-Six in May 1958 to no less than 110 mph for the new 3000 model . . .

'There is no doubt that the times taken for these tests, up to 70 mph at least, could have been improved if the gear change had not been so stiff, and if the rear wheels had maintained contact with the ground on initial take-off. As soon as the clutch was fully home and power applied, each time a test start was made, it was difficult to avoid axle hop.'

The next month Bolster tested the same car, YOJ502, for *Autosport*, and managed a better 0-60 time of 10.8 secs with a similar top speed, and a standing quarter mile of 17.6 secs, supporting *The Autocar*'s contention that the gearchange needed loosening up. Even a month of hard testing later, former Grand Prix driver Bolster said the gearlever was still stiff. 'In the past I have sometimes criticised BMC engines for their lack of "bottom end" performance,' said Bolster. 'The designers have now found the trick, and this big new six has all the torque in the world almost down to zero revs. It does tend to pink, and runs on when the ignition is switched off, which makes one hope that an aluminium head may later be offered as an extra. It is a power unit which joins in the fun when hard driving is afoot, and though it is fairly audible inside the small car, it never becomes rough when driven hard . . .

'It is fair to say that the present suspension set-up is ideal for 90 per cent of customers, but the remainder would applaud a little stiffening up here and there . . .

'The Austin-Healey 3000 is a genuine 115 mph car which will yet appeal to many drivers who never exceed "eighty". It gives a wonderful feeling of reserve power which is perhaps one of motoring's greatest enjoyments. A touch of the pedal sends it flying uphill, and one never seems to be overdriving it. In spite of its great performance, the car employs no unusual components, and there is nothing to worry the most remote country garage.'

Road and Track had a wonderful time with their road test 3000. 'All of *Road and Track*'s previous road tests of Austin-Healeys have been performed in California under practically identical conditions. In the case of the new 3000 model, a slight obstacle presented itself. This obstacle was some 2,800 miles of road between New York (where the only two 3000s in the country happened to be at the end of May) and California, where the test crew waited with anxious eyes on the deadline for this issue.

'Quickly our small, but enthusiastic, New York staff, consisting of Harvey B. Janes, Eastern Editor, and David E. Davis, Eastern Advertising Manager, offered a solution. They would drive one of the new cars non-stop from New York to the *Road and Track* offices in California. Thus we would have our test car in plenty of time and they would be firmly established as heroes, having set all sorts of coast-to-coast driving records.

'They got underway in the early evening of a Monday and, with the aid of a package of innocent-looking, but highly-potent, pep pills, pulled up at the *Road and Track* offices a little over fifty seven hours later, full of praise for the car, and for their own powers of endurance. When we informed them that a certain French economy sedan had covered the same distance in roughly fifty hours, they were only mildly impressed. The drivers of this French car, they told us, had cheated: they had not stopped to eat along the way. Of the total elapsed time of fifty-seven hours in the Healey, at least three and a half hours had been consumed in various restaurants along the route.

'In addition, they had been forced to drive through a wild rainstorm and flood in Ohio and had wasted nearly an hour in a bootleg sports car garage outside of St Louis trying to replace a silly little rubber grommet that had fallen off the throttle linkage and into a sealed compartment under the instrument panel. In view of all this, our drivers steadfastly and with glassy eyes claimed the following coast-to-coast records: fastest trip in an English car; fastest in an Austin-Healey; fastest in a three-litre car; fastest in a four-seater roadster with detachable hard top; fastest by a bearded and moustachioed two-man crew. We might add that it was also the longest distance ever covered in the course of a *Road and Track* test.'

And so the test went on, full of good spirits. Everybody who drove the Big Healey agreed that in the matter of performance and smoothness it was pleasantly similar to the original Jaguar XK 120, praise indeed from the dedicated American sports car fans. *Road and Track* had difficulty in finding a straight long enough to

reach top speed, but finally came up with this chart comparing various Big Healeys
they had tested:

	3000	*Mille Miglia*	*100-Six*	*100*
Time 0–40	5.2	5.2	6.1	6.2
0–60	9.8	10.4	12.2	11.7
0–80	17.5	19.2	22.5	20.8
Standing $\frac{1}{4}$ mile	17.1	17.4	18.2	18.1
Top speed	112.5	109	105	102

And their conclusion was: 'The new Austin-Healey 3000 is a real enthusiasts'
sports car: fun to drive, with lots of performance and good handling and braking
characteristics. It could have better cockpit ventilation and seating position, and we
still wish that the manufacturer would return to the cleaner styling of the older four-
cylinder cars, but these are only minor grievances. Dollar for dollar this is still one
of the top sports cars on the market.'

Soon after, *The Motor* tested a hardtop overdrive version, recording similar
performance figures except for top speed, which worked out at 115 mph average,
117 mph best. which was strange, as it seemed unlikely that they could have found
a longer straight than in America. Perhaps they were less observant of the 5,200 rpm
limit which *Road and Track* refused to exceed in deference to the car's handbook.

The Motor went against the usual trend in defending the Big Healey's driving
position. 'The close conjunction of windscreen and driver is reminiscent of older

The Motor's Mark II test car posing
serenely in a side street. Later it suffered somewhat on rougher roads
following the Alpine Rally.

sports cars and, despite a low seating position and a long broad bonnet, provides excellent visibility and a view of the road surface surprisingly close ahead. In addition, dirt or rain on the glass reduce visibility much less than with a distant screen and better protection is obtained from the wind when the car is open; in this form the Austin-Healey is a very pleasant machine, and with the sidescreens erect it is possible to cruise at speeds in the region of 80 mph without undue buffeting or turbulence, although with considerable wind noise as must be expected in an open car.'

The Motor went on to point out that one of the disadvantages of the 6 lb extra tyre pressure needed for consistent speeds over 85 mph was scuttle shake, although everything else benefited from higher pressures at speed. They also found the gearbox's ratios satisfactorily close, and suggested that the brakes might benefit from a servo.

'A little attention to seating comfort and a few modifications to some of the minor controls would still further improve a car which now offers quite extraordinary performance in relation to its cost, taking performance in its broadest sense to include acceleration, maximum speed, roadholding and braking. The winning of the team award amongst other striking successes, in the recent Alpine Rally, shows that durability is another attribute that must be added to the list,' said *The Motor*.

Almost as soon as the 3000 was announced AC racing ace Ken Rudd from Worthing started trying his hand at tuning a Big Healey, which he had also raced from time to time. The results were spectacular with a claimed 178 bhp being produced without resorting to an extra high lift camshaft and dark threats of 200 to come with a wild cam. Bolster was the first to test the 'fire-eating monster' as he called it in *Autosport* in March 1960. The beast had a polished cylinder head with oversize ports, special cam and triple SUs on Rudd-designed finned alloy short stub manifolds. A works-style exhaust system completed the engine ensemble and normal works-style suspension modifications were offered separately with Michelin X 6.40 × 15 tyres in relieved arches.

The normally-imperturbable Bolster was of the opinion that these chassis modifications were 'absolutely essential' and with Rudd's road test car 9380PO duly recorded 0–60 in 9.4 secs, 0–100 in 21.6 (against a generally-accepted 32 secs), a standing-start quarter mile in 16.8 and 125 mph top speed with hood and sidescreens erect on the new M1 motorway. 'The hood stands up to this great velocity remarkably well, but the sidescreens tend to bulge outwards,' said Bolster. 'The work on the suspension eliminates the flap and patter of the front wheels, and the rear axle does not bounce during acceleration.

'It is unlikely that the average owner will ever exceed 120 mph, but above that speed he would be well advised to exercise some caution,' said the man renowned for his feats in a fearsome special called Bloody Mary. 'The machine is short and has a rather conventional chassis which becomes a little lively at the top end even in this improved form. Bumps and gusts of wind tend to deflect the car somewhat, but under suitable conditions it is safe to attain 125 mph.'

Six months later Dennis May managed to get 9380PO up to 126 mph on the speedometer for *SCI* but could not match Bolster's acceleration figures. He appre-

Cornering hard in the fearsome Rudd-speed Healey.

ciated the car's brake servo and said that although Rudd was still working towards 200 bhp, reliability upwards of 180 bhp would be conjectural; 'and the requisite practical development work has not yet been essayed and won't be in the foreseeable future.' It seems it never was, despite claims of this amount *at the wheels* later by Abingdon. Experienced tuners have reckoned 175 bhp to be the top reliable figure and pointed out that Abingdon's dynamometer was renowned for its optimism!

As it was, May said that the performance of 9380PO over 3,000 rpm was quite exceptional and Rudd himself said he could have matched Bolster's acceleration figures had the road been completely dry. *Motor Sport* tried 9380PO soon after and commented on its cockpit heat in London traffic, despite the liberal use of asbestos around the bulkhead and cooling slots cut in the body. The inch or so of play on the accelerator pedal that 'becomes so annoying' on the standard model had been eliminated and acceleration was 'truly prodigious.' So was the top speed: the speedometer needle went right off the clock along the Missenden by-pass! In fact, *Motor Sport* could not find a road long enough to check the top speed, but estimated it at 125 mph with 0–60 in 9.6 secs. 'In modified form, the Austin-Healey showed little refinement compared with, say, a Porsche or Jaguar,' they said, 'and it is undeniably a "man's car" as defined by vintage car enthusiasts. The steering is fairly heavy, the suspension is definitely stiff, the exhaust note is on the throaty side . . . and the gearbox needs a strong left arm. But on the basis of excitement per mph per £1 this car

Ken Rudd extracted 178 bhp with the help of his special finned manifolds.

is undoubtedly tops.'

The Motor managed to try a similar car in February 1961. They knew they were in for some excitement when Abingdon's dynamometer showed 145 bhp at the wheels of the car, John Gott's old rally wagon SMO746. The official flywheel figure for the engine was 180 bhp, so presumably the power was about the same as that of Rudd's car, with triple SUs on long manifolds. The rally car weighed in at $\frac{1}{2}$ cwt more than the standard $22\frac{1}{2}$ cwt for an early 3000 but, nevertheless, gave The Motor 'tremendous fun to drive in a way which has almost vanished with the passing of the bigger sports-racing cars of the post-war decade. The exhaust, which has a deep bathplug gurgle at tickover develops the most purposeful hard and hollow ring as soon as the revs start to rise, almost drowning the crescendo howl of straight-cut gears. A clutch which is immensely positive, not unduly heavy and yet needs only the token movement of a pre-war Austin 7, a gearbox with very close ratios, powerful synchromesh and short, light movements and a carefully arranged progressive throttle linkage all combine to provide the most enjoyable gearchange we have encountered on a large-engined car and one which we used far more than necessary just for the fun of it.'

Unfortunately *The Motor*'s test runs were spoiled by bad weather that even whipped off a sidescreen and they did not take a top speed reading, only estimating the terminal velocity at 125 mph, with a 16.7 sec standing quarter mile under full test load of $26\frac{1}{4}$ cwt on a wet track and 23.9 secs for the magic ton. They also commented on the steering, saying it was 'remarkably light for such a car wearing Dunlop Duraband tyres, and there is no very obvious reason why this should be so. It has the benefit of skilled assembly, careful maintenance and frequent greasing, but the steering box is the standard one made by Cam Gears, the castor angle is not reduced and the general geometry is altered only as a by-product of the suspension raising.' It did have the old 12.6:1 ratio, though . . .

The Motor and *The Autocar* were predictably just about the only magazine's which managed to fit in a test of the short-lived triple carburetter Mark II. *The Motor*'s test was the most comprehensive, carried out over 4,000 miles in France, Italy and Switzerland while reporting the Morley Brothers' win with XJB876 in the Alpine Rally. 'One might say that 85 per cent of what we felt was keen enthusiasm for this car; it is capable of well over 110 mph on level road, has acceleration and braking to match its top speed, is quite pleasantly controllable, and delights both driver and passenger by providing a really comfortable ride in two excellent seats. The remaining 15 per cent of our reaction was dismay that a company which has big resources and has been developing this series of Austin-Healeys for eight years is still delivering cars with two familiar and quite serious, but demonstrably curable shortcomings in respect of ground clearance and heat in the cockpit.

'From the fact that differences between a Mark II Austin-Healey and its immediate predecessors centre around a third carburetter and a high-lift camshaft, one might be forgiven for expecting this version to put all emphasis on high performance. In actual fact, whilst an ability to reach 100 mph from rest in 36.4 secs and less than $\frac{3}{4}$-mile of road testifies to the reality of its performance, smooth running and easy riding are the characteristics which really distinguish this model from other fast cars. Its primary appeal may be sporting, as appearances suggest, but the comfort and driving ease which accompany a delightful power to accelerate clear of obstructive traffic could make this a better "executive's car" than are many more cumbrous saloons . . .

'Should the weather be even moderately hot, some cockpit surfaces become fairly warm (despite a substantial amount of asbestos sheeting, visible only when the car is raised on a hoist), and a most unwelcome volume of hot (but not smelly) air from the engine blows into the body through concealed bonnet hinges, around the doors or past the corners of the facia panel. Using our test model to follow and report

the French Alpine Rally, which was won by a factory-entered Austin-Healey 3000 fitted with neat-looking additional hot-air outlets alongside the engine and additional air inlets and outlets for the cockpit, we wondered very much why production cars could not be similarly equipped: our test car's engine did not overheat, but its passenger's (who had retained the removable hard top as an anti-theft protection for their photographic equipment) certainly did.

'A contrast with the team cars was also very evident in respect of ground clearance, and whilst a great increase could not be obtained without sacrificing some of the spring travel which lets production models ride so comfortably, it would not be difficult to eliminate vulnerable projections below the flat underside of this model's sturdy chassis. The low-set exhaust pipes have already been arranged and mounted so that frequent use of them as toboggan runners does no harm, as a moderately well laden car will ground them occasionally even on main road undulations, and very frequently on bad roads; but during our test mileage the electrical wiring to all the rear lights was severed and there were visible signs of abrasion on the clutch operating hydraulic pipe, the main petrol pipe and the steel sump of the engine.'

The Motor returned better figures from 70 mph in top with the triple carb model than their earlier 3000 but it found it to be inferior on acceleration below that with 2 mph less in top speed. From standstill to 60 mph took 10.9 secs, to 70 took 14.3, to 80, 19.2, to 90, 25.9 and 100 came up in 36.4. The standing quarter mile took 18.3 secs and the top speed turned out at an average of 112.9 mph with a best of 113.6. Fuel consumption on what was undoubtedly a hard test worked out at 20.8 mpg, with an estimate of 23.5 for more normal driving. They wound up by saying: 'We have felt it necessary to criticise some aspects of this Austin-Healey quite strongly, and we know many owners of slightly earlier models are equally critical about the same faults of cockpit overheating and underside vulnerability which could and should be cured. We also know that despite these complaints many an Austin-Healey is changed only for a later model of the same car, because owners would rather put up with the faults than forgo the unique combination of comfort and high performance which this car offers at a very reasonable price. Despite its short-comings, many other people . . . will find that this model ranks as their best buy.'

After that what was there left to say about the Mark II? *The Autocar* reckoned it was comfortable, immensely strong and rigid, when they tested it in December 1961. It cruised all day at 90-plus and gave a feeling of great confidence, even at 100 mph hands-off. The car displayed acceptably slight understeer and occasionally needed a little opposite lock, but *The Autocar* said that it would be difficult even for an inexperienced driver to get into trouble with this car. Their chief complaints centred around lack of automatic support for the bonnet and boot lids—a point which had been raised as long ago as 1957 by *Motor Sport*. Other points which struck *The Autocar* scribes were sharp clips on the hard top. They considered them bad for the head.

In October 1962, they tested the convertible a couple of months after it came out and complained of the sharp edge on the quarter light frame which has been catching out Healey owners ever since. They also thought it was about time the Big Healey was given a steering rack like the rest of BMC's sports cars and wondered why the steering wheel was so big. To complete their grouses they missed taking performance figures because the car had a 3.91 axle instead of the standard 3.55 for overdrive and commented that the wind noise at 80 was the same as ever.

SCI's American successor *Car and Driver* described it as an 'aerodynamic Edwardian with roll-up windows' in March 1963. It was 'a nearly perfect exposition of the pre-war two-seater brought up to date' by virtue of its massive masculinity and a hood that could be raised from inside the car.

Patrick McNally was also happy about the car when he tested it for *Autosport* in August 1963. He liked almost everything about it and managed comprehensive performance figures: 0–60 in 9.8 secs, the standing quarter mile in 17.5 secs and 118.5 mph flat out. 'The most impressive figure, however, is the 0–80,' said McNally, 'which is 17.8 secs—this gives a very useful turn of acceleration. The 100 which tends to be an everyday feature of this car, takes just over 27 secs, figures which show a big improvement over the earlier 3000.' He said that the new windscreen cleared up previous blind spots, but complained of scuttle shake, caused by lack of rigidity while under power and cornering fast. 'It must be stated that this scuttle shake had no apparent effect on the handling of the car—it was just annoying,' said the un-flappable McNally, who was doing rather well racing at the time. His performance figures were rather good, too, because 'when one waited for the synchromesh, the acceleration figures suffered by a second or so!' *Autosport* writers could be relied upon to get the best out of a car.

Similar comments were made and similar figures recorded—except for an off-the-clock 122 mph average—by *Cars Illustrated*, successor to the British edition of *SCI*, who found the occasional seats of 'real value,' although their extra leg room rather cramped the driver. *Cars Illustrated* also pleaded for quarter lights in the hood to alleviate a blind spot, said an oil cooler was a worthwhile investment, and defended the Big Healey against 'an unfortunate reputation for bad roadholding that it has acquired for no very apparent reason.' Their car handled very well—obviously drivers of elderly and hard-used examples were running into problems with worn suspension by the 1960s and running all Big Healeys down as a result.

Finally, *The Motor* wrapped it all up for the last of the Mark IIs on test. They said: 'Some enthusiasts feel that the modern, refined, open two-seater is insufficiently masculine to qualify as a sports car. There are, however, some manufacturers who have not yet started making velvety, all-independent sporting machines with a sort of unobtrusive high performance. BMC turn out the Austin-Healey 3000 which, despite a number of up-to-date attractions is a strong-willed survivor of a more hairy-chested era. It has a big six-cylinder engine which revs lazily in a sturdy chassis and gives lots of smooth power and an exciting performance. Cornering is good without much body roll, the steering is light, and the brakes with the optional servo are first-class. The new hood is easy to fold away, although it does not stow completely out of sight, and the winding windows and more deeply curved screens are useful concessions to comfort. It is a pity the concessions do not extend to an

First of the Mark III's on test with *The Motor* in 1964.

improvement in driving comfort, but the old problem of cockpit heat seems to have been alleviated, although the persistent Austin-Healey shortcomings of restricted ground clearance remains. This is surprising as seasons pass with further rally successes by the works Austin-Healeys whose spectacular wins have demanded better clearance than the standard machines. One wonders why the rather obvious modifications necessary to give something more than a niggardly $4\frac{1}{2}$ inches have not been made. Of the masculinity of the Austin-Healey 3000 there is no doubt; whether taming 130-odd horsepower is actually *liked* or not depends on the driver possessing the necessary skill and a certain amount of stout-heartedness. Certainly, on a performance/price basis, the car has few equals.'

The Motor were feeling much the same when they tested one of the early Mark IIIs in March 1964. 'Makes and models come and go while the Big Healey still gathers momentum,' they reported. 'Within a production run reaching back twelve years to 1962, the car must surely be approaching the end of an unusually long and successful line that has bred international competition winners, earned a lot of dollars and above all, provided relatively inexpensive high performance for enthusiasts throughout the world. In its latest form, the combination of speed, refinement and character is still outstanding value . . . It is now a unique blend of vintage sports and modern GT. A little of the original Healey 100 still remains: the classic looks; firm ride; only marginal ground clearance; the vintage driving position and a take-off that few cars can equal regardless of price. In other respects it has mellowed with age, reflecting the changing tastes of its ardent supporters—or perhaps a new more sophisticated generation of sports car drivers. Popular demand had turned the original stark cockpit into a snug and fashionable office with polished wood on the facia and a driving console down the middle that looks good but gets in the way. Even the passenger's grab handle has been replaced by a glove box. Gone, too, is the loveable bark. Two exhaust pipes and four silencers have subdued the noise to a pleasant grumble that is drowned at high speeds by the whirl of fan, intakes and wind.

'Yet this is no cissy sports car. A top speed of 122.5 mph is fast by any standards and quite exceptional for £1,200. Moreover it will accelerate to 120 mph in little more than a mile in satisfying surges that whip it across country at high average speeds. Handling and steering are by no means outstanding by modern standards but better than first acquaintance and many old hands would suggest, and the car satisfies the sporting tradition by being great fun to drive even if it takes time and knowhow to make friends.

'In a nutshell, you now go faster in greater (but by no means sumptuous) comfort on no more petrol—a fair return for long-term development.'

Only Bolster could follow that eulogy in Britain and he sensibly concentrated on performance figures with his Mark III, commenting only that 'now it has winding windows and a really good hood it can be regarded as a practical coupe rather than a "hairy" sports car, yet it is still primarily for the he-man.' His figures were: 0–60 in 9.9 secs; 0–80 in 15, 0–100 in 24.3 and 17 to 19 mpg with a top speed of 118.4 which he considered he could have bettered with a longer road.

Cars Illustrated had much the same thing to say about the Mark III, almost unremitting praise, but made the interesting observation that 'the boot also houses a

Does it bite? *The Motor* had fun with their Mark III in 1964.

battery master switch. Since no locks are fitted to the doors, it is possible to operate this switch and immobilise the car by cutting off the supply of electricity, the boot lid then being locked. Unfortunately, the switch also cuts off the supply for the side-lamps, so that one's field of parking after dark may thus be limited.' Surely it was not the first time somebody had said that, although it certainly seemed to be the first time in print. Perhaps that is why Big Healeys were one of the most popular cars for the thieves of the time.

The Autocar found the lack of locks rather incongruous now that the Big Healey had wind-up windows and a plush interior. But they liked the hood's zip-out back window and found it an aid to ventilation. Other good new points included the diaphragm spring clutch as fitted to the later Mark IIs, which was 'nice and light.' *The Autocar* were rather sad, though, that they could not test the Mark III on their usual pave track for fear of wiping off the exhaust system, while they found this early model tricky to handle even on a moderately bumpy side road. 'Despite some dated features, the Big Healey is still terrific fun to drive,' they said. 'Tractable, capable of an immense amount of hard work with reasonable economy, it will still have its devotees long after production has ceased.' Prophetic words, indeed.

In the September of that year, *The Autocar* managed a test in one of the last Big Healeys build for rallying, DRX258C, campaigned by the Morley twins. It came complete with seven headlights, side-swiped rear wing and dust from the Dauphi-nois, and went like nothing else they had ever driven: 'Whatever the cause, it gives immediate confidence and makes one want to go straight out on a circuit and get the car *drifting*. As it was, we had to make do with some pseudo rally routes around the Home Counties, but even so we found ourselves driving on well into the night just for the sheer exhilaration of it.

'With a flood of light boring a tunnel for miles ahead there is no need to reduce speed after dark. Thundering between hedges and grass banks one is forever at work;

'Driving for the sheer exhilaration of it . . .' *The Autocar* test the Morley Brothers' battle wagon in 1965.

up through the gears, lift off for a curve, back on the throttle, into overdrive then out again, hard on the brakes for a sudden hazard, back on the throttle—that's the way it goes. In between tweaks at the wheel, stabs on the throttle and brakes, and thrusts with the gearlever (forward, back across, up and down with the switch for overdrive), there are flicks at the light switches for better illumination or reducing the glare as a courtesy to other traffic (what are they doing here at this time of night?)

'And all the time there is that pulsating beat in the ears, rising and falling as the rev counter needle springs towards the red line and then falls back as though bouncing on a rubber stop. It's a real case of *son et lumiere* without the history attached, just the present as we can live it now for fun, a man's motoring that saps up adrenalin and leaves one flushed at the end like sailing through a storm or ski-ing in a blizzard.'

Obviously the rally Healey deserves to be one of the all-time classics. *Cars and Car Conversions*, the successor to *Cars Illustrated*, felt just about as emotional when they tested a Mark III in October 1965. 'This is something of a he-man's motor-car, Pat Moss Carlsson aside,' said Triple C. 'It is heavy, rough, slightly crude, noisy, and at high speed takes a bit of driving. In fact, it's almost vintage, really, and you might think that there is no excuse for this sort of car nowadays apart from the trifling fact that it still sells as fast as they can make it, and it is still more than capable of winning any international rally you care to mention . . .

'The power unit is a pretty unrefined slab of iron—four main bearings for the crankshaft, cast-iron head, push-rod overhead valves and so forth—and once the needle goes past 5,000, is almost terrifyingly rough in standard unbalanced tune. But, of course, it never has to work terribly hard, produces an adequate amount of surge and in general keeps the Healey lolloping along at a brisk old trot in fine style.

It isn't desperately economical and few owners mind that. If you can afford the insurance premium you ought to be able to pour in the go-juice alright.'

And so the test by the magazine that was to cater for the new brand of sports car, the Mini-Cooper and Lotus Cortinas went on. Triple C just loved the Big Healey. 'At just over a thousand pounds, including purchase tax, the Big Healey probably offers more urge per pound sterling than nearly any other motor.' Some admission by the Mini men.

The last road test of a Big Healey at the time of writing was by Michael Bowler in *Thoroughbred and Classic Cars* in March 1974. Bowler, who had been a *Motor* road tester when the last model was introduced ten years earlier and helped the David Dixon team with the renowned Big Healey racer DD 300 at Le Mans in 1961, said: 'Was the car really as good as you remembered or had time and development changed standards so quickly? I'm pleased to say that memory wasn't at fault having just driven a genuine 1971 Healey with 16,000 miles on the clock. It was like new and just as I remembered from ten years ago. How it came about is an interesting story.

'Three years ago John Chatham was having a lot of success in a big Healey in modified sports car racing. During this time he had acquired sufficient spares—chassis, body panels, mechanical parts, etc—almost to build a complete car and indeed had nearly started to do so. A Mr Pinell had called on Chatham, seen the bits and insisted that the car be built up as new for him: this was done during 1971 and it was registered on 1st August 1971—a new car. Subsequently he used it as a fun car, even to the extent of going on holiday with two children in the back seat: a luggage rack sits on top of the boot. The only non-standard items are the Minilite wheels with Michelin XAS tyres, a headlamp flasher and a small Motolita steering wheel. Pinell's children have become too big and now the car is being offered for sale . . .

'Finished in the standard Healey red with a fawn hood it looked in first class condition; on the road everything felt as good. The engine was nice and taut but free-revving; gearbox and overdrive flicked in and out with ease and I didn't find the close first and second upsetting. There were no rattles in either body or hood on most roads and it was only over a badly broken surface that its vintage ancestry was at all apparent; certainly the dampers were still working and the car felt nice and responsive even on the wet roads around that day. Actually the big wheels and the small steering wheel worked very well; there was little kickback and it was no great effort to steer even at low speeds. Michelin XAS gave rather better wet grip than the old Dunlop RS5s so it is quite a practical modification, but for the sake of originality I would rather revert to the original road wheels and larger steering wheel.

'The exhaust system didn't ground at all and still had the characteristic resonance around 2,500 rpm, the urgent sound of a car that is ready and willing to be driven far and fast.

'Faith was thus restored; faith in Healeys and faith in my own memory. It is still a tremendous fun car; all right, it doesn't have the ride and roadholding of a Lotus Elan or even of its eventual successor, the Jensen Healey. It doesn't quite have the acceleration of either but it is just faster in top speed than both.'

I doubt whether John Bolster would have been disappointed if he had driven that original Healey 100 again at Jabbeke twenty-five years later.

V
The Competition Healeys

Facing page: The start of a fantastic career: DD300 in its original green paint, registered UJB143, racing at Le Mans with Jack Sears and Peter Riley in 1960; it also competed at Sebring in the same year and was driven by Pat Moss in the Tour of Corsica in 1961.

Below: DD300, still green, at Silverstone in 1961 after competing again at Le Mans.

Right: DD 300, by now Healey blue, fights it out with the Sapphire at Castle Combe in 1966.

Below: DD 300, rebuilt by John Chatham and sprayed fire engine red, leads John Quick's E type in the AMASCO modsports championship of 1967.

Left: DD300, green again, still with Chatham driving, leads a historic field at Silverstone in 1976. Hard on its tail are the XK120s of John Harper (PCY189L) and David Preece.

Below: Still in the lead, DD300 fights it out with David Preece's XK120 at Castle Combe.

THE BIG HEALEY was a competitive car right from the start. Only a few days after its debut at the London Motor Show, Donald Healey took one of the prototypes back to his favourite piece of motorway near Jabbeke to break Belgian class records at 111.7 mph with a top recorded speed of 113 mph. It more than confirmed to any doubting Thomases that the Bolster road test was no freak. Much of that winter was spent preparing for production, but the three special test cars were put to good use as soon as the new season started.

One of the lightweight cars was given to *Autosport* editor Gregor Grant to compete in the tough Lyons-Charbonnieres Rally with Peter Reece. The car showed great potential until the savage mountain roads ripped up its back suspension. The gallant Grant and Reece worked wonders to struggle on to the end but the car's rally potential was obviously limited in standard form.

The Healey family took this setback in their stride, though, and were quietly confident of a good run in the 1953 Mille Miglia road race. The special test cars were driven down to the start at Brescia and desultory inspections were made of the Italian autoroutes in the area because they could not afford to practice the whole route. Instead they relied on pace notes supplied by their Swiss distributor, Count Johnny Lurani, who knew the course well. Besides, the Healey family had competed before and Donald regarded the 1,000 mile thrash as an excellent, but un-daunting, test for vehicles. As it was, the first stage was too much of a thrash for Bert Hadley's 100, which retired with a broken throttle linkage. Heartbreak struck the other Big Healey only sixteen miles from the finish, when it, too, had to retire;

1953: Gatsonides and Lockett's 'special test car' leads a Cunningham and an Aston Martin DB3S at Le Mans.

with clutch trouble. Needless to say these two faults were promptly rectified and the experienced passed on to the production cars.

All three cars were prepared for the Le Mans race soon after with 103 bhp engines. Suspension was uprated in a similar way to that of the 100M kit to come. A high-ratio rear axle and overdrive was fitted to keep the revs within the critical 4,500 limit for reliability and a large fuel tank was incorporated to reduce pit stops. Alfin drums were used on two-leading shoe brakes, but did not prove so good as the discs of the winning Jaguars. Only two cars were entered, and it was a good job there was a spare as the third was wrecked in a road accident before the race.

Nevertheless, the race was a triumph for the Big Healeys. The two cars, complete with alloy bumpers, finished twelfth and fourteenth, lapping with great regularity at around 90 mph. Despite their lightweight specification they were the cheapest and least modified cars in the race and looked it. Everybody was impressed, particularly *Autocourse*, who said: 'The performance of the two Austin-Healeys in the hands of Becquart/Wilkins and Gatsonides/Lockett, probably the cheapest cars in the race, was remarkable.' Others thought so, too, and the two special test cars were only beaten in their class by an exotic Gordini driven by Grands Prix aces Trintignant and Schell. It was a wonderful boost to the car's already soaring sales.

That wasn't enough for Donald Healey, though. He wanted to impress the Americans on their own ground, so he followed the example of the Austin Atlantic in 1949 and annexed every American stock car record from five miles to 3,000 kms and one to twenty-four hours. The standard car's average speed never dropped

1954: The Macklin/Huntoon 100S prototype is prepared for its twelve-hour ordeal at Sebring.

below 104 mph on the Bonneville Salt Flats with a fuel consumption of 21 mpg; proof enough of the car's speed, economy and reliability. At the same time, NOJ391, veteran of the Mille Miglia and Le Mans achieved 142.64 mph over a flying mile, although it was readily admitted that she had been modified. Between them the drivers, Castrol director Capt. George Eyston (famed for his knowledge of the salty course), film star Jackie Cooper, Donald Healey himself, Roy Jackson-Moore and Gordon Benett took 130 records.

Then it was back to Britain and one of the special test cars took eleventh place in the Goodwood Nine Hour race in the hands of Lockett and Ken Rudd, a reserve at Le Mans who was later to produce his own astonishingly fast Big Healey. A few British private owners managed to get their hands on Big Healeys including the renowned Betty Haig and David Shale. Shale was happy with his car and enjoyed some success, but Betty found her machine, NUE854, a bit of a handful after her lithe MGs. Years later, she said in *Motor Sport*: 'The car had a shocking three-speed gearbox and was practically undriveable due to rear axle wind-up. Healeys did try to help, though. With a Barwell-tuned head the car really flew and a 3.2 axle was put in to enable them to uncork bottom gear. But the front end really was terrible and on snow this Austin-Healey wouldn't steer even with chains on all four wheels. It was too high-geared for the Paris–St Raphael rally and by getting dug into snow banks on the corners choked its radiator and boiled. It was pleasant enough on the road, but I sold it because I was so frightened of it.' Obviously, the Big Healey was ideal for road races, but needed a lot of development for rallies.

Another early competitor was an American, Bob Cottam, who took delivery of his 100 in Germany in October 1953 as he prepared for a season of rallying. Cottam did so well that he received works Porsche backing, but kept the Healey for smaller events, winning the Hockenheim International Gymkhana, a gold medal in the Trifels Rally and second place in the Trifels hill climb, plus a first in a Nurburgring sports car race. The only trouble encountered was from the exhaust system and loose shock absorbers. Cottam eventually took the car back to America and drove it 80,000 miles with little trouble before selling it.

Despite the success of the lightweight special test cars, it was obvious that the works would have to find more power and lose more weight for the 100 to be really successful against the racing sports cars which by 1954 were becoming increasingly specialized. The special test cars were further modified to form the prototype 100S with one being completed in time for the American endurance race at Sebring that spring. The drivers were Lance Macklin (son of Sir Noel Macklin, who had backed Donald Healey before the war), and an amateur from Florida, George Huntoon. As the twelve-hour race wore on, the specialized racing cars destroyed each other, leaving only Stirling Moss in the lead in a brakeless OSCA and Rubirosa, in a Lancia, ahead of Macklin. Despite a broken rocker arm putting the 100S on to only three cylinders, Macklin hung on to third place, a 'truly phenomenal result' for a car bearing such a close resemblance to a standard production machine, according to American witnesses. The Big Healey was going from success to success in America.

Naturally replicas of the 100S were in great demand after that and the works prepared themselves for a production run. They also entered three 100Ss for the

1954: One of the first of the Big Healey rally cars in action in the Tulip.

Mille Miglia, with Macklin, Louis Chiron and Tommy Wisdom as drivers. Macklin doggedly outpaced the rival Triumph T R 2s and the other 100Ss retired; but Macklin's overall placing was not high—23rd—and a disappointed Donald Healey announced his withdrawal from racing, complaining that international regulations were not giving his team a fair break. The motor racing public were horrified, pointing out that although the 100S cars looked standard they were far removed from normal production machines. Nevertheless, Donald Healey, who had issued his statement jointly with Austins, stuck to his guns and withdrew his team of 100s from the Le Mans race, which was mopped up by the triumphant new D type Jaguars. It is ironic that the Jaguar went on to become the basis of one of the most successful production sports cars ever: the E type.

Then it was back to Bonneville in August for more record breaking. Once again, NOJ391, now up to 100S specification, plus sixteen-inch alloy peg drive wheels as used on the D type Jaguar, smashed numerous records—fifty-three in all—including the 3,000 miles at 132.1 mph, 5,000 kms at 132.2 mph, and 24 hours at 132.2 mph (a total of 3,174.9 miles). The Healey family also took along a highly-supercharged streamlined car with extended nose and tail with fin, bubble top and built-in fire extinguisher. This car with an incredible 224 bhp engine broke numerous records at 192.62 mph—and Donald Healey was at the wheel! Throughout the record attempts, the Healeys had the benefit of the vastly experienced MG record team led by Syd Enever and Alec Hounslow, who had by then been brought into the BMC camp.

Soon after, the 100S went into production and two cars were entered in the Pan-American road race, a contradiction to Donald Healey's decision to turn his back on motor racing. At least this event was well away from Europe, but it was still potentially beneficial to the all-important American sales. The five-day event was

Above: 1954: George Abecassis revs up ready for his drive to eleventh place in the Mille Miglia.

Right: Lance Macklin and Les Leston's ill-fated 100S prepares for Le Mans.

one of the toughest and most dangerous ever devised, using 2,000 miles of central Mexican roads. The two 100Ss were driven by Macklin and the rapidly rising Texan star Carroll Shelby, who had helped with the Bonneville record-breaking. He was to remember that race well, as he later recalled in *The Cobra Story* (Motorbooks International): 'I started racing with those big Lincolns and was really giving 'em hell. In fact, I passed all of them except Crawford. I had just gotten by Vukovitch and Verne Houl and taken off after Crawford when I came around a corner a little too fast and suddenly there was a big rock standing in my way. The rock never batted an eyelash, but I went end over end four or five times like the daring young man on the flying trapeze. Only it was a lot more painful . . . To put it briefly I was in a mess when the Indians picked me up and threw a blanket over me.' Fortunately Shelby recovered after eight months, but the car was a write-off. Macklin was disqualified for arriving late at a control and later recounted in *Safety Fast*: 'The 100S was a tough reliable motor car and was about the only car that you could start off in something like the Mille Miglia or Pan American and be pretty sure to finish. In fact, in the Mille Miglia, although I had troubles, I think I finished every time I was driving a Healey. It was a frightening car to drive in the wet—it certainly oversteered rather violently—and it was difficult to keep on the road at 130-140 on those slippery Italian roads, probably more so than contemporary cars such as the Aston Martin. It was a car that always amazed me; considering that it was only an old taxi engine it was remarkable how fast it could be made to go.'

After the Pan American race, Macklin was expected to drive the 100S 3,000 miles to Nassau for the speed trials there, but he hitched a lift on a plane and 'Donald was horrified when I told him I'd flown as I thought it would be quicker. He thought I'd run him up an enormous bill.' In the event, the 100S broke a stub axle, which could have been very difficult en route to Nassau by road!

Meanwhile the 100M conversions were starting to filter out to private customers. J. C. Morland from Kenya reported in *Motor Sport*: 'My Healey with Le Mans modifications was slightly faster than my Frazer-Nash Le Mans Replica—but what was wrong with my car, most unexpectedly, was the chassis. There was a good deal of scuttle shake when cornering on rough roads and this shake led to splitting and cracking of the front end of the body.

'My car was incredibly badly turned out by the local agents, so I complained to the Donald Healey Motor Company, who got cracking with Austins, and profuse apologies were forthcoming. The car went back to the agents for three weeks, after which it was rather worse than before!

'As a touring car I liked the Healey and it made fastest lap of the day at the Eldoret grass track races on Boxing Day 1954 before being written off by a police van while parked.' Service manager Geoff Price confirmed years later that shroud cracking was a serious problem with the early 100s.

The first six production 100Ss went to Sebring in 1955 as private entries for owners including Jackie Cooper, Briggs Cunningham, Bob Fergus of Ohio, Fred Allen of Pennsylvania, and a Dr Ferguson from Toronto. Macklin and Moss drove a works car, one of the two ageing special test vehicles! They took sixth place behind the winning D type Jaguar and a bunch of Ferraris and Maseratis, and with four of

1955: Donald Healey, Stirling Moss and Lance Macklin have something to cheer about at Sebring. Macklin and Moss have just driven their ageing 'special test car' into sixth place.

the other 100Ss close behind.

Macklin was again entered for the Mille Miglia with Grand Prix drivers Ron Flockhart and George Abecassis, and Donald Healey, who was by then fifty-six years old! Stirling Moss, who had been released from the Mercedes team for Sebring, won the Mille Miglia sensationally with *Motor Sport*'s Continental Correspondent Denis Jenkinson as navigator, and Abecassis in eleventh place. Macklin finished 35th with a variety of troubles including stopping to help Flockhart, who crashed into a river. But Healey was happy; he vanquished his deadly rivals, the Triumph TRs, in the production class.

The 100S returned to Le Mans as a private entry—the French had not forgiven Donald Healey for withdrawing his cars at the last moment from the previous year's race—for Macklin and 500 cc star Les Leston. Macklin was going well when he had the misfortune to become involved in the tragedy in which Pierre Levegh's Mercedes crashed into a public enclosure, killing eighty-two people. The repercussions were terrible for motor racing; horrified governments banned the sport and the attendant publicity did neither Austin-Healey nor the winning Jaguars much good either.

Three months later trouble struck Macklin again, when his 100S became involved in a seven-car smash in the Tourist Trophy on the difficult Dundrod circuit in Ulster. Two drivers were killed, and once more the publicity was bad for Healeys and although he bore no blame for the accident, a dispirited Macklin was to run only one more race.

By this time Triumphs were starting to mop up international rallies and BMC, who had decided to start racing that year, tried to do something about it with a works

100S in the 3,000-mile Liege-Sofia-Liege rally, which was more like a rougher version of the Mille Miglia road race. The 100S was to be driven by Peter Reece and Dennis Scott, but the unfortunate Scott crashed it soon after the start, before Reece had a chance to drive. Private entries fared little better in big rallies with the RAC Rally going to a Standard 10 with a TR2 second and the only 100S nowhere!

Far away, Ross Jensen was having considerable success with one of the first production 100s to reach New Zealand. The entrants, Auckland's Austin-Healey distributors, had one of the new 100Ss on order for Jensen and decided to offer the 100 to an up-and-coming young Austin 7 special driver called Bruce McLaren. The offer was accepted with alacrity by McLaren and his father, and Bruce said later in his book *From The Cockpit* (Motoraces Book Club): 'Pop decided to enter himself in the Healey for the 1955 New Zealand Grand Prix and for the next few months wrapped himself up in the car, having little time for anything else. When he finished, it was quite a sports car. After running it for 1,000 miles, he completely stripped it down and embarked on a big souping up session. Everything that moved was polished and balanced. Chrysler pistons were fitted, along with Buick cam followers and pushrod gear and Chrysler exhaust valves. The ports were opened out and highly polished and a special twin-pipe exhaust system made up.

'A full-length undertray was made and the cast-iron brake drums were refitted with plenty of cooling holes and big scoops on the back plates to draw in the air; they proved to be superb brakes with the aid of Mintex M20 linings. Finally the spring rates were changed to improve the Healey's handling and Pop could hardly wait to try it out at Ardmore. It performed to expectations and for the next three years was a class winner at nearly every event in which we entered it—even beating the 100S Healey five times at sprints!'

Illness forced Pop McLaren out of the cockpit and Bruce starred in most of those victories before moving onto Coopers for international events. By this time the Healey family were moving on too, to the six-cylinder, but the 100S and 100M continued to do yeoman service for the clubmen, notably John Dalton and David Shale, who were placed first and second in the *Autosport* championship in 1956. However the Healeys could not resist Sebring where they had had so much success and sent over two special 100Ss. It was Macklin's last race and he did not last long, for the Weber-carburetted 145 bhp cars both shook their exhaust systems to pieces. However, one of the leading Healey distributors in America, Ship and Shore Motors of Florida, managed to put a private entry for Huntoon and Phil Stiles into eleventh place.

The 100-Six of 1956 was heralded by another of the wonderfully-successful record breaking runs. The Healey team took a pair of six-cylinder cars back to Bonneville; a long-nosed BN2 with 150 bhp six-port head and the 1954 streamliner with 250 bhp supercharged C type engine. Shelby and Jackson-Moore scooped yet more international and America D class records, including the 500 miles at 153.14 mph and the six hours at 145.96 mph. Donald Healey was even more successful in the streamlined car; in one howling run he broke the magic 200 mph barrier by 3.06 mph.

The next year, 1957, was to be the start of the Big Healey's most successful competition era. Donald Healey's long-time friend and *Daily Herald* motoring correspondent, Tommy Wisdom, persuaded the Austin publicity department to let him have a 100-Six for rallying. The result was the immortal UOC741, now owned by Dave Jeffery, of Southern Carburetters. Tommy took it to the Sestriere Rally in March with his daughter Ann as co-driver. The car was near-standard and finished 83rd overall and tenth in class, but the Wisdoms had learned enough to make suggestions that Marcus Chambers, BMC's new competitions manager, realized could make the car a winner—and trounce the Triumphs.

Meanwhile, in the same month, Warwick entered three 100-Sixes for Sebring with the hope of scooping more vital publicity for the peak spring sales. These cars had long noses and Weber carburetters, but rather like the earlier and similarly shaped C type Jaguars at Le Mans they ran into engine trouble; only one managed to limp home second in its class. Tommy Wisdom shared UOC741 with Cecil Winby in the Mille Miglia that year—the last in which the classic Italian road race was run—finishing 37th with a prototype six-port head. This was the car tested by Dennis May for *Sports Cars Illustrated*. At the same time Dalton continued to wipe up club events with his 100S, RWD132, and Tony Lanfranchi—who was still racing in 1977—was going well in his 100, EVV106, formerly raced by Shale.

But the BMC works rally team captain, John Gott, had not forgotten the 100S

1956: David Shale heads for second place in the Autosport British championship. John Dalton's sister car finished first and was later raced by Dick Protheroe. Tony Lanfranchi was also successful in EVV106 later.

he had persuaded BMC to use the previous year, and he had noted the performance of UOC741 in the hands of Tommy Wisdom. So he reminded Chambers of it, who said later: 'That winter I happened to run into Geoffrey Healey and said: "That was quite a nice car you lent us. Do you think it is possible to run 100-Sixes in long-distance events?" He said: "Yes," if we carried out modifications to the chassis which they had done when they ran similar 100Ms. I said: "They're a bit low aren't they, for Alpine events?" and he said: "Jack up the springing and armour the sump." So in 1958 we started a serious attempt to run Healeys in events. The Alpine was probably the most interesting. This was the first Alpine in which we were really determined to have proper servicing facilities. We had a number of A90s equipped with one driver, two mechanics and spare parts in two categories. The parts which could be fitted before the event started, i.e. parts which were replaceable for something that might have gone wrong during the recce or practice and parts which could be fitted in the very slender time allowance during the event itself. Organizers were getting to the stage where they were giving a 60 kph average speed for the easy sections, and those easy sections were purely liaison sections which joined the difficult bits which were against the clock to the nearest second. So one had to drive over a thing like Russe or Stelvio, which had probably hundreds of corners at racing speed, where one mistake meant you might have a drop of over 2,000 ft. The Gaglio

1957: John Dalton's 100S hard on the heels of one of the Big Healey's greatest rivals, the Mercedes Benz 300 S L, in the British Empire Trophy Race.

Above: 1958: Lovely exterior of the Sebring car of that year.

Right: 1958: Stark interior of the Sebring car.

1958: John Gott before he lost a
wheel from the pioneer works rally
car, UOC741, in the Alpine.

for example—they say that if you come over the top too fast, the first bounce is about
4,000 ft down, so you have to be rather careful. There was always the possibility that
something might break and John Gott knew this to his cost in that event. In 1958 he
was going down a mountain pass at quite a reasonable speed, something like 70 mph,
when the car became uncontrollable and went into a spin. Fortunately the road was
wide enough and he came to a stop, and his co-driver said: "What the—— did you
do that for?" and he said: "Didn't do it on purpose." Just then there was a great
crunch and something hit them on the roof. This was the back wheel that had gone
up the mountain, down again and funnily enough actually hit the same car. This
was due to the fact that the Rudge-Whitworth hub on the Healey was modified—
as you know they had bolt-on wheels in the first cars and wire wheels were optional
extras; and they bolted on to a flange which was rather slender and so it wasn't a very
clever modification . . . the part was modified immediately, which meant that the
production cars got much stronger hubs.' And the car? It was the gallant UOC741 . . .

Stirling Moss's sister Pat went on to finish fourth in that rally despite trouble
caused when a well-meaning journalist tied a knot in the engine's breather pipe
thinking he was helping to tidy things up under the bonnet. Pat's co-driver was
none other than Ann Wisdom; they were to become one of the most successful
partnerships ever. The other Big Healeys were driven by Gott and Chris Tooley,
Jack Sears and Sam Moore, Bill Shepherd and John Williamson, and Nancy Mitchell
and Gillian Wilton-Clark. Between them they collected an Alpine Cup for Shepherd
and Williamson, and a Coupe des Dames award for Pat Moss and Ann Wisdom and
various other placings, plus lots of good publicity. Fired by this success, the BMC
team declared war on Mercedes, currently the top rally men with their exotic

300 S Ls. 'We set about them on the Tulip rally and beat the 300 S L in at least three events,' said Chambers. 'They were the Liege-Sofia-Liege, the Alpine and the Tulip. I always think this was a great credit to the Austin-Healeays—that we took on a car like the 300 S L and knocked hell out of it, especially when the price of the Healey must have been about a third of the Mercedes.' Again Pat Moss and Ann Wisdom were the stars, leading the team to a Coupe des Dames, manufacturers and team awards in the Liege rally.

Meanwhile the clubmen were still having a glorious time in their 100Ss, with Dick Protheroe prominent in R W D 323. He took third place in the *Autosport* championship, winning the over-1,600 cc class from other Healey drivers such as Sears and Shale. In South Africa, a rising young star called Tony Maggs made his debut in a standard 100-Six, racing with considerable success before selling it to finance a trip to Europe and the Grands Prix circus. From then on it was a steady programme of development for the Abingdon Healeys with constant modifications being homologated in conjunction with the circuit racing programme at Warwick, plus a little bit of record breaking. This took the form of a Cambridge University team lapping the Montlhery track in Paris for four days and nights to annex seven international class D records including the 10,000 miles at 97 mph.

The Healey family took a team of three 100-Sixes to Sebring to win the manufacturer's team prize with 14th, 17th and 22nd places overall despite oil on the clutches from old-fashioned scroll type seals, which were promptly modified. The capacity of those cars was significant—2,912 cc—a bored out 2.6 litre which was to become the basis of the 3000 production model next year.

The next year started very badly, as often happens with cars later to become famous. Sear's single R A C Rally entry came to nothing in the snow, while a complete team suffered the indignity of being beaten by the T R 3 As in the Alpine. Only the grim and determined Gott finished in that event. Chambers said: 'After that we thought we'd better build a really strong Healey and decided we could jack up the car about three inches, strengthen the front suspension and armour plate the sump and then we wouldn't have any more broken springs or spring hangers. We built a back spring with fourteen leaves and this had a nice shock absorber effect because of the friction in the leaves so the shock absorbers had less work to do—a brilliant piece of work by Enever. We had some trouble on the Greek rally with outriggers coming adrift at the back so we improved on these and the front springs. Pat Moss had felt that Healeys sometimes went round left-hand corners faster than right-hand ones, and sometimes vice versa. We thought we'd get to the bottom of this, because to have a rather unpredictable car with about 135 bhp on a wet road was rather unpleasant. Terry Mitchell, who was a brilliant young designer at M G, suggested that we check the specification of all the springs in our stores. We did this for both the standard and heavy duty springs. The matched sets we obtained were fitted to the cars and this improved the handling considerably.

'We were running overdrive on all four forward gears, which was awkward because it needed unlatching before going to reverse from first. We had been suspicious that, as the power went up, the overdrives were becoming sluggish, which could lose time on a mountain climb. Laycocks made a better overdrive with the

1958: Bill Shepherd in another early rally car now owned by Dave Jeffery, PMO202, in the Alpine.

right bite, which we used, but only on second, third and top. They also made a brake servo with a better and more evenly progressive action which we welcomed.'

The car which saw most of this development was the much-rebuilt UOC741 which became, in effect, one of the first 3000s in company with production proto-types at Warwick. There was no substitute for loving care and attention and the Abingdon mechanics under Duggie Watts certainly gave this to the cars. Years later Jeffery still marvels at his machine with 'everything wired and even the core plugs covered by screw-in alloy plates to prevent blow-outs.' In fact the engine currently fitted to UOC741 (now registered 2422DD) is the original unit from another early rally car, PMO202, also owned by Jeffery.

One of the most notable events of 1959 from the BMC point of view was the winning of the Tulip Rally by one of their rivals—a privately-entered 3.4 litre Mark I Jaguar saloon driven by Don and Erle Morley, twin farmers from Suffolk. They promptly signed them up and the Morleys started an illustrious career in 3000s by winning the GT class in the RAC Rally. Peter Riley and Rupert Jones had given the 3000 its first international class victory in the Liege, and Pat Moss and Ann Wisdom managed second in the German Rally—the highest overall placing then in

Right: 1958: Jack Sears laps Brands Hatch (in reverse direction) in a rally 100 in the R A C event.

Below: 1958: The brave young men from Cambridge in their flying Healey. From the left, the students who broke seven international records at Montlhery: J. A. B. Taylor, from Birmingham; G. Horrocks, Northampton; T. J. Threlfall, Stourbridge; R. S. R. Simpson, Harrow; R. S. Jones, Parkgate; J. M. Clarke, Bolton; and W. H. Summers, Burton.

1959: Big Healeys were already having a hard time! Gerry Brugess on the right has to grin and bear it in the Liege-Rome-Liege Rally.

an international rally by a women's team. Three of the cars used were registered SMO744, SMO745 and SMO746, and were to feature in Austin-Healey lore for years to come.

The next year, 1960, was to be the greatest in Austin-Healey competition history. It marked the wonderful win of Pat Moss and Ann Wisdom in the toughest international rally, the Liege-Rome-Liege and the debut of a car which is still thrilling crowds today: DD300. It started life as a lightweight racer from Warwick and went to Sebring with two others, UJB141 and UJB142. Two other cars were prepared, one for Austin's Canadian team, and the other as a spare. Two of the cars managed to finish, both handicapped by trouble with their gearboxes which left only top gear operable. Later UJB143—the only Big Healey entered at Le Mans that year, for Sears and Riley—crashed while 12th in the second hour. It was an inauspicious start to what was to be a glorious career.

Not that BMC were really worried. The rally cars were going really well. The year started with a class win for the private 3000 of Bobby Parkes in the Circuit of Ireland in which Pat Moss and Ann Wisdom retired SMO744 with gearbox trouble, calling it a 'pig of a car'. Poor 'SMOie,' as Pat called it, was crashed by almost all the works drivers in one event or another until sold to Parkes to whom it gave no trouble at all. Now it is the beloved 'shopping car' of that great Healey enthusiast, Thelma Segal. Not that the other SMOs were without their misfortunes. In the Lyon-Charbonnieres rally SMO745 was prepared for Pat and Ann but crashed on the way to the start; SMO746 was hurriedly taken down to the wrecked car and the mechanics worked all night transferring bits from 745 including the number plates. Then Pat had a spectacular crash at Solitude and everybody thought she had wrecked 745! Graham Robson was later to recall in *Autosport* that: 'When a Healey had completed a Liege or an RAC Rally, it was a thoroughly battered hulk, particularly if you were brave enough to take a look underneath. Even all that skid-shielding and the massive chassis members couldn't disguise the terrific pounding taken by the cars on the rough tracks, and rebuilding for the next event was a long and painstaking process. There would be no question of the ten-day build-up jobs that a modern Escort seems to accept with ease—two months was more like it. A Healey stripped down for a rebuild was a sight to be seen, for little more than the chassis, scuttle and basic inner body panels remained. But the strength and the rugged reliability could be built in; it came from years of practical experience . . .

'Pat Moss usually hogged the same car all season, gave it thoroughly feminine touches, and invariably a pet name. Her 1960 Liege winner was URX—after its registration number—and there was a rather less loved one called 'Orrible 'Orace. It was Pat who gave the car its early successes, and that never-to-be-forgotten outright win in the 1960 Liege.'

Pat and Ann had started the year well with the Coupes des Dames in the Geneva Rally and Tulip Rally. They also finished second overall in the Alpine, before winning the Liege, with fifth place being taken by David Siegle-Morris and Vic Elford. Gott and Jones were tenth to complete the winning team. Chambers recalls: 'We were running Weber carburetters on Healeys by 1960. This was grand because we were getting 150 bhp all the time and the cars were then much faster than we needed. It was the first time after four years of hard work that the drivers actually wrote on their reports under "power", "Enough". That was fantastic, since for years before it had always been "More."

'We hadn't solved the terrible overheating which was so fatiguing to the drivers. Pat found that if she took a sidescreen off the girls got choked by dust. If they kept the sidescreens on they died of heat. We tried all sorts of things, like ventilating the sides of the bonnet, and found that, as so often happens when you cut a hole in the coachwork that what you think is going in, is really coming out. So you've got to be very careful where you have ventilation. The pressure point on many cars is in front of the windscreen and that's where modern cars have their air intake. The low pressure outlet point is at the sides just in front of the scuttle, where the swirl area helps suck the air out. We noted that the 300 SL had its air extraction for the engine on each side, so we did the same thing on the Healey, or at least we did as much as we could in that way. Unfortunately there is a large square box bulkhead where your feet go and this upsets the amount of air you can get out of the engine compartment. We did improve matters a bit when we put the exhaust system higher and further up, but when you are producing that amount of horsepower and you've got a six-branch exhaust manifold, its difficult to get rid of the heat, especially as it's a car where the engine is very much shoe-horned in. There isn't much space around for the air to get out. It just heats up the floor boards and the bulkhead and then it heats up the crew. When you realize that the average temperature in the Alps in the summer is always up in the 70s and 80s, you can imagine what it's like, even if the car was properly cooled.

'In 1960 we felt that we had improved driver comfort and our servicing arrangements. We went in for both the Alpine and the Liege with a great deal more confidence. I don't think the management at BMC were happy about the fact that we were running nothing but Austin-Healeys because that wasn't the way to sell Morris

Left: 1960: It's amazing where road test cars turn up! *The Motor*'s 3000 of 1959 is hammered into third place in the RAC Rally by the Morley Brothers.

Below: 1960: Pat Moss with the famous URX727 in the Alpine Rally. The car is now owned, in exactly the same condition as she left it, by Peter Butt.

1960: There's a lot more to rallying than just driving: mechanics weld the exhaust of a works 3000 in the RAC event at Inverary.

Cowleys and things like that, but they hadn't produced a motor car which was likely to be successful then . . .

'We produced a stronger gearbox for the Tulip and found that the only crown and pinion which would fit the Healey axle and suit Pat's requirements for the Liege was either a 4.5 to 4.9 unit from a London taxi. This set-up produced a 0–60 time of six seconds. Pat's car was the only one fitted with this ratio because I couldn't risk all the cars blowing up from over-revving. Pat swore she wouldn't take it over six thousand.

'As it was she had clutch trouble but had made up so much time we managed to cure it with the help of her husband-to-be Eric Carlsson in Pat's old Liege Morris 1000.' The year closed with Pat and Ann being showered with honours including Ladies European Rally Champions. The Austin-Healeys which had carried them to victory also came in for their fair share of publicity with ten international class wins out of the fourteen possible.

In the same year a twenty-year-old garage proprietor's son from Bristol, John Chatham, had been saving hard for a battered BN2, SAL75, which he managed to purchase for £365—nearly £200 below the normal price, and another young man called Paul Hawkins had been equally impressed with a 100S in Melbourne, Australia. Chatham bought SAL75 and Hawkins spent his savings on a one-way ticket to England so that he could work for Donald Healey! For Chatham it was the start of a long career in club racing with Austin-Healeys and for Hawkins the beginning of a career in which he became one of the greatest Austin-Healey tuners and eventually a Grand Prix driver.

'I was involved with Frank Walker and the Healey club in Bristol,' said Chatham, 'and started using SAL in a few sprints and driving tests. In those days you just took your standard car along and pumped up the tyres and you were competitive and you drove your car home at the end. I just put bigger carbs on the car—that was before there was lots of sticky tape to make them go faster.'

The BMC team were not so keen on sticky tape either. They continued to do things properly—indeed they did so well that the Morleys won the Alpine in 1961. The five Big Healeys entered for that event were at the peak of their development in relation to other cars. Gott realized that these were the cars to beat and took the only Coupe for a penalty-free run. Chambers said: 'The Morleys couldn't do the Liege each year because it coincided with their harvest period. The Alpine was really something—they liked doing it because they could go on an Alpine race in June, the rally was in July, and it didn't interfere with their farming. It always amazes me that the first time the Morleys won an Alpine cup I didn't think they would even finish the event because they had lost second gear before the last special stage before Cannes. It's quite a long twisty one called the Cap Shelmont. I was the only service car that was anywhere near, and it was vital that they should do this section within the time set, which was 65 kph or something quite high. The road was very narrow, almost exactly the same width as a Big Healey is long, and you can imagine reaching 40 to 45 mph in the mountains on a road that wide. We got to the control at the beginning of the stage. There's one very steep patch, which I was wondering if they could get up, because I thought they would probably have to use second gear. If they had

1961: Scrutineering at Le Mans for Dickie Stoops and John Beckaert's Healey, TON792.

stuck the only thing we could do was to take the barge, as we called our service car, and give it a push up the backside. The Morleys wondered how we were going to get into the stage, as there was a policeman at the beginning of it. I had an Alpine service plaque on the front of the car, but service cars weren't allowed on the stages, so as soon as the Morleys started we followed. The policeman shouted and blew his whistle and we took no notice. I looked in the mirror and he was just drawing his gun as we went round the corner—we often wondered if he would have shot us. Anyway we'd gone by then and I'm glad to say we never caught the Morleys up . . . when we got to Cannes we asked spectators if they had got in and they said they had won the rally outright!'

Sadly, Pat Moss and Ann Wisdom could not repeat their previous year's win in the Liege, their car broke its chassis. But Dave Siegle-Morris and Tony Ambrose won their class, and followed up with a similar success in the Monte Carlo Rally. Pat and Ann managed a class win in the RAC Rally and once more it was a highly-successful year for the rally cars. On the circuits, UJB143 was re-registered DD300 by its new owner, David Dixon, and ran impressively at Le Mans until eliminated near the end with engine trouble. The entrants were the Ecurie Chiltern and the drivers Dickie Stoop and Johnny Beckaert. DD300 then passed into the hands of Bob Olthoff who had a fabulous South African season with it. On 3 November, 1962, for instance, Olthoff and Tony Maggs finished second in the Rand Nine Hour race, only two miles behind the winning Ferrari 250GTO, which covered 691 miles. It was a truly remarkable achievement for a machine not far removed from production sports cars against an out-and-out racing car. Meanwhile Chatham continued to modify SAL75.

He fitted the front discs from a 3000 and reduced the rear braking balance to

Above: 1961: The Big Healey with a gaggle of rival Porsches, Sprites, an Alfa, and MG and an Elite.

Left: 1961: The Morley Brothers get ready to win the Alpine Rally.

Above: 1962: Foot hard down, tail scraping the road, Pat Moss hurls her Healey into third place in the Alpine Rally.

Right: 1962: David Seigle-Morris finds a handy escape route on the Alpine Rally.

Above: 1962: Healey 100Ms were still proving a handful in club events! The other car pictured at Snetterton is a Daimler Dart.

Left: 1963: Timo Makinen on the road to Sofia in the Liege Rally.

1963: Paddy Hopkirk and Don Morley prepare to overtake the Bolton/Rothschild Triumph TR4 at Webster Turn, Sebring.

match before boosting everything with a servo. By this time SAL had covered 80,000 miles and needed an engine rebuild—which promptly took it up to 100M specification. The clutch from a scrap taxi behind the tiny garage in Gloucester Road took care of the extra power with a 3000 gearbox. Chatham tried everything from autocrosses to driving tests, from hill climbs to rallies, with the Derbyshire, Exeter and Land's End trials thrown in. 'He treated each hill as a pure speed trial,' said one local journalist. 'The stones and the grit were still rattling down minutes after his dramatic passing.'

In America, Hollywood Sports Cars of Los Angeles race-prepared two Big Healeys, a 2.6 litre for John Christy, editor of *Sports Cars Illustrated*, and a three litre for the proprietor, Chick Vanderziff. This latter car recorded nineteen straight wins out of twenty races with its triple-carb engine giving 205 bhp at 6,000 rpm on the dynamometer. Christy also did well in production classes. At Sebring, Olthoff

and Ronnie Bucknum finished fourth in their class behind three prototype Ferraris, with Hopkirk and Donald Morley sixth.

1964: It takes a brave man (in this case Don Barrow) to ride with Timo Makinen in the RAC Rally.

The crowds continued to turn up to goggle at the BMC team in the rallies of 1962. The Morley twins finished first in their class in the Tulip with Riley and David Astle second. Ann Wisdom, who had married Riley, had retired from rallying, and was replaced by Pauline Mayman. She entered the Acropolis rally and subsequently won her first Coupe des Dames with Pat Moss.

The Alpine was again a benefit for the Healeys, with the Morleys winning the event outright for the second year running. Pat and Pauline were placed third, with Siegle-Morris and Ambrose taking eighth place and completing the winning team. 'Siegle-Morris had a six-minute lead over Bohringer's Mercedes in the Liege,' *Safety Fast* reported, 'but during this stage a rear spring mounting broke. Dave drove the car like this, with the bodywork rubbing on the tyre for 180 kilometres, dropping $1\frac{1}{2}$ hours in the process.

'At Coriza, Duggie Watts took the fuel tank out of the car, welded the chassis and fitted a new spring and replaced the tank in just over an hour, so that Dave was able to achieve a personal ambition and finish three Lieges in a row and thus qualify for a special Gold Cup—an ambition previously achieved by John Gott.'

That year also saw the introduction to the team of Paddy Hopkirk, lured from Rootes to tame the Big Healey, and the flying Finn, Rauno Aaltonen. 'Only four people ever mastered a Healey completely,' said Robson, 'Pat Moss and Donald Morley, Aaltonen and Timo Makinen. Hopkirk got himself side-tracked to Mini-Coopers with altogether exemplary results.' However, Hopkirk did manage to finish second in the RAC Rally with Pat Moss and Pauline Mayman third to again win the Ladies European Championship. This was the third time Pat had won the championship.

Chatham continued to mop up club events and DD300 again had to retire at Le Mans, this time when leading all the 'standard' cars, because of a shortage of oil. Again the entrants were the Ecurie Chiltern and this time the drivers were Olthoff and John Whitmore.

The next year was unlucky for the BMC team with two outright wins being snatched away from them at the last moment. Makinen, however, teamed up with the flying girl Mini driver Christabel Carlisle for the Monte Carlo Rally. After a magnificent drive with a great surplus of power they won the GT category and finished 13th overall, despite the fact that neither could speak the other's language—other than Christabel shouting 'Faster, faster'. She was one of the few people to ever shout that at the legendary Makinen. 'Timo was a big basic Finn and new to British rally cars,' said Robson. 'Nobody seemed to have told him that the Healey was a big car, that it had a certain reputation, that it was difficult to drive. Nobody told him that you simply didn't drive a conventional car like that—and if they had I doubt if Timo would have been listening. Timo drove Healeys like Minis, if he drove them like anything; there are those prepared to swear that he picked up his car bodily and hurled it to the end of the stage without a thought for the mechanical limits anyway! To see a co-driver getting out of Makinen's Healeys at the end of a stage was to see someone who had looked at life for the very first time; they were often silent for a time before daring to comment. To look at a sweating, grinning Makinen was to understand the effort and the pleasure it gave him.'

Tragically a broken axle put the Morleys out of the Alpine and lost them the chance of a Coupe d'Or for three consecutive penalty-free runs, an award won previously only by Ian Appleyard in an XK120 and Stirling Moss in a Sunbeam Alpine. But Makinen and the Morleys finished first and second in their class in the RAC Rally.

By 1964 the major effort of the BMC competition department had been centred on the Mini saloon with consequent effects on sales as it won races and rallies everywhere—but the Healey family came back on the scene with a car for Hopkirk and Canadian champion Grant Clark to race at Sebring. Sadly, Clark overturned it. The Morleys soldiered on with class wins in the Tulip although Robson regarded them as outright wins. 'These stupendously fast drives in 1962, 1963, 1964 and 1965

Left: 1964: Night of the Big Healey: Sir Peter Moon and Miss Denise McCluggage contest the Tulip Rally in XJB876.

Below: 1965: Sideways as ever, Ted Worswick scatters the mud in the RAC Rally in his virtually bog-standard 3000 convertible!

1965: Ted Worswick in action at Brands Hatch with his ex-works racer, PJB828.

should all count as victories,' says Robson. 'The trouble is the organisers were messing about with a complex "class improvement" scheme which robbed the Morleys.'

Three works cars were entered for the Liege, which was to be the last of the classic ninety-four-hour events. This time Aaltonen and Ambrose won by nearly half an hour. In the RAC Rally, Makinen and Don Barrow drove their Big Healey into second place overall, the first GT car to finish.

The Finn would have done at least as well in the Alpine and the Liege if he had not had a rather tired car in the former and had to 'open the road' in the latter with the inevitable accident because nobody expected the first car to appear so quickly!

Meanwhile, Chatham was burning up the club tracks, but not without opposition from the drivers of other Big Healeys. One of the fastest was an old 100-Six, PJB828, driven by a young Lancastrian called Ted Worswick. PJB828 was a former works Press car fitted with a decent engine and ancilliaries. Worswick and Chatham went on to win numerous British races between them with SAL75 and PJB828.

Meanwhile on the other side of the Atlantic, one Juan Harris did 162.74 mph with a modified 100-Six road car to take third place in the national trials at Bonneville!

The last active appearance of the works-entered Big Healeys was in 1965 when the Morleys collected class awards in the Tulip, Geneva and Alpine rallies. Makinen finished second in the RAC Rally with enthusiasts everywhere willing him to win,

but one icy slope in Wales was too much for the Big Healey's spinning wheels and Aaltonen's front-wheel-drive Mini overtook him for first place.

Makinen teamed up with Hawkins that year to take second place to a Ferrari GTO on the Italian car's home ground in the last of the great road races the Targa Florio. Hawkins also drove a 3000 at Sebring, with Warwick Banks, to a class win and seventeenth overall.

One of the last Sebring cars, 767 KNX, was sold to Worswick, who also bought Tony Ambrose's ex-works rally car, 67 ARX. They were not raced in 1965, as Worswick was tied up with the TVR works team. Chatham also sold his beloved SAL 75 in 1965 and replaced it by a pile of pieces—'She had been rolled at Snetterton five or six times'—registered DD 300! It took Chatham most of the season to rebuild DD 300.

Meanwhile Juan Harris was hitting 180.09 mph at Bonneville and saying: 'I feel if a man's car has show car looks and race car speed, plus still be in street-driving condition, it must be quite a salty Healey!'

Stuart Hands in Gary Bristow's ex-works rally car, XJB 876—the car which had taken the Morleys to their 1962 Alpine win—became the best Big Healey on the British circuits in 1966 until Chatham got DD 300 back together again. Worswick managed to get a drive in the Targa Florio in 767 KNX though, but had to retire with a broken differential.

John Gott also campaigned his ex-works car, SMO 746, with a lot of success.

Above and over: 1965: (one) The Morley Brothers start the RAC Rally; (two) Their service crew fight to keep them on the road, changing a half shaft and welding up the underside; (three) All in vain! A tree got in the way.

Chatham crashed DD300 again, on 4½ in rim-wheels and Pirelli Cinturatos, then rebuilt it with 8½ in alloy wheels; it was the start of the modsports era when sports cars were developed to such an extent they could not be driven on the road. 'The factory weren't too helpful,' said Chatham, 'because they had developed the cars for rallying and they weren't interested in the chassis tuning needed for British circuit racing.'

In the winter Worswick drove 67ARX to high placings in the Welsh Rally, then bought Makinen's old rally car, EJB806C, the last made. But in between he drove a standard 3000 convertible in the RAC Rally with only the benefit of a sump guard!

Circuit racing really hotted up in the next year, with Gott winning most of the events and Londoner Syd Segal entering the fray with a modified road car bought from Liz Jones. 'It had been used for all sorts of things, autocross, racing, rallying, sprints and hill-climbs, with the benefit of Paul Hawkins as a mechanic,' said Thelma Segal. 'It was one of the first Big Healeys to be fitted with wide wheels—up to ten inches in the end.

'John Gott had most of the parts left over at the works when the Healeys were phased out, with John Chatham buying some too,' said Thelma. John said: 'I had to stick to 8½ in bolt-on wheels in 1967 because the wires were too expensive. After that we used welded steel wheels, followed by J. A. Pearce alloys. You had to use a Sprite anti-roll bar with the ten-inch wheels or you got very bad understeer. As it was we had a handling problem with DD on its wide wheels which was only solved by removing the Panhard rod and letting the axle slide sideways, up to three inches at a time! The springs didn't last long . . . At this time all our modsports cars were going over to fibreglass coachwork, too, with enormous flares to cover the wheels.'

Chatham, Hands, Gott, Segal and company developed their cars further and further away from road specification, partly with the help of fibreglass panels supplied by another driver, Pete Smith, who had a garage in the Cotswolds. They frequently banded together to form a trio of immaculate cars racing under the banner of Team 3000. Meanwhile Worswick continued to race substantially unaltered cars and made second fastest time on the final stage at Croft in the Gulf London Rally of 1967. And the works produced one last competition car, PWB57, a fearsome rebuild of the ex-Morley Alpine car, ARX92B, then owned by competition manager Peter Browning. The driver was to be Rauno Aaltonen and the object was an overall win as the rally now included a class for group six sports cars. One of the three all-alloy engines made by the works was fitted, with a capacity of 2,968 cc and triple Webers, side exhaust and Minilite wheels, shod with 185 × 15 radials, were among the special equipment. I'll never forget the scenes of disappointment as I went to the rally headquarters as part of a television crew and learned the great event had been cancelled because of foot-and-mouth disease. Suddenly we realized that we would never again be filming a works Healey in full cry.

It was a sight and a sound never to be forgotten. The noise was incredible, brutal and searing and the car was a veritable monster as it slithered and lunged along forest tracks. The modern Minis were nothing more than an antiseptic reminder of a bygone era when rallying re-started.

The next year in the competition history of the Big Healey was bitterly fought

1966: Ted Worswick storms along in the Fram International Welsh Rally.

all round the circuits of Great Britain, with Chatham triumphant in DD 300. He drove anywhere and everywhere, and in twenty-eight victories he shattered class lap records at Silverstone, Mallory, Oulton Park, Castle Combe, Llandow, Brands Hatch, Crystal Palace and Snetterton. He took mechanical disasters and accidents with a cheerful aplomb; between practice and the race at his beloved home circuit, Castle Combe, he rebuilt a wrecked engine. This incredible story started on a Friday night with a hurriedly rebuilt engine for DD 300. In the scramble, the wrong pistons were fitted—they had been incorrectly marked 'plus 30 thou' on manufacture, but were in fact, of standard size. Subsequently, when the engine was started, ominous noises were heard. There was no time to do anything about it—only time to take the car to the circuit. Within three practice laps, DD 300 had blown all the oil out of its sump and all over Chatham—but it had achieved a grid position, albeit rather lowly. By then it was 10 a.m. on the Saturday morning, and because there was another race on the Sunday, Chatham's crew decided to scratch from the event at Castle Combe and return to Bristol for yet another rebuild. Work started at 11.15 a.m. and the fault

was soon found. By 1.15 p.m. new pistons and chrome top rings had been fitted and the car loaded up again for a frantic drive back to Castle Combe. Chatham and DD300 arrived just in time to start the race and set off in pursuit of Stuart Hands in XJB876. Driving like a man possessed Chatham passed the entire field, and in a do-or-die effort DD300 collected one door handle from XJB876, and the winner's laurels, on the last lap.

In another event, at Mallory Park, Chatham practically wrote off the red-and-white monster and fled in terror from the wreckage at the thought of being carried off on a stretcher. Within a fortnight the car was completely rebuilt and contesting both the F. W. Dixon Championship and the Amasco series. However, specialization paid, and Hands won the Dixon trophy and Gott, in SMO746, took the Amasco Championship. Chatham had the consolation of winning more events than anybody else in Britain, and it was ironic that so soon after the model was discontinued that the Big Healey should also win both sports car championships.

These extraordinary modsports cars were build to much the same specification:

Above left: 1966: Stuart Hands in Gary Bristow's XJB876 at Silverstone. See how she's changed . . .

Top right: 1966: Last of the great road races, and one of the last of the great road racers, Ted Worswick's Sebring Healey (the last made) starts the fiftieth Targa Florio in Sicily.

Above right: 1966: Hasty repairs for the Worswick Healey (a change of differential) before the long drive home to Lancashire.

Above: 1967: It's a hard road to ride for Ted Worswick's ex-works Healey in the Gulf International Rally.

Right: 1967: Last of the works cars: the ferocious PWB 57. We never had a chance to feel its bite, we just heard its bark.

Top left: 1968: Idols on parade: from the left, the ex-Bolthoff Sebring Healey, Makinen's Monte Carlo Rally-winning Mini-Cooper S, and Worswick's Sebring Healey.

Left: 1968: The Beast at Bay: Sid Segal lines up with an incredible assortment of machinery in a British club event.

the bodies were fibreglass or alloy with flared arches covering ten-inch rims carrying low profile tyres (Firestones in the case of Hands and Chatham, and Dunlops for Gott). The engines were ex-works with free-flow exhausts, triple Webers, and all the stops pulled out now that power was more important than long-distance reliability. Hands claimed 197 bhp at the wheels of XJB876 and Chatham claimed that the alloy blocks tended to let the crankshaft whip, with the result that number six rod could go through the crankcase! Needless to say, he said it with feeling.

Meanwhile Worswick soldiered on with a substantially unaltered car for road racing, although he drove a very rapid E type Jaguar when competing against Chatham, Gott and Hands on the track. Worswick went once again to Sicily for the Targa Florio with 767KNX, finishing twenty-fourth—a wonderful effort for a man who sells life insurance! 'My co-driver, Richard Bond, and myself, did not worry about the heat,' said Ted, 'we just drove in our shirtsleeves.' It must have been one of the last times that a big sports car was driven in the traditional manner in a classic road race—then driven 2,000 miles home again!

The modern modsports racing continued as fast and furious as ever in 1969 with Segal coming more into the scene in his Big Healey, now registered SYD1. And when Simon Taylor track tested DD300 for *Autosport* he found what a handful these massive cars were like: 'My respect for Mr Chatham increased further when he offered me some laps of Castle Combe in DD300,' said Taylor, 'for by comparison with light, balanced modern racing cars, the big car seems a real handful. You sit in an upright fibreglass bucket seat with the big leather-rimmed steering wheel well within arm's length—which is just as well, as it requires big elbow movements to move those fat front wheels. Over the high scuttle you see an undulating expanse of red bonnet, and within the cockpit there are the standard Healey instruments, plus an additional rev-counter. The gearlever boasts a king-sized knob with a switch built into it which operates the overdrive.

'The engine produces a rorty note which is more agricultural than racy, but the power is certainly there—provided you keep the revs between 4,500 and 6,000. There is little response much below 4,000 rpm and with this very narrow power band the overdrive is essential, and plenty of juggling with the gearlever and switch is necessary to make the best use of the engine . . . it is often very hard to remember which gear you are in.

'Quite how John Chatham gets it round Castle Combe in 1 min 13.2 sec is a mystery to me.'

Soon after, Chatham sold DD300 and campaigned an MGC for two seasons, leaving only Gott of the original trio to keep the Healey flag flying. 'John Gott went faster and faster as he grew older,' said Thelma Segal. 'I think it was the competition from the younger Healey drivers that spurred him on. But Nigel Kerr took a lot of lap records with an ex-Sebring car, ABL6, and eventually John bought it, to go with his other two Big Healeys, SMO746 and BMO93B.' The move paid off for Gott in 1970 when he had his best season on the circuits, winning twenty-two races. Syd Segal was next best with half a dozen wins. When Richard Hudson-Evans, then editor of *Cars and Car Conversions* tried SYD1 round Silverstone he was even more amazed than Taylor had been with DD300. 'Once perched in the inner sanctum,' he wrote, 'I wound away on the key, following the instructions most carefully to apply half throttle with the right foot. After various mechanical chunterings, six cylinders started to burble, followed by calico barkings from the side exhaust. The monster was alive—and I was to find out how well alive the jet car was to be, once given the all clear to venture out onto the great wide open spaces of Silverstone itself . . .

'My gawd—the gearlever was positive, or rather very stiff. It seemed to become stiffer, or my left arm was beginning to fall off. After a couple of laps of holding the beast on course, my right arm became seized up too!

'I found that the brakes needed warming up before any real confidence could be mustered. If I became too brusque with them, they would retaliate by setting up pattering and juddering. I also found the clutch a trifle woolly . . .

'The combination of noise and smell of the beast, pulling all the revs it could in overdrive top, coming down the straight into Woodcote is difficult to describe. Suffice it to say, as you might imagine, it was very, very exciting.'

And so they went on through 1971 and 1972, with £25-a-week lorry mechanic Bill Viney coming into the reckoning with his Big Healey, HAS2, frequently maintained in the street outside his home in South London! Then tragedy struck for only the second time in a top flight Healey drive . . . Gott was killed when SMO746 crashed heavily in a modsports race at Devil's Elbow on the Lydden circuit near Dover in 1972. John Gott, who had at that time devoted more of his life to the Big Healey in competition than anybody, was fifty-nine years old and chief constable of

Northamptonshire with Silverstone on his beat. He had started racing as a riding mechanic at Brooklands in 1930, with his first event the 1933 RAC Rally. He won the George Medal for rescue work in the blitz and finished every Alpine Rally from 1948 to 1951 as leader of the works HRG team. He went on to drive for Frazer Nash and lead the BMC works team until he was appointed chief constable in 1960. Soon after his faithful mechanic, known to everybody only as Jock, died. Thelma Segal took his remaining racing Healey, ABL6, and says it will stay the same forever—a reminder of the racing of the late 1960s and early 1970s.

It was the end of the era and the start of a new one. Chatham bought back DD 300, wrecked again, and rebuilt it as a historic racer now that modsports was on the decline. Year after year since then it has pulled in the crowds all round Britain as a David and Goliath act fighting it out with the aluminium XK 120s of John Harper and Martin Crowther and the Aston Martin DB4 of David Preece. Chatham has always been a crowd-pleaser with a reputation for incredible starts, rarely being led into the first corner. And now DD 300 is back onto narrow wheels and a properly-located axle she is surprisingly just as fast as she ever was in her modsports days.

October the Second 1977 was a typical weekend in the life of Chatham and DD 300. The seemingly indestructable man from Bristol was at a party until 4 a.m. He was awakened by his mechanic, John Horne, with coffee two hours later, and arrived at Brands Hatch fast asleep with Horne driving their battered Ford Granada towing a trailerful of Big Healey. A fried breakfast, three practice laps, down to 57 seconds for the club circuit, and Chatham quit. 'The car is suffering from driver fade,' he said. The others did lap after lap trying to match his speed. David Ham tried so hard that he bent the front of the often-battered Oldham and Crowther XK. (Not to worry, they have a big hammer!). Everybody else has done twenty laps by the time Chatham has parked his car back in the paddock, but only Harper looked good and he was no faster than DD 300. Driver fade, or supreme driver? Harper ought to have been a lot faster, his XK has 3.8 litres against DD 300's 2.7 for the smaller class. Then Harper got down to 56.8, but Chatham wasn't worried. Nobody else could get on the front row with the size of the dent in Crowther's XK. At 3.15 p.m. the ten-lap historic race was ready to start; it was cold and sunny. John Horne flicked a piece of tape over a raised joint between the passenger's door on DD 300 and the front wing. 'He had a brush with Harper the other day,' says Horne as twenty cars unlease hundreds of horsepower on the grid. The crowd rose with bated breath as the cars stormed away in a cloud of oil smoke and dust. Every head turned to see the Big Healey swoop first into Paddock Bend. He'd done it again . . .

With arm's full of opposite lock Chatham was down to 56.8, then it was full opposite lock round almost every corner and the XKs stole by. But there was nothing else in the same class as DD 300. The only other Healey, driven by the great enthusiast Derek Allanson, was lapped, and Reg Woodcock's famous TR parted with a con-rod for the third time that season.

'It was driver fade,' said Chatham in the post-race inquest over third place. 'Or it could have been the sun coming out and warming up the track and spoiling it for the tyres . . . I don't reckon this going for class wins. I'm going back to three litres next year and those XKs won't get a look in . . .'

VI

Strengths and Weaknesses: Part One

MOST PEOPLE buy a Big Healey now for one of two reasons: to drive it frequently and enjoy it, or to show it off, driving it only infrequently; others buy the beast for both reasons and a few simply as an investment. But nobody buys a Big Healey casually any more, just because it is a cheap and cheerful sports car. Everybody is after value. The main thing they all have to remember is to get a good car or one that is suited to their purpose. It is my opinion, at the time of writing this book, that the four-cylinder cars are undervalued. Currently, the Mark III is top of the average tree with only the odd exotic 100 in the same class; nobody seems to rate the 100-Six as anything more than an interim model, and this can make it a bargain. The 100 is the light and lovable car; the Mark III was by far the best everyday car. But Healeys are no longer everyday cars, so I reckon it is time the values of out-and-out sports cars such as the 100 caught up those of the softer Mark IIIs. After all, any Healey can be in a diabolical state after ten year's neglect, so the actual year of manufacture is not so important. Naturally BN1 spares are more difficult to obtain than those for late cars—but their rarity value ought to make up for that, and once restored they should last forever, being cosseted now instead of abused.

So how do you value a potential purchase in monetary terms, knowing they all cost a fortune to have totally rebuilt commercially, and assuming the 100 is about to catch up the Mark III? The first factor is the number made. This puts the 100S and practically any works car top of the tree, with an authentic 100M, preferably factory-built, as the dark horse. The more period competition fittings the better. The only exceptions to this rule would be the modsports cars and American V8s which nobody likes any more. Their only advantage might be that somewhere under the fibreglass lies an ex-works racer. Performance then enters into it, with the six-port 100-Six beating the four-port and the first couple of hundred Mark IIIs being left out in the cold with no ground clearance. Originality is very important, of course, with a good car. With a bad car, you are going to have to replace half of it anyway, so original parts are only important if they are in good condition or suitable for restoration rather than scrap.

The first thing to check when you are thinking of buying a Big Healey is the body—that's the most expensive part to replace. Rust attacks it almost everywhere, especially in the lower twelve inches if it has lived in a damp or salty climate. The most common corrosion points are the lower wing to chassis joints, the rear wing's lower cavity, the lower door, the sills, the lower flange on the luggage boot lid, the shut plates, the luggage boot floor, the petrol tank, the wing tops, and the alloy shrouds which suffer especially from electrolytic corrosion along the seams.

One of the first points to be examined should be the shape of the shroud around the radiator grille and bonnet. Cracks and distortion are signs of accident damage and new shrouds are expensive. Bubbles in the paintwork are the electrolytic corrosion tell-tales. The outer front wings sometimes rot under the headlights and frequently near the bulkhead. The inner front wings rot at their edges, increasing the gap between them and the outer wing. Road debris gets through this gap to accumulate behind the outer wing near the bulkhead with resultant corrosion. Again, paint bubbles are often the first sign of this malady. It also pays to check the security of the bottom of the front wing, which can become detached from its mounting. The next point to check is the sills. They often become holed at the front and soon rot away. Usually the first signs of trouble can be seen at the point where the inner sills join the floor and in the outer sill between the door shut faces. The chassis outriggers rot away in similar fashion.

Then there are the rear wings, one of the best known and most obvious corrosion points. Check where they are attached to the door shut face at the bottom; you can sometimes detach them by hand. Electrolytic corrosion rears its ugly head along the top seam as in the front wings and underseal often disguises all manner of holes in the wing itself. Like the front shroud, the rear one is difficult to repair if it has suffered accident damage.

Moving further into the car, check the door hinge pillars—they are prone to rot away below the bottom hinge. The aluminium trim surrounding the door shut areas is also often the only metal holding that area together. The passenger area floor is also prone to rot, particularly across the front of the car, along the sills and around the rear wheel arch. The same applies to the metal covering the rear axle and the luggage boot floor and rear inner wings. The petrol tank can conceal a lot of rot in the boot and don't be surprised if that is rotting away too! Doors don't escape the dreaded tinworm either, suffering in a similar way to the wings, with similar warning bubbles.

Even the chassis is not immune to rust, suffering particularly where it meets a floor section—so a rotten floor can often mean a rotten chassis, too! On the Mark III, the radius arms are mounted in boxes next to the wheel arches, which frequently suffer from rot. Check also for kinks and splits in the frame around the front suspension pillar and engine mountings, and cracks in the shock absorber mounting pillar in this area.

Electrolytic corrosion might have been present for a long time. Service manager Geoff Price recalls cars being treated for this ailment, which eats away the shroud flange, early in their lives even before rust had attacked the steel. The cars survived to rust even more because of the massive steel chassis. It is generally the best part of a rusty car, but do not be fooled by masses of underseal. Frequently there is little but underseal and the stuff catches fire around the exhaust to reveal a gaping hole when you have beaten out the flames and recovered from the acrid fumes.

Above left: The Healey's bodyshell is welded to the chassis frame and causes problems on restoration. A rusty floor usually means rusty frame members—this picture shows a Healey boot floor which has suffered from such inter-related rust. The floor member has been removed so that holes in the chassis can be repaired. Note the drilled bumper iron support brackets; these can often corrode or become bent, with resultant misalignment of the rear bumper.

Above right: The Healey's sills are notorious rust traps; the outer sill in this picture has been removed revealing the corroded inner sill. The door shut face, has been cut away revealing the cockpit floor on the passenger's side.

Most Big Healeys have ejected oil at some time, which frequently protects the exposed portions of the main chassis rails, except in the case of those cars which have been stored for a long time and sometimes rust through here. Savage jacking with small-headed implements can damage the rails and cross members, too. Look for underside abrasions and check the whole rig for truth. Healeys can survive tremendous shunts, but not necessarily unscathed. On some occasions the chassis has been known to bend quite easily. Minor points which suffer underneath can be the slave cylinder feed pipe and dangerous ones the petrol pipes and wiring. Electrical wiring tends to suffer in hot climates, incidentally—if you don't have rust you might well have electrical problems. At least they are simpler to rectify. I don't think there can be more than a handful of Healeys that haven't had exhaust trouble. The flexible connections in the system are the most fragile, and if you want to replace them alone, measure their length first before cutting their replacements. If you weld in a piece the wrong length you might have to buy a complete new system because it does not hang properly.

Having satisfied yourself that you know the state of the chassis and that the body is not a mirage or can be rebuilt, the mechanical side should be examined. It is much easier to put right than the body and chassis, but must not be neglected or the car will be terrible, or even, terrifying to drive. First look at the engine. Old Healey engines have a tendency to smoke from all the usual places and some unusual ones if they are worn. A compression check will reveal not only the state of the bores and piston rings, but the state of the valve gear. Pressures should be at least an even 100 psi and beware of smokey starts and a touch of the blues on hard acceleration: it can mean a badly worn rocker shaft. Geysers of oil when the engine is run without its valve cover confirm this and either worn valve guides or fouled plugs, or both, are another clue. Oil dripping steadily from the rear air cleaner can also be a manifestation of the dreaded rocker shaft wear, as can low oil pressure. It can also indicate bore wear, which leads to crankcase compression and a resultant oil mist leaving the breather to collect in the filter. Oil splattered around the underside can come from

Left: In this picture, the front wing has been removed clearly showing the forward end of the main sill under the bulkhead, and the front inner wing. Rust has holed the inner wing and allowed mud to build up along the sill, promoting further rot.

Below: Halfway to a restoration. The Healey in the picture is being stripped for sandblasting, reparation and re-painting. The operative is chiselling off the cockpit floor before removing the front bulkhead and sills as a unit.

Right: A classical result of electrolytic corrosion. These rear shroud flanges needed skilled attention.

Below: The bare bones of a Big Healey, halfway through a total rebuild, showing the inner wings, bulkheads and floor.

Close-up of the sill and bulkhead areas on a Big Healey, showing typical rot.

the rear main bearing oil seal (worn out) or even a crack in that area; generally speaking, the oil pressure should be at least 50 psi hot and the engine should be dry outside. Healeys will survive lower pressures for a while before they start to knock.

However, you must not be confused by knocks. They can mean a variety of things. A heavy knocking noise at fast tickover can mean that the crankshaft damper has worked loose. Get it tightened to see if it has knocked out the crankshaft as it can be very expensive if it has. At the least, a special key will almost certainly be needed to cure this ailment. A little bit of knocking, particularly on the 3000, can emanate from the little ends. The easiest way to check these for audible wear is to run the engine at about 1,500 rpm then shut the throttle quickly. If you hear a strange tapping as the engine slows down then it almost undoubtedly comes from the little ends. While the engine is idling listen for any other strange noises. If the tappets appear to rattle in an irregular fashion the cam followers are probably pitted or unevenly worn, and as they rotate, the tappet clearance varies, causing the irregular noise. If there are no strange noises from the engine, give it a road test. It should be smooth and show no sudden desire to consume oil when hammered down a motorway. Worn piston rings plus continuous high-speed cruising equals an efficient four or six-cylinder oil pump, because of the build up of pressure in the crankcase. You can blow out a gallon of oil in no time! Signs of this happening, apart from a dry dipstick and a drop in oil pressure, are a lot of oil in the vicinity of the engine breather pipe. This is sometimes extended and routed into the bottom of the front wing to carry engine fumes away from the cockpit, so make sure you know where to find it.

Providing everything else is OK in 'the black hole of Calcutta'—an apt description for the engine bay of many second-hand Healeys—and everything runs smoothly, leave well alone. Taking the head off unnecessarily means a decoke and probably a violent increase in oil consumption. Misfiring can be simply Champion UN12Y plugs (original equipment on many cars, which often lose their spark over 4,000 rpm after a few thousand miles). You can get camshafts reprofiled by people like

John Chatham at a high price, because it is expensive if done properly, or cheaply from various dealers whose products do not always last long. Alternatively, they are available in exchange from A-H Spares, the organization set up by Fred Draper when Big Healey production ceased. Water pumps squeak when they are either worn or worn and dry—there's a steady demand, says Draper. Healeys overheat, particularly in traffic when they have radiator, gasket, or thermostat trouble, although a blown head gasket should show up on a compression check.

They also misfire and pink at a constant speed when the ignition is too far advanced and they pop and bang on the over-run when the mixture is too weak. They suffer from throttle linkage wear, particularly on the BN4, when subject to heavy stamping on the accelerator and carburetter life is determined by spindle wear. Watch these items; SU carburetters cost a small fortune to replace now, although reconditioning can be achieved at a much lower cost. Exhaust manifolds are also expensive, the flanges of which are easily broken by ham-fisted mechanics or unlucky amateurs; that is supposing you are lucky enough to find replacements for these expensive items. Potentially lethal faults in the engine department can include loose fan blades and cracked or loose dynamo brackets. These are far from uncommon.

Providing you are happy about the engine, make sure you have a good gearbox; the cost of replacements can be enormous. The main points to watch are the synchromesh (which is frequently weak and noisy on pre-Mark III models), and the first and reverse gear which is often noisy. All Big Healey gearboxes whine a bit, but the noise should not be excessive or you will soon be in trouble. These expensive noises are often accompanied by a lack of synchromesh occasioned by brutal gearchanging. Badly-worn boxes jump out of gear, too. The gearboxes fitted to BN1 cars were dreadful. They lasted only about 35,000 miles and their first motion shaft was overstressed in any case even if it outlasted second gear. Beware, oil around the gearbox and along the rear frame rails that can mean a rear main oil seal has gone, which also shows up with a steady drip of oil from the gearbox housing and heavy engine oil consumption whether you use the car or not.

Overdrives do not give a lot of trouble on road cars. Failure to work properly is usually due to faulty electrics or hydraulics, which are not difficult to repair, providing the pump is not at fault. Be careful, though, anything else wrong with the overdrive can be expensive, although exchange units from A-H Spares are still something of a bargain.

Rear axles do not give much trouble except for the odd leaky seal, which is easily replaced and the very rare casing tear which should be visible. An oily back axle can be the result of a blocked breather, which can oil up the rear brakes. Brakes should be good—they are no different from those on many cars, although the drums are becoming difficult to find.

Having checked all that, make sure the car stands straight. If it is lop-sided or droopy, and the chassis has survived your checks, the suspension is at fault. More than likely this would have been evident on the test run. The biggest source of trouble in the suspension is the costly shock absorbers. They date back to the days when it was normal to check their fluid levels, and not many garages do that now. Dry shock absorbers are sometimes difficult to detect at the rear if the springs are very stiff, unless the fluid level is checked. They are all too apparent at the front: the wheels wobble in the most terrifying manner if anything like that is wrong there. Everything wears in the suspension, it takes such a hammering. Back springs crack, sag, collapse and are easily replaced. Front springs give up the ghost gradually. Shock absorbers come loose and the front suspension pillar can collapse as well if the whole front end is shaking about. All the rubber bushes wear, and anti-roll bars suffer from kerbing at the front. Kingpins clonk and are more tedious than expensive to replace if worn.

Worn hubs and splines with wire wheels also clonk—and are very dangerous. If there is any movement there the whole wheel can fly off. Wire wheels also collapse and go oval, especially the forty-eight-spoke versions now that tyres grip better. Give the spokes a tap with a pen and listen to them like a piano tuner. If they give a uniform ding, ding, ding they are OK. If you get a dong you have loose spoke trouble. Wire wheels and hubs cost a lot new, although rebuilt exchange wheels can cost less than half the new price.

Wheels which wobble along can also mean worn kingpins, swivels, bearings, ball joints, anti-roll bar rubbers, steering box or idler. More than one inch of play at the steering wheel means adjustment is needed at the box if nothing else is worn. If the box is worn it is expensive to replace although parts and exchange units are readily available.

Don't worry over much if the car won't start because of the starter motor. They were never really man enough for the job but usually it is only the bushes and commutator that need attention—about three hours work.

If the car pulls to one side when you slam on the brakes, try swopping the tyres around; it often does the trick. If you get an alarming grating noise from the region of the prop shaft when you brake it is often only the handbrake cable touching the universal joint. If this is the case reroute the cable. Then again, a vigorous vibro-massage, according to restoration expert Derrick Ross, is only the exhaust system fouling the chassis. It's common and can be cured.

Ross is a great authority on interiors, too. He wrote in the Austin-Healey Club's British national magazine, *Rev Counter*: 'Having satisfied yourself that the chassis and engine is in order and the body can be rebuilt (assuming it needs it), before you move the fruit bowl off the sideboard to make room for the concours cup, the interior of the car should be examined.

'Hoods themselves present no problems because they are still available, but if the hoodsticks are missing on some models then you may go bog-eyed searching the small ads columns and *Exchange and Mart* to find a second-hand set. Carpets can easily be made up from the same material as original and the local trimmer will sew it and bind it to improve the appearance.

'The seats can cause concern, depending on the model, but the best deal available for leather trimmed seats is offered by A-H Spares who can supply kits and many trim panels. On the other hand, it is not difficult to retrim the door panels with bulk materials: for example I have found that Dunlop Formula One adhesive is the best for sticking both leather and plastic trim.

'Now let's look at the boot. Probably the lining and floor covering will either be missing, torn or damaged. The original material, called Armourcord can still be obtained.'

Other tips include feeling for wetness under the hood drip rail on the BJ7 and BJ8, because it gets blocked easily and leads to corrosion; watching for doors that need re-hanging—they are a bit heavy for their hinges, and looking for missing boot hinges which crack and corrode and are difficult and expensive to come by. Hood frames are also hard to get; they are like gold dust and cost more because many original owners who fitted hardtops threw them away or at least did not sell them with the car. Windscreens are generally available, but side window glasses are a current problem. A-H Spares are investigating their re-manufacture, but because of their double curvature, the tooling costs are immense.

Finally, when you are peering along the wing lines for signs of bad fitting, watch your head on the quarter light top point if the car is a Mark III. The rubber protection pieces disappear, don't get replaced, and the razor sharp frame makes a terrible hole in your head.

VII

Strengths and Weaknesses: Part Two

ONCE YOU HAVE bought a Big Healey the main problem is to keep it running. Often it is a case of doing the work yourself because good sympathetic garagemen are few and far between now, and naturally, they are often expensive. You will save yourself a lot of trouble if you remember rally driver Andy Dawson's ten commandments of good workshop practice: one: cleanliness and tidyness are next to Godliness; two: safety before speed; three: keep a job list; four: never leave a job unfinished—if a bolt isn't tightened for any reason make a note of it; five: when working under a raised car, always use axle stands; six: never let a car down off a jack without tightening the wheels properly—even if you think the wheels haven't been removed; seven: after working on the brakes remember to make sure you have a firm pedal, and hold heavy pressure on the pedal for thirty seconds—movement indicates a leak; eight: always use some form of locking for suspension fixing bolts, either double nuts, Nylocs, shakeproof washers, Loctite or wiring; nine: wash units off before stripping; ten: clean your tools and put them away when you have finished with them. How many times have you mislaid a spanner?

Maintenance comes under two headings: preventative and reparatory. We'll start with preventative. Rust-proofing is the most essential work of this nature on almost every Big Healey except perhaps those that live in the middle of the Arizona desert, and providing the car is in good condition to start with. The Midland Car Restorations process is a good guide. Director Paul Skilleter, first put his ideas into practice when running a Mark III while working for *Thoroughbred and Classic Cars*. He says: 'If you wish to protect a sound mild steel body part that already has a coating of rust, the only way you can be sure that it won't rust again for many years is to clean the surface right down to bright shiny metal. Wire-brushing away loose rust and then applying rust-preventer is not sufficient. A minute's work with emery paper is more effective. The only way to do the job properly is to fix a coarse sanding disc on your drill and get to work, ending up with fine emery paper to remove the heavier scratches if the area has a visible top surface. If you can't reach the part properly with the drill you will have to do it by hand. The brush-off and wipe down the surface with rust inhibitor before priming. Let the primer dry completely, then spray on the undercoat, followed by top coat. Use a zinc-plate Aerosol for getting in nooks and crannys that your primer brush can't reach.

'Even more important is the protection of the internal hollow sections and seams. Inject Waxoyl into these sections with a syringe or oil can. It sets on the metal as a thickish wax film rather like the stuff new cars are protected with when exported.

'It has great water-chasing and "creeping" properties, and according to the makers, does not lose effectiveness with age if not subject to constant abrasion. The sills and outriggers are the prime recipients of this treatment, through drillings on the inside which can be blocked later with grommets. And when all that is done and the underside of the car cleaned and primed where necessary, coat it all with Waxoyl —it's much better than underseal which can trap moisture between itself and the metal with disastrous results.'

Each expert has his pet way of preventing rust. Dave Jeffery says: 'Ideally you should take the wings off a Healey every year for cleaning, but even I do not go to those lengths. So far as rust removal is concerned I consider that sand blasting is the only real answer.' Hank Leach, founder and past-president of the Austin-Healey Club's Pacific centre, told his avid audience in their magazine *Healey Highlights* that they ought to drill holes in the bottoms of their precious cars. Hank's advice made sense. One area of the Big Healey that must be kept clean is the lower rear wing cavity. Dirt and damp accumulates between the outer wing and its triangular internal suport. Then the dreaded rust bug eats away from the inside out, destroying metal on both sides. Much the same can happen behind the front wing in areas where a lot of salt is used on the roads. The cure at the back is to drill a half-inch hole next to the extreme tip of the triangle, as near as possible to the striker plate, through the bottom of the outer wing and inner sill. Keep the passage clear by frequent blasting it with fresh water when you are cleaning your beloved car. Do the same at the front, just forward of the door pillar if you have a salty dog—and a good tip when you are drilling those holes under the car is to impale an old plastic coffee cup on the drill's bit. It will catch any particles of metal that might be about to fall into your eyes as you writhe under the car. The front drainage hole must be on the very edge of the compartment to work properly. It also pays in salty areas to thoroughly blast clear any accumulations of debris along the underside of the stainless steel wing beads, otherwise your Big Healey is running the risk of electrolytic corrosion between the steel rear wings and the alloy shroud. What is this electrolytic corrosion? It strikes when that joint between the steel wings and the alloy shroud is exposed to a saline solution —such as is found on the roads on a murky winter's day. The saline spray coats the insides of the wings, starting an electrolytic reaction. As it happens the electrical difference between steel and aluminium are considerable and the alloy flanges on the shroud crumble away, especially at the back. So swill it all out every time the car is driven on salty roads.

Corrosion strikes most other places, particularly the exhaust system, which rarely lasts more than three years if it is made of standard mild (rusting) steel. The resonance from the engine can also split silencer boxes. You can try changing the exhaust system for something of better quality, such as stainless steel, and hope that it lasts that much longer. No matter what it is made of, though, it will still suffer if scraped on bumps. Springs suffer from corrosion, too, and benefit from regular cleaning. Keeping the back springs clean helps with spotting hairline cracks in the

Plate 1
Left: The heart of a works car: SMO744's triple SU powerhouse.
Plate 2
Below: The car for all seasons: Thelma Segal's ex-works rally car, used later on the circuits and for shopping!

Plate 3
Above: The Big Healey today: a car for leisure.

Plate 4
Opposite page: Brutal reminder of the modsports era: Thelma Segal's ex-John Gott 3000, with the Alpine Rally winner XJB876 and SMO744 creeping into the picture.

Plate 5
Opposite page: Last of the 'un-refined' Healeys, the early 3000 showing off its sidescreens.
Plate 6
Left: Flat out for a fortune: a US-specification 100-Six undergoes high-speed tests at the Motor Industry Research Association's track at Lyndley, Warwickshire.
Plate 7
Below: Happiness is two Big Healeys: his is the sporty basic two-seater 100-Six with disc wheels, hers is the 'luxurious' two-plus-two 100-Six with trendy wires.

Plate 8
Above: Just to prove that you can seat four people in a Big Healey, Austin hired these models in 1959. How the girls' hairstyles would have lasted in the (optional) rear seats is open to conjecture!

Plate 9
Right: An early, and rare, picture of the Austin-Healey 100's engine compartment, showing the A90-based four-cylinder engine which began the Big Healey story.

Plate 10
Above: A contemporary photograph of the Austin-Healey 100's luggage boot, showing the trim and spare wheel stowage, plus the painted instrument panel and big-spoked steering wheel.

Plate 11
Left: One of the 100's best-known features, the fold-flat windscreen, photographed in 1953.

Plate 12
Overleaf: The one that got away: the 3000 Mark III phase two, built by John Chatham in 1971.

Plate 13
Above: The star of any show: Derek
Buck's 100 lines up for a concours.
Plate 14
Opposite page: Farewell Big Healey:
there will never be another quite
like you.

Plate 15
Opposite page: One of the greatest
Healey racers, John Chatham, with
the immortal DD300, and his 'fun'
car, the rally-replica GRX884D.
Plate 16
Above: Archetypal Healey enthusi-
ast Derek Allanson fights it out with
Reg Woodcock's rapid TR3.

Plate 17
Last of the Sebring cars: Ted
Worswick's mighty 3000 on its
return from the Targa Florio.

Plate 18
Rare colour picture of a rally Healey
in action: Ted Worswick howls
along sideways in the Gulf International Rally of 1967.

Plate 19
Above: Liege Here We Come! Tim Holder recaptures Pat Moss's epic win of 1960.

Plate 20
Right: Grrr! Would anybody trifle with a Big Healey?

leaves around the U bolts and rivets. Don't let rust on axle bolts fool you into thinking they are tight, either. Check with a spanner and see if you can get a bit of a shiny thread. Shock absorbers and handling are much improved if the fluid levels are checked regularly, at the same time. Watch carefully for any suspension wear; it can ruin the handling of your Big Healey.

So can a lack of servicing, and there is an awful lot to do. The Big Healey is a car that was designed in a bygone era when mechanics thought nothing of attending to a couple of dozen grease nipples every 3,000 miles and there was a blacksmith in almost every town to reset your rear springs. Labour was cheap and oil cans were used frequently in those days and still should be on the Big Healey. The drop of oil on the throttle spindles where they emerge from the carburetter casings is vital to reduce spindle wear. Worn spindles cost a fortune in excessive petrol consumption, especially on the triple carburetter cars.

Beware against overfilling the dashpot reservoirs. Excess oil will clog free movement of the carburetter pistons, and cause poor running. Don't neglect to wash the wire mesh air filters in petrol at least every 6,000 miles either. Do it thoroughly because dirty filters cost a lot more in wasted fuel than the little bit you slosh about. When you have finished, springle a little oil into them, then clean the fuel filters in the float chamber unions and check the float levels.

Keep a close eye on the tappet clearances and take great care when tuning as top dead centre is difficult to find. Engine oil is best changed at 3,000 mile intervals despite the claims of some multigrade manufacturers, and it can be quite difficult because of the low ground clearance. This is also a problem associated with the gearbox and rear axle. Never put additives in the overdrive and gearbox, although they do no harm to the engine or rear axle. Dampers can benefit from topping up more frequently than recommended if they are suspect. Nevertheless they may have to be replaced for legal reasons now that they are part of Government tests in countries such as Britain. The back ones can be reached more easily by removing the eight captive bolts securing the rear seats in the two plus two—that is providing they come out easily. Often they are extremely difficult to get out without breaking.

While you are poking around there, make sure the axle casing breather is clear to prevent oil being forced out through the axle seals onto the brakes.

Brake and clutch hydraulics need only routine attention if the car is used daily with a change of fluid every 18,000 miles or eighteen months, whichever is the sooner. But if the car is laid up, say in the winter, pump the brakes and clutch once a week to help keep the rubber seals lubricated and stop the possibility of the clutch seizing.

A new brand of trouble is developing with brakes now that cars are being pampered. When they were hammered every day the brakes and clutches wore down at a regular rate and the operating pistons stayed fairly clean. Now they are used only infrequently, especially in the winter, the pistons spend long periods immersed in the hydraulic fluid, which absorbs water. As a result, the pistons go rusty on the unused section and when the car is driven again the rusty parts pass through the seals, which promptly wear and leak. This is especially applicable now that brake linings are hardly ever worn right down—more of the piston spends its time immersed in the fluid. One solution, apart from dismantling for the duration of the lay-off, is to have the calipers or cylinders reamed out and fitted with stainless steel sleeves. It should be remembered, also, that the manufacturers are now recommending frequent renewal of the brake fluid.

Longer term preventative maintenance includes renewing the brushes and springs on the starter motor. These units hardly ever survive more than 50,000 miles-worth of cranking over the massive engine—and it is worth overhauling them before they give up the ghost. The worst part about the job is getting the motor's bottom securing bolt on and off. You need patience and long slim fingers, and 'you'll cry with happiness when you get it back on,' says Rich Locasso, *Healey Highlights*' technical correspondent. He wrote an excellent series how to make your Healey run further and faster. Basically he said:

Gap the plugs at .025 in, or .035 in if using a hot coil—this helps starting and gives more spark to ensure ignition under running conditions. Do not waste time on plugs more than 10,000 miles old—fit new ones for ultimate performance. Make sure the points are in good condition, clean off any protective coating from a new set, and do not get any grease or oil on the surfaces during fitting or when measuring the gap—it decreases their life. Condensers rarely go wrong providing they are changed with the points. Use good quality copper plug leads with a proper terminal, not the crimp-on type. 'It is possible to develop a high-speed miss from a spark leak between the number six cylinder plug wire and the heater hose running from the block into the heater on the later Healeys,' he says. 'The solution is to cover the last three inches of the plug wire with a similar piece of rubber hose.' So far as the rest of the wires are concerned, check the primary leads from the control box and distributor to the coil to ensure that the contacts are clean and solid and that the wires have not deteriorated.

Check the distributor cap for signs of cracking. This is happening more often now that people are washing down their engine bays and getting moisture on or in the cap. If the engine starts with the distributor in this condition the heat frequently cracks the cap. The distributor's centre carbon contact should also be in good condition and free to move up and down. If it is not, clean it or replace it.

Timing on a Big Healey is always somewhat empirical with no conventional markings. Make marks at $\frac{1}{4}$ in intervals on the crankshaft pulley. They equal approximately five degrees at a time. 'Sometimes the timing notch on the pully is inaccurate from the factory,' says Locasso. If this is suspected, and you have not got a dial gauge, remove number one plug, insert a rod, turn over the engine and determine top dead centre that way. But don't be fooled—there is an awful lot of movement on the crankshaft either side of top dead centre which will only move the rod a fraction. The distributor should be kept immaculately clean with everything properly lubricated. Check the centrifugal advance springs to see if any are broken and that the weights can open to full advance. You can check the vaccum advance diaphragm by disconnecting the vacuum tube at the carburetter, sucking on it, holding the vacuum with your tongue, and seeing if the vacuum remains in the tube or disappears from air leaks in the diaphragm. A diaphragm will increase fuel consumption because it cannot advance the spark when the engine is under low load. Make sure, too, that your battery or batteries is good enough to give the proper voltage to the coil.

Check the curburetters as instructed in the workshop manual and suspect the SU fuel pump or fuel lines if you have high speed starvation. They should be no smaller than $\frac{3}{8}$ in outside diameter with a large bore and not too long a flexible section so that they restrict flow. It is also advisable to route the lines away from the exhaust. When the pump is suspect, the first test should be to disconnect the outlet pipe to the carburetters and check the delivery rate. This should be at least one gallon every four minutes. If the pump fails to work, check the electrical lead with a test light. Never spark it to earth; there could be a tremendous explosion. Providing the pump has a proper electrical supply, but still does not produce, check its points, a much-neglected job. Then it is a case of following the workshop manual as far as possible, but don't try to go too far because there are some tricky adjustments and the old pump is worth quite a bit in exchange against a reconditioned unit.

Clutches are straightforward on the Big Healey providing you can get the slave cylinder off the six-cylinder models. You need patience and another pair of hands to get at one of the bolts. Whenever working on the slave cylinder it is worth replacing the flexible tube which hangs down below the frame member and frequently suffers from being in this position. Tape it up to the frame for safety, but don't kink it in the process.

Gearboxes cost a fortune to overhaul and they are painful to work on. 'Some times even works mechanics had to rebuild them three times to make them work properly.' says John Chatham. 'This was mainly through lack of experience,' says Fred Draper. 'With the 3000 gearbox out of the car and the bell housing removed, if one selected a gear it would drop out the selector ball and spring. Then the box would have to be partially stripped again to replace it.' You can save yourself a bit of money, though, by removing the transmission yourself and taking it along to be reconditioned. 'One or two people can handle the job,' says Hank Leach, 'and there are a few tips which aren't in the workshop manuals. After removing the seats and interior around the transmission housing, remove the four universal joint nuts. Reach back into the propeller shaft tunnel, unscrew the cap at the end and slide the universal joint off the propeller shaft. Don't replace it until after the transmission is back in the car. Be sure to remove both the bolts on top and the two from underneath the frame at the back of the transmission housing. Remove the stabilizer while you are underneath and note the condition of the rubber grommets. They will almost certainly have to be replaced. Then lift out the gearbox and when replacing it use a small hydraulic jack under the engine to help line up the two components. This is best done with an old first motion shaft. When everything except the transmission tunnel is replaced, bleed the slave cylinder—it is a lot easier than doing it from under the car.'

It is quite practical to overhaul a BMC gearbox following the workshop manual, but the job will still be expensive because of the high cost of remanufactured parts. The overdrive is much more difficult and best left to the experts, although spares are still readily available and reconditioned units proportionately cheaper. Providing the unit has not been abused trouble is usually traceable to external components such as the wiring or solenoid. One Big Healey owner has had two new units fitted to his car because of intermittent operation, only to discover later that the fault was in the overdrive switch! The way the fault was found is worth remembering: a wire was fitted to the power lead at the solenoid and connected to a bulb inside the car with an earth wire to the chassis. When the overdrive suddenly cut out the bulb went out, too, proof enough it was the switch causing trouble. If the switch is not the problem check all electrical connections followed by the solenoid operation, and external valves. After that get the unit pressure tested. If the reading is OK, the fault could be a sticky sliding member which can sometimes be cured by letting the clutch in with a bang at about 40 mph on the over-run after re-wiring it to work like that. Other than that it means removing the unit from the car and stripping or fitting a reconditioned overdrive. But at least it can be removed on its own like the gearbox.

Rear axles rarely give trouble, but if they start to whine, act quickly, for they do not usually last long afterwards. Sometimes the axle seals leak, but they are easy to change providing you have a special locknut tool or can get a twenty-four inch crescent wrench. If the shock absorbers are leaking they must be replaced, but you can try a heavier oil in them to give you time to save up. Reconditioned absorbers are not much use; the mating of old and new parts does not seem to work. You can adjust the shock absorbers for stiffness by grinding the surface of the internal valves— but it is essential to keep the front dampers stiffer than the back or you will be subject to a dangerously-swinging tail. The work involved is usually beyond the average enthusiast's skill and patience, though. In the same way it is better to fit pairs of new rear springs than have them reset. Old springs wear where the leaves rub together, so they lose their temper quicker when reset. A good way to keep a check on the car's ride height is to stand a cigar packet under the appropriate point, slide it out to touch top and bottom, then remove the packet for measurement. It is a lot easier than using a ruler!

Front suspension wear is easy to diagnose on the Big Healey. It shakes, shudders, vibrates, wanders, knocks and bangs. Almost anything can cause this condition. One of the prime suspects should be the wire wheels if fitted. Check them for truth and balance. Tyres go out of balance, too, when there is suspension trouble. When getting the tyres changed with wire wheels, try to get it done by hand if the firm fitting them is using an American machine. These pneumatic tyre removers exert so much pressure they can weaken the spokes. The machines used in Britain do not use the same pressure to break the tyre's and are quite safe.

King pins and swivels wear, especially the lower bushing. Follow the workshop manual carefully, or you could have wheels flying off if the components are not reassembled properly. Wheel bearings are easily checked by rocking the wheel. Worn ball joints can be easily detected by looking for movement of the ball joint within its housing. Play in the steering can usually be adjusted out at the box by following the workshop manual. Otherwise, a reconditioned unit is expensive although readily available, as are several component parts. A worn idler can be detected in a similar way to a worn ball joint. Worn anti-roll bar rubbers are easy to spot.

Electrical problems are chiefly a case of donning a Sherlock Holmes hat and patiently eliminating one suspect at a time. The bodywork benefits from keeping immaculately clean. Hoods can be expensive and they usually last only a few years, less if folded when wet. Brasso, followed by Silvo, works wonders on opaque rear windows and you can fit household draught excluder to the top channel of rattling sidescreens to turn your old Healey into a modern luxury liner (nearly!).

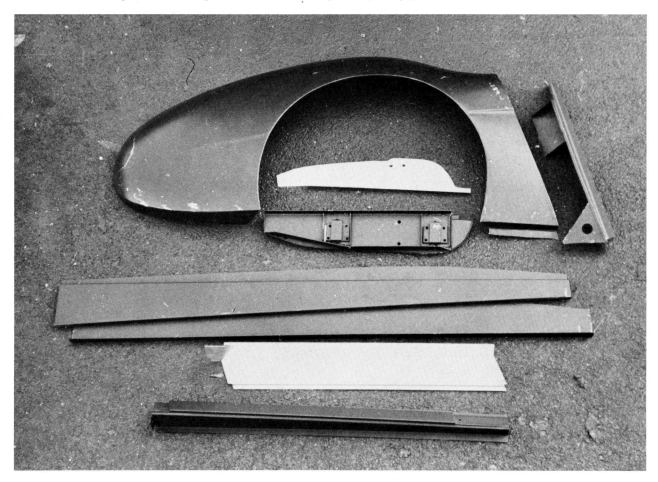

Body spares in the metal: a rear wing, alloy door shut trim, a steel door shut face, the alloy kick plate trim and inner and outer sills.

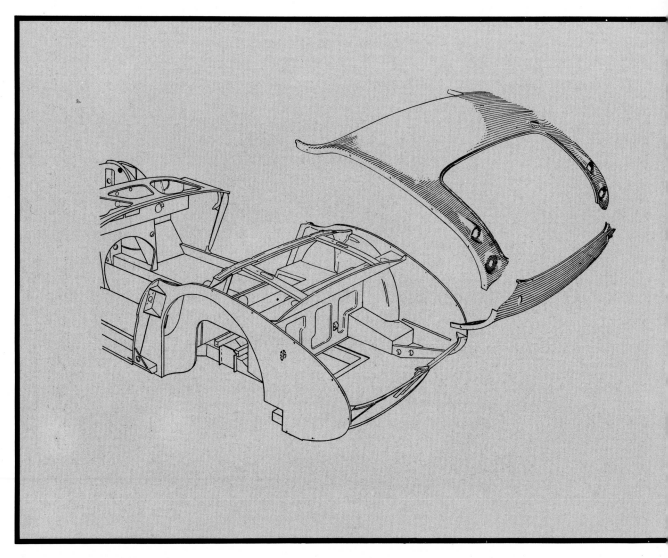

How the rear shroud fits onto the chassis and inner wings.

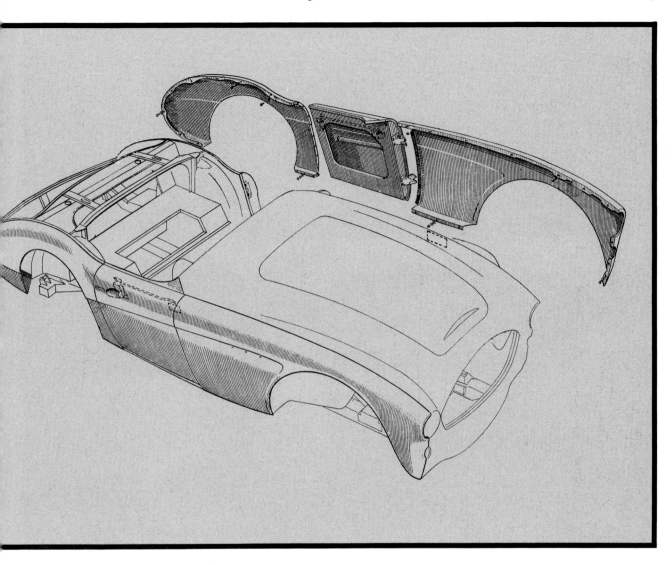

The outer body parts (from a 100-Six, other models similar).

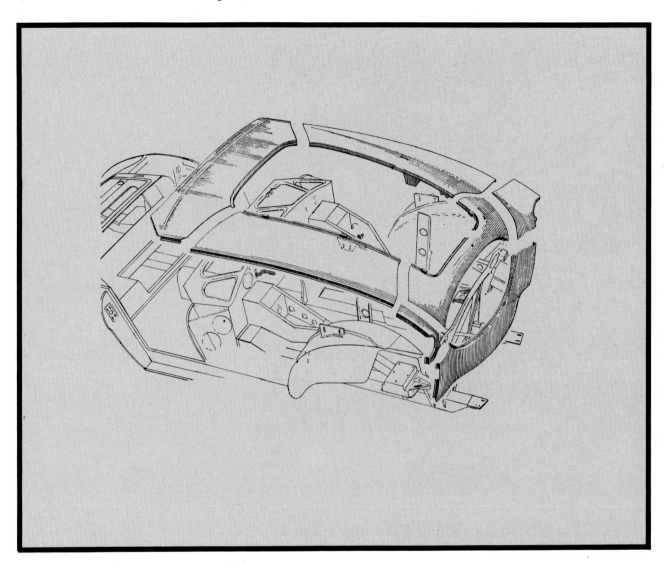

How the front shroud fits onto the chassis and inner wings.

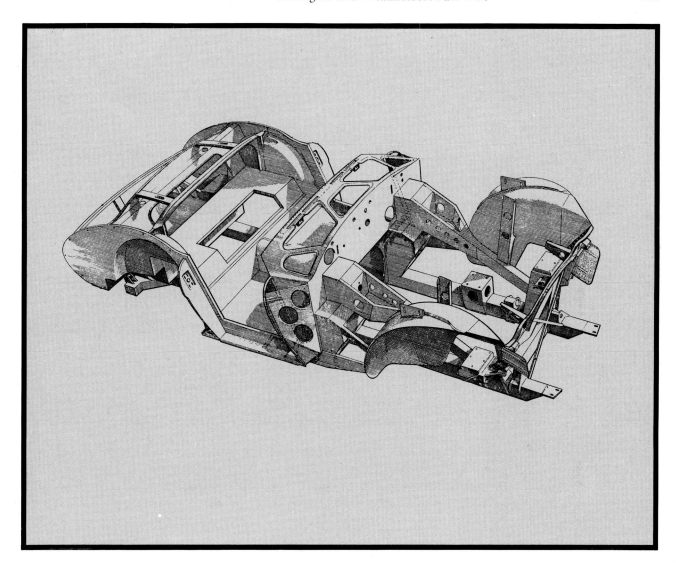

The basic chassis with bulkheads and inner wings fitted.

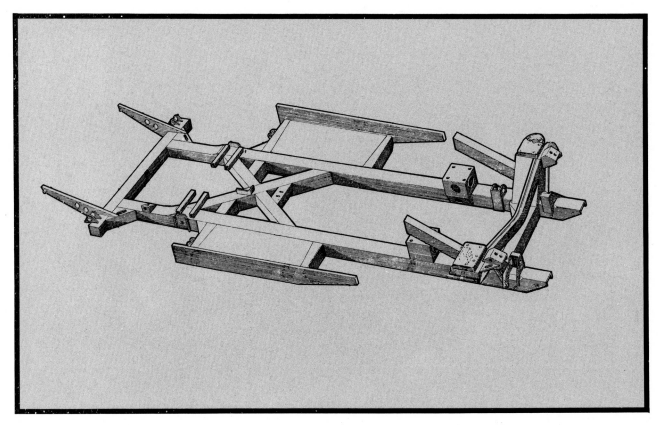

The bare chassis.

Use a cigar packet to check your rear
suspension height—it's easier than
using a ruler!

VIII

Common Problems

ONE of the chief problems about running a Big Healey today is using it enough. They simply lap up the miles with great reliability if they are looked after properly. But what was it like in the good old days before Big Healeys became a costly investment and the price of car spares generally accelerated? Photographer Dave Kennard, who works for *Hot Car* and *Car Mechanics* among other magazines, used to drive a Big Healey 24,000 miles a year, much of it in the London rush hour, plus frequent fast trips to the South Coast for *Boat* magazine.

'I bought my first four-cylinder Healey for £100 after smashing up an MGA,' said Dave, 'simply because the Healey was a sports car. With the sort of mileage I was covering and the price I paid for the car, there was always something that needed doing. I used to spend practically every weekend under the car repairing something —but it was possible to drive a classic sports car everyday and use it as a working vehicle because you could go to any BMC dealer for spares.

'After about a year I had a confrontation with a Rover 2000 and the Healey needed a bit of repair work. Initially damage to the Healey appeared to have been confined to the offside headlamp, but on further investigation it was found that the vulnerable aluminium shroud around the bonnet had crinkled, so this needed replacing as well.

'As a new one was rather expensive, we found a chap who had a rather nice line in fibreglass parts and bought a new shroud and a couple of wings. They were a bit of a fiddle to fit, but the overall effect was very good, only the original bonnet being retained at the front. Later I fitted fibreglass rear wings and sills, and a luggage boot lid of the same material as the old ones were getting a bit ragged round the bottom.

'Later I really went upmarket and bought a 1963 Mark II, paying about £400. Eventually this needed fibreglass panels, too, and a rebore after 120,000 miles. We got that done at home and the gearbox rebuilt. While all this work was underway I spent hours of back-breaking work preparing for a respray, which is none to easy with a combination of fibreglass and metal panels. Preparation of fibreglass is even more important than with metal as imperfections are more likely to show up. However, it is possible to get a good finish with fibreglass; it just takes a lot of work.

'The chief problems of driving the car so much in heavy traffic, apart from cockpit heat and the like, centred around the clutch and gearbox. The thrust race bearing used to wear out at about twice the rate of the clutch. I put this down to the lack of a return spring on the clutch. I reckoned that the lack of pressure on the race when the clutch was let in allowed it to move out only slowly. In London traffic it never had time to free itself properly.

'I tried fitting it with a very light return spring, but it pulled so far back that you used to have to pump the pedal every time you used the clutch—which was frequently, and turned out to be impractical.

'The shock absorbers used to wear out fairly quickly, too—lasting about 30,000 miles on average. You adapt to the gradual deterioration and don't really notice the wear until you feel it at the front when they get really worn out. I remember I was once stopped on Westminster Bridge by a policeman who informed me that I had hardly a wheel on the ground. He had never seen anything like it before! I also fitted steel instead of phosphor bronze bearings in the synchromesh and have never had any trouble since. (None of the experts recommend this modification): Of my two Healeys, the 100 seemed much more solid than the Mark II.

'Now spare parts are difficult to get in some cases and expensive, and I use the Healey only at weekends, hammering the company Cortina all over town. Life will never be the same as it was in the 1950s and 1960s when you could run a Big Healey every day.'

Why are the spares so expensive? I asked Fred Draper. Fred, who has lived with the Big Healey every working day for twenty-five years and survived to build up an unparalled reputation among the fanatics, said: 'It's chiefly the cost of tooling. You have to order in such large quantities nowadays to get anything made, let alone bring down the price to something realistic. We feel that our efforts have been worthwhile when we are able to market many parts at a lower price than British Leyland did three or four years ago. One of our chief problems with the Big Healey is the failure of first gear. We got over that by sweating a new gear onto the old laygear cluster and managed to produce a reliable replacement part for about a third the cost of having them remade.

Sometimes you can buy up a quantity of redundant spares to keep the price down. In one case, we re-imported Healey parts from Singapore. On another occasion I bought up a dozen or so gearboxes for the Westminster used by the British police in the mid-1960s, knowing they had the same gear train as the Healey gearbox, unlike other Westminsters. But, of course, their mainshafts and overdrives were of no use, being Borg Warner . . .

'Overdrive parts are not a problem at present, though. Back axles are readily available, except for the 100, although we have a few spares for that. Shock absorbers used to be relatively cheap, but they have soared in price now that few vehicles are using the old lever pattern. There's no problem over brake parts, except sometimes the drums. Springs are easy to get and so are most engine parts, although sometimes there are hold-ups. Steering box parts are getting rare, although reconditioned units are still available.

'Body parts used to be a problem when several different people were making them. The wings, for instance, hardly ever fitted. But now we have got the original makers to reproduce them we have had only one complaint in 200 sets sold. This is

Left: Shock absorbers must be in good condition if a Big Healey is to handle at all well. Pictured from the left are a standard Armstrong rear shock absorber; a competition unit with a wide range of adjustment; and a front shock absorber.

Below: What a power train! A triple-carburetter Healey engine, gearbox and overdrive ready to drop into a Mark II.

because they are pressed out now, whereas they used to be made by hand in three parts and then welded. Shrinkage from the welding caused the problems, allied with the fact that Healey panels are difficult to fit anyway. The shrouds, which are made in seven pieces, still need highly-skilled assembly, though.

'The wings are all basically the same, except for those on the 100. The early 100 cars had a different wheel arch depth of course, and no swage on the front wings. The later 100 wings are basically the same as those on all the rest of the models, except that again there was no swage. In this case, you have either to beat out the swage or lead it in. The three basic doors, 100; 100-Six and early 3000; and the late 3000, give no problems.

'Lucas electrical spares and Autosparks looms are in good supply. But any radiator grille for other than the Mark III is like gold dust. And because we have to use small manufacturers for remaking such items, the cost of reproduction is frightening. The same sort of problem applies to hardtops, although it is possible that one of the specialists will start remaking them soon. Bonnets and boot lids give no problem and we are remaking the fragile luggage boot hinges in better material; plus locking door handles and boot lid handles in a higher quality material than was used originally.

'Wheels give no supply problems and we are reproducing hubs, but this is a very expensive business. On the other hand, reproduction luggage racks are surprisingly cheap! Naturally we get hoses remade in quantity, but like all rubber parts they seem expensive. Radiators give no problem for exchange in the case of the 100-Six and 3000, although supplies for the 100 can be difficult.

'Suspension parts wear, of course, so we can stock up on those—but in the case of rarely-needed items such as the side glasses on later cars, the unit cost of reproduction is fantastic. Complete windscreens are in good supply for the 100-Six onwards.'

As he wrestled with more problems, I asked Fred which was his favourite car. 'The four-cylinder BN2 for sure,' he said. Another man who has wrestled with a few Big Healeys in his time is Dave Jeffery, of Southern Carburetters, near the world-famous Wimbledon tennis stadium. Dave used to be one of those exclusive breed of people who broke up Big Healeys for their second-hand parts as a dual line to retailing carburetter parts dating back to the early 1900s and sorting out problems on his rolling road. Mind you, Dave didn't break up all his Big Healeys—he still has a fine collection down at his farm in Surrey, including one of the first works cars, bought as a wreck for £90! What were the chief problems with the wrecks, I asked, apart from the obvious corrosion? 'Camshaft and rocker shaft wear were other common problems' said Dave. 'Running-on gave a lot of trouble, too, with the higher compression engines such as the Mark III. Sometimes you could only stop the engine by opening the throttle wide and switching off.'

Dave, who normally drives a Mark III or a 100 to work, says he prefers the 100. 'It's a much better balanced car and better performing,' he said. 'Do you know, you can even take-off in overdrive from 750 rpm?'

One firm whose business is taking off and has seen a fair number of Big Healey problems in recent years has been MCR in Birmingham. I asked them what was the worst job on a Big Healey and they said servicing the steering. 'You try and get the grille off without damaging it . . . it's very difficult. And fitting the exhaust system. That's so time consuming.'

I then asked John Chatham what was the worst job on a Big Healey. 'Fitting the wings and shrouds are a real problem,' he said. 'Nothing of this sort ever fitted properly for a start and it's no different now. You need to use highly-skilled bodymen for assembly. Replica parts vary wildly. It's best to get the same man to make and fit the shroud and wings.'

They say that no two Big Healeys feel the same. Much the same can be said of the specialists. They all love the handsome brute—and all feel differently about the problems of keeping them on the road.

IX

The American Scene

DONALD HEALEY'S 100 hit the United States like a bombshell. Its fresh sensational lines, ample power, and very attractive price created overnight queues of eager buyers everywhere. 'Thanks to the post-war automotive revolution begun in the colonies by MG's TC and Jaguar's XK120, Americans by 1954 were buying British sports cars as if there was no tomorrow. Merchant marine convoys which a decade earlier crossed the Atlantic eastbound laden with war material, now sailed the opposite direction to disgorge thousands upon thousands of Jaguar, MG, Triumph and Austin-Healey sports cars on US piers,' says Dave Ramstad, one of America's greatest Healey men.

Dave, who now lives in Washington, was turned on by a friend's 1955 Healey 100 in 1957. It rapidly became his favourite car although it was not until 1962 that he was able to afford one. That was when he bought his first Healey, a brilliant red and black 1957 100-Six. A few years later another 100-Six followed, this time a white 1959 four-seater with hardtop, and he now enjoys a golden beige Mark III bought new in Cocoa Beach, Florida, in 1967.

"The British sports car boom of the 1950s and 1960s poured so many cute and sexy two-seaters into the affluent American scene that any vestige of uniqueness or exclusivity was quickly lost. Well-to-do high school and college students drove them to classes, upper middle class housewives drove them to the supermarket, and hedonistic, upwardly-mobile young singles and couples drove them everywhere. E type, TR3s and TR4s, MGAs and MGBs and Healey 100s and 3000s were seen on American streets, highways and parking lots to such an extent that they simply melted into the panorama of the times. A great many British sports car owners were merely interested in the way the car made them feel, or the image it helped them project,' says Dave.

Mike Markey from Washington frankly confessed that he bought his first sports car, a 100, in 1956 'because it was the next best thing to a Sunbeam Alpine, which I wanted. It was pure whoopee! An emotional mixture of Fangioism, wind in the collar, Hey! Look at us, and a feeling of mechanical better than a Ford Sedan. It was an excuse to go motor racing . . .'

Bob Maioroff, from Berkeley, California, became a Healey person as soon as he saw one in 1954. The car fitted in with his ten-handicap golfing, surfing, fishing,

Candid camera shot of Donald Healey in America. The scene is the Austin-Healey Club Pacific Centre's second annual West Coast meeting in 1976. The maestro arrived at Patrick's Point State Park, California, in Kevin Faughnan's 1967 BJ8 with Kevin's wife Agnes in the back seat, for the club's car show, barbeque and awards presentation. 'I had just had our Healey resprayed and had not had time to replace the interior door handles,' said Kevin. 'Consequently, when we three arrived at a site, I'd have to rush around the car, or Agnes would have to open the door for Donald! Also, because Donald prefers to ride in an American sedan, we would stop about a mile from the site we were visiting and Donald would switch to the Healey. Then we would drive in to the wild cheers of all the other owners who didn't know our secret. Of course, Donald Healey would eventually tell everybody and we would all have a good laugh about it.'

ski-ing, and motor racing ambitions. And like many American owners, he found time to do his own tuning and repairs . . . another sportsman, Ron Pfeifer from Fremont, California, scoured the sixty miles from San Jose to San Francisco to find his Mark III 'in better shape than its former owner, a member of the fair sex . . .' Student Tom Albright from Washington, DC, divided his spare time between surfing and tinkering with his 1960 BN7; German-born Rusty Hanewacker from San Francisco numbered diving, photography, hunting and fishing and collecting coins as alternative hobbies to his 1963 Mark II; mechanical marvel Dave Giampetro occupied his time playing with his clarinet, saxophone, flute and 100-Six and telling fellow owners how to keep them going; sixteen-year-old student Edie Mayntz divided her time between training horses and dogs with driving her birthday present 100-Six; Blake DeLuca ran the Pacific Centre's parts service; Jerry Tibbetts from Maine preferred his two Big Healeys and mobile home to a house; and Joe and Judi Coffman did 200,000 miles in their 3000 two-seater. Joe also found time to become a professional musician in San Francisco and edit that wonderful magazine *Healey Highlights*. And Rich Locasso from Washington contributed really good technical articles based on his experiences in taking his BT7 to pieces.

Meanwhile Dave Ramstad was thinking about buying one of the last Big Healeys to land in America. 'It was mid-September in 1967 and I had become involved in a small way with the fantastic NASA adventure unfolding at Florida's Kennedy Space Centre, having coaxed my reliable, but well-worn 100-Six there in the winter of 1966–67. This machine had transported me and all my worthwhile possessions south from my native Washington State to California, then east via Albuquerque, Kansas City, St Louis and Birmingham to my balmy destination in the Sunshine State. Such travels are certainly not unusual in highly-mobile America, but this trek was accomplished on that BN4's 4.125 axle without benefit of overdrive, and with a dramatically-clanking first and reverse gears, which added a bit of excitement.

The voice of the American Big Healey owner today: Dave Ramstad with his wife, Kathy, and '41578' at the inaugural West Coast annual meeting at Grants Pass, Oregon, in September 1975.

I received an unforgettable education avoiding much of the famous interstate highway network, whose speed limit was then 70 mph, and meandering over secondary routes out of necessity—I was too slow—a method often followed today out of choice by serious auto and cycle tourers.

'That old 100-Six and I got on quite happily in the months that followed. Weekends were spent journeying three directions out of Brevard County: Fort Lauderdale to the South, St Augustine to the north, Sarasota on the Gulf Coast opposite, and the great endurance racing spectacles at Sebring and Daytona were merely the high spots. The BN4 received regular maintenance, of course, and it was during one of my visits to the local BMC agency when the saga of my current Big Healey started. Exiting the parts department via the showroom (which required passing between shiny new Renault R10s, Sprites, MGBs and huge Dodge sedans), I was accosted by a Good Ol' Boy salesman, who suggested that he could make me a "right nice" trade on a new 3000.

'I was not interested in this proposal then, with the 100-Six doing just fine, but mainly because the heavier-looking BJ7/BJ8 convertibles did not create any special personal excitement. Curiosity alone, though, saw me follow this gentleman outside to the agency's Austin-Healey "demo." It happened to be a new Mark III finished in ivory with a striking red interior—a commonplace arrangement at the time—but the car was being regularly and thoroughly thrashed about the area by potential buyers of questionable driving skill, and I wanted no part of it. He was not finished. A short walk out back to the storage lot revealed a sight which was totally new in my experience.

'There lay what was obviously an Austin-Healey, but in the most forlorn and woebegone state imaginable. It had heard how export automobiles were prepared for their Atlantic sea voyage, but I was not ready for the actual sight of such a creature. With all the brightwork coated liberally with cosmoline, the convertible

Big Healeys as they used to be. UJB141 (centre left), UJB142 (centre right), and UJB143 (later to become DD300) extreme right, in the thick of the action as the field roars away at Sebring in 1960.

top sealed in clear plastic, shipping labels slapped on much of the glass, a filthy lacklustre finish, and a pronounced list from one nearly flat Road Speed tyre, this particular 3000 Mark III looked very sad indeed. Its singular apparent distinction was an unusual metallic tan finish.

'This car was truly a mess, but, of course, all those layers of grime and grease were removeable. I still didn't like the bulky, long convertible top, the inside view out through the new curved windscreen was too close to that experienced in a fortified pillbox, and the revised exhaust system was unsportingly quiet for my tastes. On the other hand, two rather positive factors became quickly apparent. First the metallic sand finish was one I had never heard of, let alone seen; and the second, the car was practically untouched by human hands—the odometer registered an impressively virginal twenty-two miles!

'Still not highly aroused, I left the agency in old reliable and resumed life as usual. That old four-seater, and its always handsome works hardtop, all dressed in white, ran even better than before; could it have been my imagination? In any case, an event that was to change my life that fall occurred soon after. Spotted in the back pages throughout the world's automotive Press was the announcement that production of the big Austin-Healey would cease with the end of 1967. It was as if a switch had been turned in my mind—suddenly the simple prospect of buying a new car took on an historic aspect. Within days, serious discussions with Good Ol' Boy took place with the eventual goal putting the old BN4 in their care, and the curious metallic tan BJ8 in my hands. I considered with great timidity the prospect of three years of car payments on this, my first new car purchase. The longest contract into which I had previously entered was one of only eighteen months duration for the purchase of my first Big Healey five years earlier.

'This particular Mark III, chassis number HBJ8L/41578, carried a window sticker indicating that it had been imported through Miami by one Ship and Shore Motors of Palm Beach, and, more to the point, its base price was $3,565 and the only included option was a $44 tonneau cover—the top boot was standard equipment. The grand total including tax and license just broke $3,800 and deducting $1,000 for the BN4—a respectable figure in 1967—left me with a thirty-six month balance payable in $92 installments; a very sobering thought at the time as I recall. My sole request prior to delivery was that a swap of knock-off caps be arranged with the white "demo"; 41578 carried the new octagonal "safety" caps while the white car featured the earlier and more traditional eared type. A totally cleaned and quite transformed 41578 was delivered into my nervous and highly-excited possession at the end of that week.

'Anticipating a long relationship with 41578, its run-in took place the very next weekend during a leisurely 500-mile tour to northern Florida and back. That big three-litre six was kept strictly below 2,500 rpm (the owner's handbook stipulated a 50 mph maximum), an extremely frustrating task considering the potential of the 150 bhp BJ8. The first actual attention by the owner was an adjustment downward of the throttle pedal to allow a more relaxed leg position (done in the first twenty-four hours), and an upward adjustment of the headlamps. Shortly after 41578 returned to the agency for its 1,000-mile service, the installation of a BMC AM radio, one aerodynamic Talbot mirror for the left front wing, and a pair of nice MG-Austin-Healey crested seat belts. One of the first tasks carried out by the new owner was the respray of the wire wheels, since the rigours of the car's shipment and storage had reduced their once bright appearance to a dull grey. The first actual failure in my memory was a burst upper radiator hose. This triviality would not merit mention but for the fact that it ruptured merely two weeks after delivery, caused most likely by a manufacturing defect.

'41578 spent the period from October 1967 to December 1968 commuting a total of forty-eight miles daily to work at Kennedy Space Centre, while weekends were involved with treks about the Sunshine State, much as its predecessor had done. Twenty-five thousand miles were recorded over those fourteen months, 90 per cent of which were of the easy highway variety. The car returned excellent reliability and touring pleasure. Mechanical attention during this period consisted of a clutch slave cylinder replacement and the repair of a leaking rear axle pinion seal. Strictly voluntary additions included the installation of a Lucas sports coil, triple air horns (unobtrusively located on the right of the radiator), Lucas Fogranger lamps, a pair of Amco rubber floor mats, countless coats of Classic Car wax, and a luggage rack.

This latter item was of immeasurable value during a pleasant tour north to Great Smoky Mountains National Park, the occasion being the doubling of 41578's ownership through marriage in the spring of 1968. My new wife, Kathy, took quickly to the Big Healey, helped, I'm sure, by her experience in a succession of family Volkswagen Beetles, although she has never quite felt comfortable behind that big wheel to this day.

'It must be added that while the original equipment Dunlop Road Speeds offered top-notch sporting performance appropriate to the Mark III, their life expectancy was remarkably brief. Even considering the rather conservative touring use to which they were applied, the disappearance of tread on the rear pair at 15,000 miles and on the fronts by 19,000 miles was difficult to accept. 41578 received its first of several sets of Pirelli Cinturatos early in 1968.

'The Christmas season took the form of a crossroads for both 41578 and its owners. With the downturn of employment in the Apollo/Saturn moon rocket project, Boeing saw fit to offer paid transfers for many Cape Kennedy employees to the company's Seattle, Washington, home base. Having accepted, we watched all our major possessions packed away in a huge transcontinental moving van before packing our personal gear in the Healey and excitedly plotted a course westward. It was mid-December and surprisingly cold in the American South. Passing through Montgomery, Vicksburg, Shreveport, Dallas, Amarillo and Los Angeles, car and crew covered 3,000 trouble-free miles before reaching incomparable San Francisco where an extra day was spent riding cable cars and climbing hills. After nine days and some 3,800 miles we eventually arrived in the North West at our destination and my home town, the pulp, paper and 747-producing city of Everett. 41578 digested the whole trip without drama, the only annoyances being well-soaked carpets from a mysterious rain leak, and laboured starter cranking due to thick 40 weight engine oil which had suited the Florida environment well.

'Fully broken in now at some 30,000 miles, 41578 began its second phase, a span of five years when as sole family transport, it took its owners to work, carried the weekly groceries, and hit the open road for the expected weekend and summer holiday pleasure trips. When the Ramstads increased to three with the arrival of baby son Christian early in 1970, the big tan Healey was there to carry that tiny bundle from hospital to home in style. These years witnessed 41578 in totally dependable daily service through all seasons and in every form of weather found in the great Pacific North West. Modest snowfalls were taken in its stride, thanks to the Healey's slightly rearward weight bias, ample torque, and its efficient Pirelli radials. The only collision ever sustained by this car occurred during just such a snowfall, when $100 of damage was done in the right headlamp area due to sliding into a Mustang on a hard-packed surface.

'Areas of special attention in this radically different climate included defence against corrosion, sealing of wind and water leaks, and an increase in the perennial cleaning and waxing schedule. This second phase saw a continuation of periodic general maintenance plus replacements of the original fuel pump at 45,000 miles; first brake pads, 38,000 miles; and rear main bearing seals, 55,000 miles. It was at this time that 41578 received its side air vents *a la* works rally cars, a modification

which actually made more sense in the previous heat of Florida, but which has proved beneficial through the years in spite of Washington's temperate climate. Having received top service and performance from the Pirelli Cinturato tyres, it now seemed desirable to fit the slightly larger 175 × 15 Cinturato, a size which is now quite elusive.

'It was well before this time that the true scarcity of late Healeys in metallic golden beige became obvious. Possibly a total of half a dozen similar cars had been spotted in the South East, and maybe a dozen and a half were encountered in 41578's new home. Correspondence with Fred Draper and Leyland's Abingdon, Cowley and Longbridge offices have shed no light on the origin or reason for this peculiar finish.

'This Big Healey's work load decreased sharply in November 1972 with the addition of a stablemate, a large Dodge van, and when relative prosperity in spring 1975 allowed the purchase of a restored 1961 Austin Mini, 41578 finally earned a well-deserved rest. It has spent much of its time since, which we call the third phase, patiently waiting under cover for use in strictly pleasurable pursuits. That includes

Keeping the British flag flying in the US, the Big Healey of Bob Olthoff and Ronnie Bucknum howls past the Morgan of Dick McNeil, William Clarens and Joe Ferguson at Sebring in 1963.

carrying we four Ramstads, daughter Erin arrived in July 1974, to local and regional Healey club functions and tours during the warmer months, as well as the three annual and immensely enjoyable United States Healey owners' meetings which have occurred since 1975.

'The long periods of relative inactivity which now mark 41578's existence most assuredly do not indicate a lack of attention. Rather, the care and maintenance programme continues as previously, but with the positive distinction that lengthy projects may now be accomplished in a rather leisurely fashion. This was simply not possible in those earlier years when, regardless of what was attempted, the entire thing must be completed by Sunday night since the Monday morning drive to work was lurking just ahead. This third phase, which began for 41578 at about 60,000 miles, encompasses more general upkeep requirements such as brakes, radiator hoses, fan belts, and silencers. More substantial jobs include the replating of the bumpers and overriders, replacement of the soft top's window and zipper, and adding another pair of auxiliary lights, Lucas Square Eights beneath the bumper, have also been completed. Not being subject to daily exposure to road grime, this 3000 since 1975 has experienced a much higher level of fresh paint, polish and general detailing in its engine bay, chassis and suspension components. The original sixty-spoke wire wheels have been totally rebuilt and trued, contributing to a much smoother ride, and summer 1977 saw 41578's fuel tank removed for corrosion repair while the entire boot was stripped, heavily painted, rust-sealed and detailed to match as new appearance.

'At ten years of age, and having covered over 70,000 miles, 41578 yet carries its original clutch, showing no decrease in performance; an engine yet to see a tear down or head removal, but returning cylinder pressure readings of 140–150 psi plus touring fuel mileage of 22 mpg; a smooth and quiet gearbox/overdrive unit; tight suspension, steering and healthy dampers; and most obvious, the original convertible top, exterior paint finish, and interior woodwork, upholstery and carpeting. To say that we are proud of this achievement is an understatement. While there are other unrestored Big Healeys about with half the mileage or with slightly more pristine appearance, no apologies are offered for one which combines a great many pleasure-filled, dependable miles with a remarkable state of preservation. I've owned and driven many cars in my two decades of motoring, but this Big Healey is the finest of them all.

'You ask what is the secret? There is none. I'm convinced that each and every one of the Big Healeys could do the same as our 41578. I've found that our experience seriously disappoints those whose egos seem to require a belief that the Big Healey is a delicate, easily-broken automobile needing all sorts of expensive and finicky treatment.

'We've all heard that theme bandied about through the years, and I'm here to tell you that it is simply not true. Much closer to the truth is this: the Austin-Healey, in company with the many of its British contemporaries, responds ever so well to the *involved* owner/driver, the one who finds satisfaction and enjoyment in the continual preventative maintenance these cars appear to thrive on. This does not necessarily include heavy mechanical jobs, but does consist of minor component replacement, tuning, cleaning, adjusting and lubricating—light duties easily handled by the most amateur yet enthusiastic Saturday mechanic. As in most other areas of life, there are some rules to live by, however. The formula utilized in the nurturing of 41578 included its planned and methodical break-in when new; consistent use of the same high quality fuel and lubrication products; motor oil and filter replacement as well as chassis lubrication at rigid 3,000-mile intervals; brief engine warm-up before driving (just till the coolant temperature needle leaves the peg); keeping the car covered whenever possible; and finally, using a bit of wisdom behind the wheel.

'So, while never again will be offered the opportunity to drive home in a shiny new Austin-Healey, all is not lost. Hundreds, 100-Sixes and 3000s in similar or better than new condition after careful restoration roll out of the shops regularly, and on several continents as well. I firmly believe that the Ramstad experience with 41578 does not have to be seen to be unique—any Big Healey will return stimulating, relatively trouble-free service if given the proper care. Why not commence such care as soon as your cherished machine emerges from its rebuild—or better still, right now?'

There's no doubt about it, Dave Ramstad is the voice of the American Big Healey owner today, having been through the three typical phases of ownership.

X

Healeys Round the World

FOUR out of five Big Healeys were sold in America and the balance, something over 14,000 cars, had somehow to help satisfy the rest of the world's hunger for sports cars. As a result they led charmed lives, particularly in Australia and New Zealand. Every Big Healey that reached the Southern Hemisphere was special and survived so much better as a result. There are even eleven of the exotic 100S models still going strong in Australia and New Zealand, probably as many as there are in the rest of the world. Also, for sheer dedication, the Australians and New Zealanders are hard to beat when it comes to restoring and running their cars. Big Healeys are a way of life there. 'We all meet socially every Easter and competition wise in the Six-Hour Relay Race in early spring,' says Jim McConville, one of the leading enthusiasts in Victoria. 'Racing our cars within the historic racing movement has more recently brought us together in competition and the all-Healey races (Big Healeys only) are considered to be the best competition of the day. The first two Big Healey races in Australia have been held this year (1977) at Amaroo Park, near Sydney, and in June at Winton, in central Victoria. Both weekends were extremely successful with respect to promoting the marque.

'So far all the cars racing have come from Victoria, New South Wales, and Southern Australia, and it is teams from these states which meet every year in the relay race at Melbourne. The Easter Rally involves a lot of travelling for the Queenslanders, for instance. The hazards are enormous: attacks by wild aborigines, dry water holes, flies, not to mention punctures on the gibber plains.

'Our cars are probably in a similar state, rustwise, to those on the West coast of America. In Victoria we have seasons of a sort, but no ice or snow except in the high country and nobody throws salt around here. However, cars that have been garaged in Melbourne and especially those near the seaside towns around Port Phillip Bay exhibit rust in the subframes and lower sections of the panels. Members rebuilding their cars usually obtain new subframes and panels from another member, Morris Rushton, when the need arises. Most of our cars are 100s, although we have quite a few 3000s, a Rolls-Healey, and five of the 100S cars.' McConville owns one of the 100Ss and his opposite number in Sydney, Pat Quinn has an even rarer Big Healey, the only BN3 prototype, to keep his 1953 100 company. 'I had to drive a long way last year for the national rally,' said Pat, 'including more than six hundred miles from

Brisbane to Sydney with only one gear, although, luckily, that was top.

'We don't suffer from any major problems in Australia. Heat can be a problem, but only in the summer traffic. Rust is a small problem, nowhere near so bad as it is in the United Kingdom and the Eastern coast of America, and Canada. The only real problem is that of spare parts. They are very few and far between and what you can get is very expensive. When restoring their cars, most people buy in bulk from A-H Spares. We are currently thinking of buying parts from the west coast of America, especially for the 3000s, which are far harder to find parts for than the 100s.'

Pat's club in New South Wales meets the Queensland Big Healey owners half-way at Coffs Harbour for an annual festival, attended in 1973 by Mel Nichols, then editor of the Australian magazine *Sports Car World* and now editor of the British magazine *Car*. Mel wrote in *Sports Car World*: 'The cars were lined up every-where. Many were superb. Most were immaculate. A few were a little rough: still being repaired or restored, or just plain hard-used. I told them I wanted the best examples of each model from the BN1 to the sixes, that we'd take them out in convoy along the Pacific Highway and then up into the mountains. No problem, they assured me. The boys wouldn't mind taking their Healeys over a bit of dirt.

'There was the 1953 BN1 of Joe Jarrick, from Brisbane, Adrian Hart's BN2 from Sydney, Barry Birch's 100M, also from Sydney, Ray Jorgenson's 100S from Sydney, Queenslander Stuart Lutton's 100-Six and Ben Seller's ex-Ross Bond racing 3000. Soon after I was leading the convoy in Joe Jarrick's BN1, twenty years old, immaculate, red with original black enamel dash and 97,305 miles on the speedo.

'It sang, that car. We were clipping along at 85 mph, its big four loping and strong and free from any of the weariness I'd expected to find in a car twenty years old that had probably been thrashed most of its life . . .

'It was so tight that I was poking it along much more quickly and much sooner than I had planned. Don't worry, I was prepared for all kinds of idiosyncrasies, turning the motoring clock back as if I was stepping from the technological sophisti-cation of my Citroen GS into the 100 which even the Healey people will agree is getting close to a vintage car underneath.

'There were a few funny things, of course. Separate key and tiny black press-button starter. The weird across-the-tunnel gearstick. The gigantic steering wheel almost rubbing on your chest. The jouncing and jigging across the gutter as we left the motel and burbled out into the street.

'But my fears—and you really could call them fears—that the car would be a now-unsafe relic, better left to its die-hard supporters and their dreams, were dis-patched with the steady throb of the engine, the sure feel of the fat radials on the road, and the swish of the air past my head on that humid, sunny afternoon. This car knew what it was about. It was showing me a very real and still potent character.

'The driving position, which for the first couple of miles had made me feel insecure, was now cosy. I was enjoying it, and I started laughing as we went into a long, sweeping curve with the double yellow lines spearing bright down its centre. I was laughing because I noticed that I was sighting down that little metal bead that runs along the top of the Healey's mudguard; looking along it to the road like Ascari and Nuvolari and Behra had once in those furious old cars they drove, arms pumping on a wheel the size and location of this one.

'I peeped in the mirror, expecting to see the other Healeys strung out in the sun behind me. There wasn't one in sight. They hadn't expected me to get cracking so quickly . . . then they came, and Healeys seemed to be everywhere as we stopped, their drivers still not knowing what I was up to. I thanked Joe, who was laughing at my obviously developing enthusiasm, for something I had forgotten; for that matter, never really known, and trotted along to Adrian Hart's red 1956 BN2.

'His bird, Chris, a delectable blonde, cotton-shirted over her bikini, bravely decided to stay in with me.

'The four-speed, plus overdrive, BN2 felt lighter than the BN1, somehow more spritely, but still bulldoggy. The road we were on now was bumpier and more coarse than the highway, but the car rode it well; very well. I was quite surprised, I had expected the traditional boneshaker bit but this was about what you'd get from a Falcon GT on wide tyres.

'Trees started lining the road, giving it the appearance of an English lane. We flashed along it, settling down after I learned the correct technique for cutting the electric overdrive in and out, to a nice steady cruise.

'I was getting in tune with Healey motoring; old sports car driving in the traditional sense where you just sort of motor alone, slowing down for corners then gradually building up speed again when the road straightens. You aren't aware of any turbulence or buffeting, just that there's only you and the road and the sky over your head and all the smells of the country. You are going fast, but you are in no real hurry. The big, lazy, torquey engine makes it seem all the more relaxing.

'About the time I'm thinking all this Chris talks about how her parents used to have a Healey twenty years ago and isn't it strange to think that she and Adrian are doing the same things her folks once did in the very same sort of motor car. I smile . . .'

Another stop followed and Mel changed to Barry Birch's 100M. 'I'm right into this Healey thing now,' he continued, 'and I set about using the extra power of Barry's M. This engine runs to six grand, is fully balanced and immediately feels that way. It's lively, and much cleaner feeling than the other fours have been.

'The car has a new steering box, too, so it hasn't the slight slack or vagueness of the BN2. But still the steering isn't heavy, something else I'd expected to find in the Healeys.

'So I start driving a bit harder; pushing pretty quickly through a few bends, one of them a fairly tight S coming onto a little wooden bridge. I allow for the car's aged suspension design, don't ask for too much, and it does the job very well. Nice. So I'm getting pretty confident, and coming down a long, mildly sloping hill I get into overdrive again (I've got that down to a smooth, quick movement now) and keep pushing down on the M's throttle. The noise deepens, hemmed in by trees, picked up and repeated by the cars behind us.

'We are pulling hard. The Healey feels good, strong. I study another one of the road's small wooden bridges coming up. Yes, it's okay, no need to slacken the pace much. I see Barry stiffen in his seat. He knows what is going to happen. Crash! I've forgotten how low slung the Healey is. The slight dip onto the bridge makes it bottom, thumping the exhaust pipes hard, and, I was to find out later, ripping off an

John Swann, fresh from burning up the track in Canada, with the chequered flag for a souvenir!

overdrive wire.

'Barry grimaced painfully, but didn't look at me and didn't say a word. I knew what he was thinking, and cursed hard for being so stupid. Hadn't my Melbourne friend who once had a BN2 had to inch into service station driveways; the car was so low?

'I slowed down, and for the next bridge I stood hard on the brakes, crawled across. I stopped soon after. Barry merely nodded when I thanked him, rather shame-facedly, for the drive.

'I went back and climbed into Stuart Lutton's red 100-Six. My hand was hardly on the wheel when it started pouring. The clouds that had been gathering to the south for the past hour opened and we all took off to get up some speed. If you keep the pace up, you don't get wet. But then we came onto a dirt section and we had to slow, so were soon sodden anyway.

'The six, a 1957 model with 114,00 miles up, had a lustiness not there in the fours. It was even stronger low down, and felt smoother and, well, less agricultural than the fours.

'This impression—it's more than just an impression, it's a fact—carried over to the car's road feel. It felt bigger and stronger, more sophisticated, more attuned to open-road loping and when we were going fast I was pleased to note that it felt about 30 mph less than the actual speed. Big brother.

'On the dirt road, which the car handled very capably really, it rode well, had

Gavin Gullery and Dave Young with
Gavin's fantastic 100 arrive at a jamboree in New Zealand.

few rattles, and offered a lot of fun, tail-out stuff. Like they said, no worries about the
dirt.

'Looking in the mirror one time as we cracked along the twisty, undulating
miles of dirt, in the dry again now because the patchy rain had passed on to the north,
I was amused to see the nose of the ex-Ross Bond racing Healey poking through the
dust. Its fat, flared guards were moving and weaving in a way they never did on the
track as corrugations flicked the tail way out of line and Ben Sellers, big in the seat,
caught it and hauled it back again.

'A couple of miles past the end of the dirt lay a little town. We stopped . . . and
I switched into Ben's car, the legendary 1961 Mark I 3000 that, in Ross Bond's
hands, had swept all before it for almost ten years. When Ross retired, Ben bought
it, detuned it and fitted road wheels. You didn't sit in this one with the wheel rubbing
your chest. The seat was right back in the longer 3000 cockpit, and stuck there. The
wheel wasn't the normal wire-spoked monster either, but a small leather-bound
MotoLita that was a full arm's reach away . . .the 3,250 cc engine didn't feel very
mean at all. It had that typical bhp feel of the quick, fast rev rather than the low-down
slow heft of torque. The power, Ben reckoned, was just under 200 bhp.

'I felt immediately at home in the car. Didn't hesitate about cracking along as
soon as we took off—and we were now into the best part, the twisty, hilly, forested
part of our road.

'The 3000 felt tight and firm on the road, imparting that impression through
the seat of your pants, the soles of your feet and the rim of the wheel, even though
there were a scad of rattles from the bodywork and plenty of thumps everytime we
hit a ripple in the roadway.

'From the word go, you sense that the car is an inherent oversteerer. You're not going to need lots of lock going into bends; you're going to be driving pretty much on the throttle, and using just small wheel movements to keep it in trim.

'And that's exactly the way the car was. Within a mile I was fairly flying along the road, clipping apexes perfectly, swinging in tight with the solid brake pedal pushed hard on to bring the nose in real close and then hoofing the power back on to exit out in spitting power oversteer. Nice. Ben Sellers loved it too . . . The race breeding showed . . .

'There was only the 100S left for me to drive now. When it pulled up, I went back and slipped in beside Ray, adjusted the seat to get comfy in the close-up driving position once again. We told the others they might as well go back to the town now. We'd probably be half an hour.

'Then Ray and I turned, and went back to the hills. From that first U-turn, from the first touch of the throttle, the release of the clutch and the shift of the stick, I knew that this one was something very special. It had that priceless feel of pure breeding, of every part being honed and worked until it aproached perfection.

'Oh sure, a lot of it was the car itself. But it owed an awful lot to Ray's painstaking restoration which went all the way to original brake pads for the four-wheel discs and the closest Dunlops he could get to the original 5.50×15 crossplies . . . the Healey people doubt that there is a better 100S in the world than this one. And what a masterpiece it is to drive. Everything about it is crisp and sharp and pure, each function a classic in itself . . .'

What a way to spend a jamboree . . . and how do the other Big Healey people spend their time in Canada, South Africa, Spain, Germany, Denmark, Norway, Sweden, Rhodesia, Italy, Portugal, France, Sri Lanka, Hong Kong, Singapore, Holland, Switzerland, Fiji, Japan, Hawaii and South America? In not such an ambitious way as the British, Americans, Australians and New Zealanders, because they haven't got the facilities and organization. But they have every bit as much enthusiasm and they are making headway. The Canadians are among the most advanced with Vancouver as the chief centre of interest. 'The climate is very similar to England's,' says Dave Birchall, one of the leading clubmen in Canada. 'Consequently the major problem with our cars is rust. This can be got round in two ways: first, by obtaining replacement sills, shut pillars etc, or second, by shunning British Columbian cars altogether and going to Southern California for a car. Apparently 60 to 70 per cent of all the Healeys produced went to California and with the dry, warm climate down there most of them are in a remarkable state of preservation.

'I own a 100M that I bought from a farm south of San Francisco. The car is about 50 per cent restored and I hope to race it in historic races next year. Getting parts has been relatively easy for me since I work as an airline steward and make regular trips to England.

'The president of the British Columbia club, John Swann, has raced a 3000 in the vintage race meetings this year with considerable success. His car was originally put together by a professional mechanic in San Francisco for use in SCCA D production racing. John bought the car in May 1977 and the first time he drove it was in his first race! He spun on the last lap but he's doing well now, mixing it with the Allards and Jaguars.' Meanwhile, a new centre in Toronto has celebrated its first

Above: The Swedes and the Dutch have always been among the great Healey fans. This picture was taken during the 1958 Tulip Rally.

Right: Healeys as they used to be: storming the Grand St Bernard Pass.

Facing page: Bring back the Big Healey: this message meant everything to thousands of enthusiasts all over the world who bought the poster drawn by David Kerr of the New Zealand club.

anniversary.

Times are tough in South Africa though: 'fuel restrictions are very stringent,' says leading club man Bruce Caw, 'and in Rhodesia they have petrol rationing. As it is, in South Africa we have rigidly-enforced speed restrictions, 90 kph on all roads except built-up areas, where a 60 kph limit applies. All motoring activities are strictly controlled and as a result the club tends to concentrate on rebuilding and restoring cars although we do manage the odd Tulip-style rally and lots of social occasions. We are particularly keen on keeping in touch with Rod Wells in Rhodesia . . . he's got a lovely 100S!'

The rest of the Healey people abroad operate in a similar way, with club meetings, usually monthly, visits to race meetings, touring and restoration as the main interests. Some, particularly the Germans and Scandinavians, are especially keen on concours events and achieve outstanding results. This is despite the high cost of spares when local taxes are paid. But they all say the Big Healey is worth anything . . .

BRING BACK THE BIG HEALEY

XI

The Men Behind the Big Healey

Donald Healey as he was when he visualised the Big Healey.

'CARS OF TODAY are so boring. Design has degenerated to such an extent that they all look the same. Take away their badges and bogus radiators and they all look alike.

'Modern sports cars are getting away from their purpose. Today a sports car is filled with radios and tape recorders and has winding windows. It is a tycoon's idea of getting from place to place. My idea of a sports car is one in which you must brave the elements.' Those were the words of one of the greatest car designers, Sir Alec Issigonis in 1977. It is significant that the man who made the marvellous Minis and Morris Minors had so much in common with Donald Healey. Healey's cars were never boring. They never looked like anything else . . . and it was not until the marketing men took a hand that they got winding windows and a tycoon's interior.

The purists agree that the first Austin-Healey—the four-cylinder—was the best. 'It was designed by a real driver, Donald Healey,' said one of his oldest friends, service manager and former test driver Geoff Price. 'I'd been a boozing pal of his since 1936—and joined him after leaving the Army in 1947. In fact, I helped build the first Healeys when I was on leave. We were the old gang and we went everywhere together: to the pub and to the Mille Miglia!' (Donald Healey and Geoff Price finished fourth in the touring class behind Tommy Wisdom and son Geoffrey Healey in another Healey in 1949). 'Everybody called Donald Healey the Skipper,' said Price. 'He was the power behind everything.'

The first Big Healey started as a glint in Donald Healey's eye soon after the war and the project became a reality in 1951. He had been paying frequent visits to the States to deal with affairs concerning his current American Nash-powered Healey sports car and could see which way the wind was blowing. The sensational new Jaguar XK 120 was wiping the floor with everything else in the expensive sports car class. What was needed was something fast and reliable, like the Nash-Healey, and a lot cheaper. Donald Healey could scarcely hope to match the Jaguar's performance for the price, but he could see a market for something not much slower somewhere between the Jaguar bracket and that of the cheap and cheerful MG T series. There was also a whisper that the Riley running gear for the current European Healeys would not be in production much longer. It was also obvious that Leonard Lord at Austins had more engines and transmissions than he could sell in his Austin Atlantic coupé. So Healey went to see Lord early in 1951 and told him of his ideas for a new

Far left: 'My idea of a sports car is one in which you must brave the elements.' Sir Alec Issigonis.

Left: Sir Leonard Lord in 1953.

sports car powered by the A90 engine and running gear from the Atlantic. Lord thought about it for a while and gave the project his blessing. The initial production run was visualized at five cars per week!

Work started soon after this date, the overall conception of the new car being that of Donald Healey, with Barry Bilbie as chief chassis designer, Gerry Coker as chief body designer, and eldest son, Geoffrey Healey as chief engineer. Meanwhile chief experimental engineer Roger Menadue obtained a second-hand Austin A90 engine and gearbox.

The engine had an interesting and rather unlikely history. It was developed by Bill Appleby at Longbridge as a four-cylinder Jeep version of a six-cylinder Army truck design. It eventually found its way into the Austin 16 saloon and was developed in 2.2 litre form for one of the first true post-war Austins, the A70 saloon. The same unit was also used in taxis and light trucks. Soon afterwards it was bored out to 2.6 litres for the Antlantic coupé, producing 88 bhp with Vokes air cleaners. As it happened they wouldn't fit under the bonnet of the new Healey-to-come and Burgess pancake filters were fitted, allowing another 2 bhp.

But what about this new Healey? Few people had had more experience than Donald Healey—first British winner of the Monte Carlo Rally in 1931—of trying to make fast cars stay on the road. 'He has come to the conclusion that good roadholding is 75 per cent frame rigidity and only 25 per cent suspension,' said *The Motor* in 1953. 'He therefore insisted that the frame for the new car must be the most rigid his company has yet built.

'This has been achieved by designing a car which is mid-way between the old type with a simple chassis frame, which depended so largely on its massive side and cross members for strength and the integrally-constructed modern saloon.'

The Skipper laid down the basic principles of the chassis, Geoffrey Healey did the complicated calculations, such as working out torsional rigidity, and Bilbie turned their visions into reality. 'Geoffrey was not much good at drawing, but he was an awfully good engineer,' said Bilbie. 'I did everything under the car's skin and Gerry did everything you could see, with Donald and Geoffrey Healey constantly at our elbows.'

All this took place in the attic of the Skipper's home for fear that representatives

Geoff Price, still at the Donald Healey
Motor Company.

from Morris Motors, who made the Riley units in the current Healeys might find
out what was going on. Years later, Geoffrey Healey retained this passion for secrecy
with signs at the works in Warwick, saying: 'No visitors allowed past this point unless
accompanied by a director,' and frosted glass in the experimental shop's windows.
One of the signs, and the frosted glass, are still there today although the Donald
Healey Motor Company sells Renaults now. 'It really was a joke,' said Geoff Price.
'You couldn't keep anything secret in the Midlands; everybody in the motor industry
used to go on the booze together.'

It was probably a good job that the first Big Healey was being designed in
Donald Healey's attic, though, for at the same time, Lord Nuffield had John Thornley's team at Abingdon designing a rival sports car, the MGA, Jensens were dream-
ing up another at the instigation of Lord, and Frazer Nash were trying to make an
A90 unit work in their current sports model to make it more competitive on price.

As work went ahead on these four rival projects, the Healey team sweated blood
in the Skipper's attic. Bilbie was bang on target with his chassis and the first prototype was started early in 1952. At the same time, Austin and Morris were linking up
to form BMC and there was less need for secrecy now that Morris Motors were
coming into the same camp as Austin engines! John Thompsons produced the first
chassis using Land-Rover welding techniques: the Big Healey already owed a lot to
utility vehicles, when you remember its Jeep-based engine. Later many panels were
made from Birmabright, an aluminium alloy much favoured on Land-Rovers.

Menadue fitted the engine and firms like Girling supplied experts to fit suitable
brakes. 'Whenever we needed specialist help, they just sent a couple of people over,'
said Price. Mintex supplied the appropriate brake linings and Borg and Beck the
clutch. Lucas worked on the electrics and the body went out to Tickford's at Newport Pagnell. This specialist coachbuilder made up an alloy body to Coker's design,
which had the Skipper's blessing, as he did the test driving and chassis development
with Geoffrey Healey, who used experience gained with Pinin Farina while working
on the Nash-Healey, to mount the body. 'The first body had sides based on the Nash-
Healey, with small fins at the rear and the swage line continued through the rear
wheel arch,' said Bilbie. 'But the Skipper didn't like the fins and they were taken off,
with the swage on the rear wings. On the whole we were very pleased with the prototype, except for the nose. Nobody liked it. That's why we parked it behind a pillar
on the stand at Earls Court in 1952. We hoped nobody would notice the nose.

'The design weight of the first 100 was one ton all-up; with 100 mph. It turned
out at 21 cwt with 110 mph, so we were happy! It had to have a very clean floor and
to be very low for the Skipper. The chief problem was what to do with the exhaust,
and we ended up just hanging it on the bottom.

'We wanted to use rack and pinion steering on the first cars, but the only unit
available was the Morris Minor one, eventually used on the Sprite, and it was not
man enough for our job. As it was, the first prototype had its steering box mounted
well ahead of the axle line and we moved it back when we realized the danger.

'It's a pity we could never do anything about that rack, but we had to use existing components to cut costs and we couldn't afford a specially-engineered job like
Jaguar's.'

Geoffrey Healey said later in his book, *Austin-Healey: The Story of the Big Healeys* (Wilton House Gentry) that the original layout was rather spongy, and was redesigned on the basis of the system used on current Ferrari Grand Prix cars. The result was a great improvement and worked well when everything was brand new. Manufacturing tolerances had a tendency to develop a high spot in the steering box which did not coincide with the straight-ahead steering wheel position with the result that straight-line steering deteriorated. Wear in other steering parts made the problem worse and it was never really solved. All this made it even more of a pity that Healeys couldn't find a rack to fit their car.

Nobody knows the Big Healey like Fred Draper.

The other chief problem with the first 100, apart from the sheer weight of the components, was the rear axle ratio. The Healey family—the Skipper and Geoffrey Healey—located all the components necessary for a car and couldn't find a ratio high enough. Eventually Ian Duncan, who had built special bodies on earlier Healeys came up with a Laycock overdrive, which, with modifications, solved the problem. The first prototype, KWD947, was painted in an Alvis blue which had caught the Skipper's eye and was completed just in time . . .

'Healey got to Lord three days before us,' said Thornley, whose men had been making the MGA at the same time. 'Lord had made a deal with Healey that he would produce the Healey 100, and in Lord's eyes the two cars were so similar that the MGA couldn't go ahead.' The decision to shelve the MGA in favour of the Healey 100 caused a lot of disappointment at Abingdon, especially as there was no going against it now that the parent Austin and Morris companies had merged. It was to be another three years before the MGA went into production, and five years before the Big Healey went to Abingdon—where the MGA's brilliant designer, Syd Enever, was to do much to make it a better car.

Meanwhile, Jensens were hard at work on their new sports car. They already used Austin components in their other cars and, although they were using a $1\frac{1}{2}$ litre MG unit in the new model, they felt they stood a good chance of getting it accepted by the new BMC. 'At the time of the 1952 London Motor Show there were three sports car designs for BMC to view,' said Peter Browning and John Blunsden in the *Jensen Healey Stories* (MRP). 'Lord Nuffield had already seen the MG by the time the show opened, but no decision had been made to go ahead with Abingdon's design. Jensen's new sports car, which no-one at Longbridge had seen, should have appeared at Earls Court, but was held up at the last moment due to a shortage of brake parts. Donald Healey's new car, however, was ready just in time for exhibition, although it arrived too late to enjoy most of the pre-show publicity. But immediately the Healey 100 was rolled on to the stand and unveiled it became the sensation of Earls Court.

'It was only then that Nuffield, Lord and BMC's George Harriman saw the car for the first time, and they were all mightily impressed, not only with the orders which were being placed for it—orders which the Donald Healey Motor Company could not possibly hope to fulfil. Leonard Lord immediately offered to build the car at Longbridge, knock £100 off the Healey's price, and market the car under the name Austin-Healey. Donald Healey agreed, was retained as a consultant, and overnight the Healey 100 became the Austin-Healey 100.

Too ashamed to show its nose, the
Healey 100 makes its debut at the
1952 London Motor Show.

'It was an arrangement that suited both sides ideally, but it created one problem; what was Lord to do when Jensen produced the sports car prototype which he had commissioned? Conveniently, a solution was found when it became clear that Tickford, who had built the original Healey 100 prototype, would be unable to build the 150 bodies per week which the anticipated Austin production rate would demand. So, faced with an acute body-building problem, Lord arranged a meeting with Richard and Alan Jensen and asked them to quote for the job.'

Lord also asked to see the prototype, which was hurriedly completed, and was most embarrassed to see that it bore a close resemblance to the Healey 100 and the MGA! He also owed Jensen something, having 'lifted' one of their designs for his Sheerline saloon, so they got the Healey body-building contract and were 'well pleased.'

That left only Frazer Nash of the great rivals, and they couldn't get their car to handle, or sell, so they made only one.

The first couple of hundred Austin-Healeys had alloy bodies partly because of the steel shortage which decreed that steel permits would only be issued for exports, but once production was under way there was no trouble getting supplies. 'The Skipper was a tremendously popular man in the motor industry and could get almost anything he wanted,' said Price. 'He also had a wonderful eye for fashion.

'It was the Skipper who was responsible for bring back the wire wheel. Nobody else was using them by 1951, and he had considerable trouble in getting anybody to make them. Eventually Dunlops agreed to produce forty-eight spoke wheels for him on a long-term contract. And he had to stick to forty-eight spokes for a long time—despite the trouble they used to give—because of his contract. Eventually, when

The men who made the Big Healey at Abingdon: John Thornley (left) and Syd Enever.

they started making sixty-spoke wheels for MGs we were able to change them. It was really a question of building cars out of what you could lay hands on.

'I reckon the Skipper would have liked to have had retracting headlights on the 100. He wanted them on the first Healey prototype in 1946—the lights were fitted with covers—but he couldn't get anybody to make them at the right price, and he had also wanted them on the first Austin-Healey Sprite after the 100, but the same problem remained, plus wind resistance which stopped the lights popping up.'

Meanwhile development work proceeded under Geoffrey Healey who Donald Healey described as 'very much one of the backroom boys who did the work and shunned the limelight'. Harry Weslake, the great freelance cylinder head expert, who had been responsible for the A90 engine's gas flow with such good results for performance and economy, worked through the 100M conversion to the 100S engine, but Healey's couldn't afford to produce it at the right price in quantity, and so turned to the first new product of Morris Motors since the BMC merger: the C-series six-cylinder engine.

Morris Motors' great chief engine research and development engineer, Eddie Maher, made the new unit sufficiently reliable for the 100-Six and produced more power from the cylinder head when it was needed. He was also responsible for the competition sixes to follow. In the same way, the Morris C-series gearbox and rear axle found their way onto the later 100s, and there was a theory that the name should have been changed to Morris-Healey! Price was responsible for building the factory 100Ms and Fred Draper for getting the parts together with Geoff Cooper of Austins. Later when the 100-Six moved to Abingdon, Enever helped sort out specialized design problems, particularly on the rally cars that were to give BMC such great publicity. Thornley, the M G chief whose name was synonymous with Abingdon, remembers Enever's solution to one suspension problem: 'I'd been discussing this point with Syd at one of our meetings and did not really feel that I had a complete answer,' said Thornley. 'But having worked with Syd for years I knew when to leave him alone . . . A few days later I was passing Oxford public library, when to my surprise, who should come staggering out, but Syd, clutching a huge volume. "What have you got there?" I asked. "It's a book on locomotives written in 1898," said Syd. "It's all in there!" Surely enough, a few days later, Syd had solved the suspension problem, and when you came to think of it, if you can keep a massive locomotive balanced on the rails and riding well at 80–100 mph, you have to know something about suspension. It's often a question of going back to basics. That's why Syd was such a great engineer. He never forgot the basic principles learned over the years. That's how he designed the fourteen-leaf rear springs that were such a feature of the works rally cars. The leaves rubbing together acted like a shock absorber, just like those on cars years before.' The combination of men such as Enever and Thornley was of incalculable benefit to the Big Healey. Thornley probably prolonged its life for years by fighting to keep his production lines full of sports cars.

Back at Warwick, the Healey family kept up their flow of design ideas and over in Abingdon, the M G men, Cecil Cousins, Reg Jackson and Alec Hounslow worked as hard at the Big Healeys as they did at their beloved M Gs, especially with competition versions. Appleby came back onto the scene as head of BMC power unit design, particularly to improve the troublesome gearboxes. The Morris C-series axle, once fitted to the Big Healey, never gave any trouble up to 300 bhp, although naturally it weighed more than the earlier Austin unit.

The Healey family were not as blind to the Big Healey's deficiencies as many thought: when it became apparent that the 3000 needed updating they were respon-

Big Healeys roll off the production line at Abingdon, alongside M G As and Frogeye Sprites.

sible for suggesting many improvements, such as better road handling, increased rear wheel movement by lowering the frame, new rear springs, larger rear shock absorbers, more ground clearance, bigger fuel tank, and rack and pinion steering. At the same time, MGs suggested an improved exhaust system, brake servo as standard, improved brakes and stub axles, a cable throttle, vacuum overdrive switch, electric rev counter, side jacking, revised anti-roll bar links, and stiffer front springs. Morris Motors suggested triple carburetters and a better gearchange. But wind-up windows and an improved hood got priority from BMC.

The first Healey 100 hood had been added almost as an afterthought, and the hood had to be made bigger. As a result it became more awkward to lower and raise, as were so many other hoods of the day. As road speeds rose above 100 mph, flapping hoods became a liability and on cars which kept them they needed to be so strong, and mounted in such a complex manner, that the raising and lowering of them quickly, became a near impossibility. That's one of the reasons the hardtop gained in popularity and it was not until the introduction of the convertible that Healey's really solved this problem.

They also experimented with rack and pinion steering but could not find suitable components. This problem was partly alleviated by improvements in the manufacture of the steering box by Cam Gears to ensure that the high spot coincided with the straight ahead position.

Dick Burzi at Austins was responsible for reworking the Mark III's interior at little extra cost after Gerry Coker went to work in the United States, apparently still sketching radiator grilles to try to improve that nose! Probably Enzo Ferrari also had a hand in the Big Healey's ultimate development; the radius arm rear suspension was based on a Grand Prix Ferrari bought by Donald Healey in the 1950s! Perhaps that gives an indication as to how long they had wanted to improve their embarrassing rear end.

Fred Draper on the left with Geoff Price outside the Donald Healey Motor Co. as it is today.

XII

Interchangeability of Spare Parts

BASICALLY the Big Healey is a sports version of the contemporary big Austin saloon, with the exception of the body chassis, which are almost pure Healey. For instance, the engine from the 100 was a straight lift from the current Austin A90, complete with clutch. The gearbox of the BN1 is similar to that of the A90 and the earlier A70 saloon and pick-up truck, with the exception of the overdrive, gearchange and gate. The gate was modified to blank off first gear and the gearchange was an adaptation for floor operation rather than steering column gear-changing. In fact, the same units were used in the Austin 30 cwt commercial range made immediately after the war and share similar parts to even earlier Austin 16 derivatives. It is extremely unlikely that any Austin 16s are left in the scrapyards or that any spares for them will turn up now, but there are still many of the A70 and A90 ranges in running order which can be bought very cheaply for spares. The same applies to the A40 car which supplied the rear axle for the BN1. Front suspension parts are shared with the same cars and the brakes with London taxis. The SU carburetters were fitted to numerous British cars after the war although needles, jets and so on are different and frequently make interchanging impractical. It should also be remembered, of course, that the Healey specialists hold substantial stocks of new spares between them in Britain and second-hand ones as well abroad.

The rear axle for the later BN2 cars was as fitted to the Austin A105 Westminster. The BN4 adopted the Westminster's engine, too, of course, shared with the Morris Isis, although the BN6 had a special cylinder head. Many overdrive parts were in common with the Jaguar saloon and sports car ranges, with the notable exception of the casing. The 3000 range used some components in common with the Wolseley 6/99 and 6/110 saloon and their Austin Westminster equivalents. The 3.545 axle ratio, for instance, came from the saloons, the optional 4.875 unit much favoured by racing men came from the Austin FX3 taxi, the 5.125 axle came from Austin's current half-ton truck, and the 5.625 axle and the 6.3 came from Austin J-type vans. The Austin and Wolseley saloon gearboxes fitted the early BN7s and their two-plus-two equivalents, but they did not fit the later Austin-Healeys which had the gear helix angle reversed; the mainshaft needs modification, however, and the ratios are different, so the change is only worthy of consideration if it means the difference between driving the car and not: it is better to save for the new parts.

One of the Healey 100's ancestors, the Austin 16.

There is more to be gained from trying to swop parts between Big Healeys than fitting components from other cars. To this end the Big Healeys divide into three categories: the short-chassis 100 cars, and the cars with and without wind-up windows. It is not possible, for instance, to fit doors with wind-up windows to an earlier six-cylinder car; they are too wide and the windscreen angle is different. But the same front and rear wings will fit virtually any Healey other than the early BN 1s, with only minor changes. The earliest BN 1s had a different wheel arch to other models. Later wings still fit, but are not quite original in appearance. Inner and intermediate sill panels will fit all Healeys, with minor changes for the BN 1 and BN 2. Outer sills are common to all cars except the BN 1 and BN 2, which have their own. Front shrouds, on the other hand, varied considerably between one model and another. All Healeys had the same boot floor, however, and all cars from chassis BN 1 221536 will accept the axle bump stop box from the Mark III.

Externally, front and rear wing beadings, front wing flashes and boot handles were identical on all Big Healeys. All six-cylinder cars up to BJ8 26704 had the same door handles, although two types of activating levers were used. Radiator grille slats for the BN 4, BN 6 and early BN 7 were the same as the current Austin A55, many of which are still in the scrapyards. Every Austin-Healey had the same front badge until the Mark II, except the BN 1, which had an Austin of England badge. All six-cylinder cars had the same bumpers, and overriders, which were shared with the MGA and were identical. Boot hinges were the same on all cars and the six-cylinders all had the same front bumper brackets, and headlamp rims. All cars up to BJ8 26705 had the same hub spinners, with a UNF thread. After that they used a UNC thread and octagonal spinners were fitted to some export cars. Throughout this list, the BN 1 and BN 2 shared components among themselves, unless otherwise stated.

There is considerable interchangeability among rubber parts, too. All four-cylinder cars had the same windscreen to body seal; and all six-cylinder cars up to the convertible had a common seal; the convertibles were all the same. The moulding under the windscreen pillar was the same for all six-cylinders up to the convertible and all cars shared the same rear bumper bracket grommets and boot lid stops; all six-cylinder cars had the same boot lid sealing rubber. All Big Healeys had the same bonnet support rubbers and overrider to bumper moulding. All six-cylinders had

Right: The Austin A90 Atlantic coupé which gave way to the Big Healey.

Below left: The Austin FX3 London taxi which shared components with the Big Healey.

Below right: The A90 Atlantic engine installation with its big air filters.

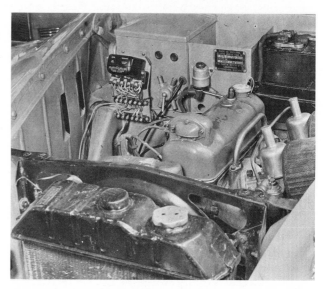

the same brake and clutch pedal rubbers and throttle linkage bush for the bulkhead.

Many electrical components are interchangeable, also. All six-cylinder cars up to BJ8 76138 have the same wiring loom; later cars, and the BN1 and the BN2 all have individual looms. All Big Healeys have the same indicator control box, battery master switch and number plate light. All six-cylinder cars have the same front side light and stop/tail light assemblies, up to BJ8 26704. All sixes up to engine number 29F 3562 have the same distributor cap. All BN1 and BN2 cars have the same distributor cap and front side light assemblies. The Mark III front side lights were different from all other models, and there were two sorts of these; they changed at chassis number BJ8 26705.

Engine parts are frequently interchangeable, of course. All standard four-cylinder engines were the same and none of their moving parts fitted the six-cylinder cars. All the sixes had the same rocker cover gasket, crankshaft, thrust washers, cam followers, timing chain tensioner, rocker shaft, rocker bushes, and engine mountings. The Mark III camshaft fits all the sixes and is a considerable benefit to the earlier engines, but they are difficult to obtain.

Brake parts are more confusing. Some were shared with the Austin saloon and commercial vehicles of similar age, but extreme care should be taken if interchanging, especially with linings which can cause premature wheel locking and out-of-balance braking if not of the correct grade. BN1 cars up to chassis number 221403 had one-inch bore front wheel cylinders, with $\frac{7}{8}$ in bore after that. All BN2, BN4 and BN6 cars had one-inch bore front wheel cylinders, which were the same when fitted with wire wheels. One-inch cylinders were also fitted to pressed-steel wheel cars, but were of different construction. All BN1, BN2, BN4 and BN6 rear wheel cylinders were the same after chassis number BN1 221536. All cars after the BN6 shared the same rear wheel cylinders. All disc-braked cars had the same calipers up to chassis number BJ8 26704. All cars with drum front brakes can use the same flexible hoses, and all disc-braked cars had the same front hoses. All cars after BN1 221535 had the same rear brake shoes, and—hold your breath—every six-cylinder car made had the same handbrake cable.

Of clutch parts, all sixes had the same slave cylinder and flexible hose; all cars up to the 3000 had the same cover assembly; the BN2, BN4, and BN6 had the same release bearing. Little else was interchangeable between individual models, although it is worth trying alternative clutches providing the splines are the same; the clutch discs used by Chevrolets between 1960 and 1969 fit the Big Healey in many cases as one instance. Of gearbox parts, all cars from the BN2 to the BJ7 had the same third and fourth gear baulk ring and overdrive to adaptor gasket; the gearbox mountings, and tie bar rubbers were the same, too.

Suspension components are frequently the same throughout the range. All rear shock absorbers were the same, fitting up to chassis number BJ8 26704. All front shock absorbers were identical. This is unless heavy duty ones had been fitted, of course, which was non-standard but desirable. All king pins will fit the same cars up to the BJ7, although according to Dave Jeffery the Mark III setting is best for all road cars. All lower fulcrum pin sets, inner wishbone rubber bushes, top trunnion

The Morris Isis which gave its power unit to the six-cylinder Healeys. They might have been called Morris-Healeys!

rubber bushes, and anti-roll bars are the same. Heavier-duty anti-roll bars from the Sprite range can be adapted to change the handling characteristics, and the anti-roll bars from 1949–53 Chevrolets, and 1967–70 Opel GTs can be fitted to the Big Healey. Rear traction bars from Ford Mustangs made between 1965 and 1970 can be fitted to the Big Healey with little modification to the mountings and many of the anti-roll bar rubbers are shared with Ford and Lincoln cars made between 1963 and 1975. All Big Healey U-bolts will fit the same and so will rear springs up to the BJ8 providing they have the same number of leaves. Coil springs can be swopped around, too, although they change the handling and ride in some cases.

All steering boxes are interchangeable, although the ratios differ on the six-cylinder cars between 12.6:1 on the four-cylinders, 14:1 up to chassis 68959 and 15:1 after that; it also depends whether the car has a fixed steering column or whether it is adjustable. All stator tube end nuts, and stator tube end olives are the same. The centre tie rods for the BN2, BN4, BN6 and BJ7 are identical.

In the cooling system, all four-cylinders have the same radiator, and hoses, and all sixes identical units, and the same top and bottom hoses either with or without heater outlets. All sixes up to engine number 29K 1027 had $\frac{3}{8}$-inch wide fan belts, $\frac{1}{2}$ in after that. The water pump changed on the BJ7 and BJ8s at the same engine number. Earlier sixes had water pumps which could be interchanged among themselves.

All Big Healeys had the same oil filter, valve cover washers and condensor in the distributor. The oil filter casings interchanged as well, every car had the same petrol tank gaskets and every standard Healey that left Warwick, Longbridge or Abingdon was fitted with the same ashtray.

First of the Austin Westminsters which shared components with the six-cylinder Healeys.

The ultimate in interchangeability of parts, a Big Healey record breaker goes on show at Earls Court.

The Wolseley 6/110 Mark II which shared components with the 3000 Mark III.

XIII

Modifications

YOU CAN improve a Big Healey quite dramatically if you do not mind departing from the original specification to a great extent. The basic thing is to make up your mind what you want to do with the car: use it only on the road, for rough or smooth circuit racing, or turn it into a replica rally car. Most of the modifications are fairly simple, although there is only one firm specializing in them: John Chatham Cars, in Bristol, England. Several other firms can supply good quality non-standard components—and fit many of them—but none are specialists in the art of making a Big Healey go faster and handle better.

For modern circuit racing you could hardly better the fastest Healey in current use: John Chatham's famous ex-Le Mans car DD 300. It has a basically-standard six-cylinder chassis clothed in alloy coachwork with a baffled box-like petrol tank sitting in the boot. This ten-gallon wonder was made by a Rolls-Royce apprentice for 'a packet of fags' and uses a filler cap from an old Bristol bus!

The suspension is softened and lowered all round, with only five leaves in the rear springs and 'clapped out' Mark III front springs rather than shortened standard springs, to give better handling. These are the springs needed for an 18 cwt circuit racer, different springs are necessary for other, heavier, cars. Back axle location is vital. DD 300 uses single radius rods above the axle line and an ingenious sliding pillar differential location which performs the same function as a Panhard rod, except better! Panhard rods work reasonably well on Big Healeys, although only reasonably, because they tend to jack up one side as the car rolls. With the Chatham modification, a long bolt is fitted to the centre of the differential casing, pointing directly to the rear. At the end of this bolt is a Morris 1000 front wheel bearing sliding in a steel pillar welded vertically to a standard-steel rear panel directly behind the differential. As the axle rises and falls it is kept in line by the 'railway track' location. The standard-steel rear panel is the only thing strong enough to hold this pillar. Lower radius links were used at one time but found to be of no help; they were more of a hindrance to DD 300's performance.

A heavy-duty roll-bar is fitted at the front, straight from a Commer 17 cwt van! This is the set-up for the current British historic racing using the mandatory Dunlop L-section six-inch tyres with heavy-duty Armstrong Mark III shock absorbers front and rear, with the rear ones adjustable. Adjustable Armstrongs are not made for the front.

The wheels are rather special. They started life as eight-inch Borranis on a Ford GT40, then the rims were cut down the centre and re-made to six inches for DD300 —'a wonderful welding job,' says one of Chatham's top mechanics, John Horne. Bolt-on steel wheels were used earlier, but suffered repeated breaking at the centres, so much so that DD300 lost a wheel just before a *Motor Sport* group track test of historic racers. The circuit that gave the most trouble with steel bolt-ons was the ultra-fast Thruxton where three wheels went in one race! This problem had not occurred with bolt-on wheels when it was permissable to use Minilite magnesium wheels for historic racing.

The braking is special, too, with heavy discs all round and massive special Girling calipers originally developed for long-distance racing. The differential is a ZF-pattern 4.1 ratio retained for all British circuits. John Gott tried the Salisbury-style American No-Slip differential and found that it was not strong enough. Nevertheless it is necessary to check the differential's pawls every year. The gearbox is a standard, but rare, straight-cut Tulip unit with Laycock racing overdrive. It is the overdrive which suffers mostly in racing, lasting only about 600 miles. If it is not replaced more often it can blow up, wrecking the gearbox mainshaft.

The engine, with its triple 45DCOE Weber carburetters is very special, of course. It comes in two capacities: 2.7 litres for the current 'small' class in British historic racing and a full three litres for the unlimited class. With either capacity, DD300 is a potential overall winner and far ahead of everything else in the 2.7 litre class. One of the most important parts of the engine is the carefully-polished ex-

A Healey 3000 Mark II fitted with three examples of the 'Rolls-Royce of carburetters'—45DCOE Webers.

Above left: Smart alloy rocker covers are available for Big Healeys.

Above right: DD 300's ten-gallon tank.

Right: Works-style side exhaust fitted for extra ground clearance.

works alloy cylinder head with compression ratio raised to 11.8:1. This is the maximum before gasket and stud trouble trouble become more than a threat. Chatham reckons this type of head alone is worth one second a lap on the average circuit— a fact that he has confirmed in back-to-back testing with a standard weight head. The alloy head saves a vital 35 lb over the front wheels and improves heat dispersion. DD 300 runs at a variety of temperatures, from 160 degrees to 210 degrees, depending on the ambient temperature. The triple Webers work best with a high-lift full-race camshaft and big valves. Needless to say, a six-branch exhaust system is fitted, exiting just in front of the nearside rear wheels. The distributor has to be changed, too, with this set-up, to a Lucas DMA 40662A. Other than a nitrided crankshaft, the engine's chief modifications are meticulous balancing and assembly with an MGB water bypass blanking plate. An oil cooler also helps keep the temperature down with outlet pipes from an adaptor on the cylinder block and the filter fitted on the chassis side member with connecting pipes. Twin SU fuel pumps near the rear axle keep up the petrol flow and a standard Mark III radiator is used. Steering is by a standard 15:1 box with a 14-inch wheel rather than the obsolete 12.6:1 box.

The coachwork and hardtop are as light as possible, of course, and a strong roll cage is fitted. This is the ultimate for current racing without 'hacking DD about,' says Chatham. He is currently experimenting with an extraordinary new circuit racer with a full roll cage rather like that of a Midget racer. The idea is to stiffen the chassis as the roll cage connects front and rear suspension and door posts. In addition, he is experimenting with the steering rack from an Austin-Healey Sprite. It should be quite some racer!

In the same way Chatham's off-road 'fun car', GRX884D, would make a great rally car. As it is, it looks just like one of the last works machines, being built up from spares left over at Abingdon when the BMC Competitions Department closed. GRX, as the car is affectionately called, has an alloy-head, nitride-crank ex-works engine with steel flywheel and Tulip box and overdrive, with triple Webers and a fantastic exhaust system exiting through the nearside front wing and under a shortened door along the old outer sill line just in front of the rear wheel. 'The time it took to fabricate . . .', says Chatham's 'professor,' Nick Pride, who builds his racing and fun cars, 'I reckon it would cost more than £500 if we put a commercial price on it.' The incredible exhaust system is a replica of that used on the last of the works cars and solves ground clearance problems completely—there's no less than seven inches between the silencer and whatever track it might be storming along. But there are disadvantages to such a modification: chiefly heat in the cockpit and the danger of people burning their legs on it, plus the contortions a passenger has to undergo when dismounting from such a formidable machine. Weber carburetters have their disadvantages, too, and the main one is fuel consumption. But for racing it does not seem as if the angular interior of an SU carburetter allows quite the same freedom of passage for air as does the interior of the Weber. For road driving, however, the SU has become very popular because its variable-sized choke tube lets it work well over a wide range of engine speeds. The rest of the running gear on GRX is standard rally specification including four-wheel disc brakes, $6\frac{1}{2}$-inch Minilites shod with Dunlop SP 58s and DD 300's long-distance thirty-gallon fuel tank hogging nearly all the tail. The suspension lay-out at the back is standard Mark III with adjustable Armstrong shock absorbers, with everything raised for extra ground clearance. The only real departures from rally specifications are the substitution of fibreglass for alloy in the coachwork to save weight (it looks the same!), and the deletion of the heavy sumpguard and myriad auxiliary lights for roadwork.

The 'standard rally specification' changed over the years, of course. Early 100-Six and 3000 works rally cars had polished heads and ports with a 9:1 compression ratio, half-race camshaft, MG Magnette ZA outer valve springs, twin 2-inch rampiped SU carbs, special distributor, and an exhaust system exiting in front of the nearside rear wheel, out under the sills—rather like that on DD 300—but with a twenty-seven-inch oval silencer. Such a system is still fitted to Thelma Segal's ex-

Pat Moss car, SMO744. This produces around 135 bhp at the rear wheels against
something like 175 bhp for DD300, GRX and the last works entry in a rally, PWB57,
of which extraordinary claims of 200 bhp at the wheels have been made. Despite
having an alloy block engine, it seems unlikely that so much power could have been
extracted from the Healey engine—a theory confirmed by Chatham who has two of
the other three alloy block engines made at Courthouse Green, Coventry. 'Two
hundred brakehorse power at the flywheel is more like it,' says Chatham.

Suspension was uprated with stiffer front springs, heavy-duty anti-roll bar to
reduce understeer, fourteen-leaf rear springs, and competition shock absorbers all
round. The individual leaves in the rear springs were not of the same thickness as
normal—they were thinner—but in total made a much stiffer spring to support the
weight of the thirty gallon fuel tank, twin spare wheels and all the spares and equipment carried on a long-distance road rally. Some attempt was made to keep the
crew cool with an air-scoop on the scuttle, a van-type ventilator flat in the roof and
the familiar triangular outlets in the front wings. Some cars had 100M-style louvres
in the bonnets—but the combination of holes in the front wings and louvres did not
work well. In fact, on John Gott's car the effect was the opposite to that expected: the
louvres were at a high-pressure point and air was forced in to the bonnet on top of
the engine and could not get out of the wing vents and underside (obstructed by a
sump guard) in sufficient quantity. So everything got hotter and hotter . . .

The wing vents helped when changing the oil filter, though, but that was hardly
their purpose. Owners such as Dave Ramstad, who have used these vents alone have
noticed an improvement in ventilation. Works cars were fitted with the Tulip gearbox and overdrive with, often, a rare 4.3:1 differential, disc brakes all round, packing
pieces in the suspension to raise ground clearance, two-speed wipers and special
uprated electrical equipment, air horns and rally instruments. There was room for
hardly anything else inside, except, perhaps, Pat Moss's handbag. Works cars, of
course, were never seen without their hardtops.

Some early cars had triple 2-inch SUs on longer inlet manifolds, later ones had
triple Webers. This meant cutting away the nearside pedal box, and alternative
strengthening, which could not be done on left-hand drive cars, where the steering
column gets in the way. The 12.6:1 steering box from a four-cylinder car was substituted for the 15:1 unit fitted to the later 100-Sixes and 3000s. This meant that
large steering wheels were retained. Hinged, or Dzus-fastened, panels were cut in
the nearside front wing tops for carburetter maintenance and bootlids bulged over
the twin spare wheels. All these rally cars were build at Abingdon and weighed
around 25 cwt. Even the ultra-lightweight PWB57 tipped the scales at 24 cwt,
because, despite the engine, it still needed heavy underbody protection.

The competition cars built at Warwick for roadracing and events like Sebring
were quite different. They weighed nearer 18 cwt than 24 cwt, using flimsy alloy
panels where possible. According to Thelma Segal, 'You could push the metal in
and out with your finger.' The best examples are the 100S cars, of course, but they
all follow the same principles—rally-style engines with full race camshaft, 20 lb
flywheel and a special gearbox. The Sebring box, as it was known, had close first and
second ratios with a big gap before a close third and top, against the Tulip box with

Above left: Works-type scuttle scoop for extra cockpit ventilation.

Above right: The boot bulges when you cram in an extra spare wheel!

Left: The cockpit of a works rally car —like something from an old-time fighter plane.

Right: A rare Universal Laminations hardtop as fitted to a Healey 100.

Below: What a wonderful hardtop! It's a Pexidome from the late 1950s. Unfortunately they turned yellow with age.

ratios to take advantage of overdrive on third and fourth. Overdrive was left off many Warwick cars to save $37\frac{1}{2}$ lb. Floorpans were changed to sheets of alloy and footwells omitted. Steel panels in the chassis were cutaway to a $\frac{5}{8}$-inch lip all round to take the rivetted-in alloy centre. Like the rally cars, fuel lines and electrics were routed along the inside of the chassis rails for protection, in this case, because the suspension was lowered as much as possible. These cars with the Sebring box were suitable only for flat circuits with long straights when fitted with axle ratios as high as 2.93:1; otherwise they used a lower axle ratio with the Tulip box with or without overdrive, depending on the nature of the circuit. Axle ratios as low as 6.3:1 (from an Austin J2 van) have been used for hill-climbs. Four wheel disc brakes were fitted like those on DD 300. Early experiments with thicker discs resulted in the car 'standing on its nose,' says Barry Bilbie, so it was vital that the brakes were not too powerful for the weight. In some cases, extensions were fitted on the wings rather than bulging them to cover the wheels as is done for historic racing today. Ventilation systems were similar to those on rally cars and oil coolers like those on DD 300 were fitted. Heaters were never fitted. Hard-worked rally and race cars did not need them. Sidescreens were retained to save weight even after the introduction of wind-up windows on the production cars.

The best modifications for four-cylinder cars are to bring them as close as possible to 100M or 100S specification, according to Chatham, although Jeffery considers that they are better in standard trim. Alternative exhaust systems similar in principle to those used on the six-cylinder cars are effective and it is possible to fit the clutch and gearbox from the Mark III; a much more reliable unit. Only six of the nine bolt holes line up when fitting the gearbox, but this has been found to be satisfactory by Chatham. The first motion shaft has to be shortened about 1 in and the small cross member in front of the cruciform removed or modified, and the clutch linkage made to fit. The chassis has to be drilled to accept the gearbox's standard rear mountings, and the chassis slightly bowed to clear the overdrive casing. A 3000 rear axle can be fitted in place of the weak BN1 unit, although the 3000 propeller shaft must be used if the 3000 gearbox is incorporated in this change. The four-cylinder car's prop shaft can be retained if the axle is not altered. Mark III radius arms work well providing the Panhard rod is removed and somebody sufficiently skilled is available to weld up the chassis. The disc brakes from a 3000 can be fitted to the BN2 and 100-Six, and Mark I coil springs used; later springs are too stiff. The 3000 servo is essential with 3000 brakes, and the 3000 front anti-roll bar can be fitted if you want to stiffen the suspension. Do not fit fourteen-leaf rear springs to any Healey other than a full works rally replica: they are so stiff they will crack the chassis without all the extra weight over the rear axle, and in any case the rally cars were completely rebuilt after every event.

Another word of warning: be careful when changing brakes to make sure that there is a good balance between front and rear, with discs and drums; Chatham recommends reducing the size of the rear brake cylinder from 1 in to $\frac{3}{4}$ in on spiral bevel drive cars. On later hypoid drive cars, use 3000 brake cylinders.

Road wheel width is the one thing that can transform any Big Healey: for the better if the wheel is increased in width and kept as light as possible, and for the worse to almost unmanageable if too big and heavy a wheel is fitted. Almost any radial tyre is a big improvement over the earlier cross-ply tyres, providing the size is not too big. The best wheel size, according to Chatham, is 165 × 15 with a 5½J rim width, for road use. Sixty-spoke wires from a late Mark II or a Mark III, or disc wheels of no more than 5J are acceptable on earlier cars and better than the original forty-eight-spoke wheels. The 5J wheels from an MGC are also acceptable. For absolute finesse in handling the best wheels, although highly non-original, are Mini-lites with a maximum rim width of 6½ ins. You can use the magnesium Minilites of this size because they are so much lighter than normal wheels. In this case, the best tyres are the 175 or 185 × 15, 70-profile Michelin XAS, with Dunlop SP Sports acceptable, but not so long lasting. Dunlops tend to be a bit on the heavy side for a Healey. Cobra rims have been fitted by many owners, but must be of no more than six-inch width or the handling deteriorates dramatically. Paul Skilleter was one owner who carried out a popular modification on his *Thoroughbred and Classic Cars* Big Healey. He fitted 185 × 15, 70VR Dunlops on six-inch rims in place of the Mark III's standard 4½-inch wires: 'I wouldn't have countenanced them had they stuck out of the bodywork or fouled the wings on full lock or something, but as it was they just gave the car a slightly chunkier appearance; the low profile "70" rating of the Dunlops certainly helped to prevent bad handling and brought back the gearing to nearly that of the standard 165-section tyres. Ground clearance therefore was about the same, or maybe marginally better than before—and the car's long-suffering exhaust system didn't ground on the office car park ramp as it did before; though new springs helped in this department, too.'

Shock absorber condition is vital to a Big Healey, and good results can be obtained by fitting the heavy-duty units made in occasional batches by Armstrong. They can be readily distinguished from the standard Armstrongs by the larger reservoir on top of the casing. A Koni conversion was marketed but these normally-excellent shock absorbers were not very successful on the Big Healey because of mounting trouble caused by the massive leverage of the suspension. In any case they cannot be fitted to the rear of a Mark III with a standard exhaust system because of fouling.

Works rally cars had re-inforced suspension mountings for obvious reasons, but one alarming fault that is coming to light on hard-used Healeys is front suspension collapse. This happened to Skilleter, and this is how he described it in *Thoroughbred Classic Cars*: 'The Healey has an upper wishbone which pivots on the shock absorber, which itself is mounted on a suspension pillar. What happened was that the top of the suspension pillar decided it didn't like the company it was keeping and peeled open like a box lid away from the pillar, shock absorber, wishbone and all.

'The result of this as it affects the driver is considerable. I was only going slowly at the time—around 60 mph on a dual carriageway—when the car began to veer left. At first it didn't appear to answer to the helm at all and I'd reached the stage of merely wondering which hedge/tree/ditch we were going to damage; then a few feet from the kerb it did respond and thereafter it was quite easy to guide it to a standstill without touching the brakes—I thought that a tyre had deflated at that stage. However, on alighting from the vehicle (as they say), it was immediately obvious that tyres were not the reason for this particular bit of drama, as the nearside front wheel was leaning inwards at a very marked angle. On removing the wheel, it took me some time to spot the actual cause as my search was directed immediately behind the wheel at the swivel pin, which I felt sure must have been broken. I was rather amazed to discover the true reason, with the damper lodged up against the inner wing panel.'

Subsequently the plate was bent back into position and rewelded, and a reinforcing plate was welded over the top on both sides. 'We never had that problem when the cars were newer,' said former service manager Geoff Price. 'We had only two front suspension collapses, once when the captive nut holding one of the four shock absorber mounting bolts broke and once when the bolt had been put in cross-threaded.' Chatham confirms that shock absorbers have a tendency to tear themselves out when they work loose and Dave Jeffery, who dismantled many Big Healeys for spares in the early 1970s, says that it was evident that many had the beginnings of severe shock absorber mounting problems. Generally, the specialists agree that the standard suspension, in perfect condition, is best for road use. Despite this 'no two Healeys feel the same,' says Thelma Segal. 'And only those in perfect condition feel right. The others are terrible.'

Engine modifications include most of the usual ones such as polishing the ports, but one of the easiest and most dramatic can be either fitting a six-port head to a four-port 100-Six or simply dropping in the entire engine from a 3000. Early 100-Six cars suffered from severe scuttle shake before they had extra stiffening incorporated on production, and a standard works modification was to fit a hoop over the gearbox aperture, which helped tremendously.

Other modifications come more into the line of temporary repairs to keep the car running apart from fitting a fibreglass fan to combat overheating; fibreglass panels to replace rusted steel ones; alternators to power extra lights; extra gauges; extra insulation; early post-war Buick back wheels and V8 or Jaguar engines.

Installing a V8 used to be popular in California where the big saloons they power populate many junk-heaps. But it is a major engineering problem, like fitting a Jaguar engine, which has been tried in Britain. If done properly, the car will handle better if the engine is lighter than the standard heavy Healey engine (remember the Six weighs more than the Four). Few of these conversions have been very successful, though, suffering chiefly from installation causing chronic scuttle shake apart from anything else.

Fibreglass fans, on the other hand, have been very successful in America. Air flow can be increased by about one third between 600-1,500 rpm (typical traffic jam revs); noise reduced at the typical Healey howl point of 3,000-3,500 rpm; and fuel consumption improved by, perhaps, a full 1 mpg. Other overheating dodges include removing the thermostat and pulling out the choke.

Fibreglass panels used to be popular, particularly in Britain, where some quite effective wings and shrouds were made, being difficult to distinguish from original metal, but now they are in little demand due to poor efforts ruining the originality of appearance on some cars.

Alternators work very well, but are expensive because many parts must be changed including the voltage regulator. Extra gauges are useful, particularly an

Below: Disc rear brakes as fitted to
DD300.

Bottom: Where the power comes
from—a big-valve alloy head for a
three-litre Healey.

ammeter. Care must be taken when fitting an ammeter, especially on a Mark III, where the obvious place is between the rev counter and the milometer. Unless you have access to a template such as that owned by the Austin-Healey Club's Pacific centre, the actual fitting on a Mark III is best left to a real professional. It is not just a case of taking care not to break the temperature gauge's capilliary tube when removing the dashboard wood; you have to know exactly where to drill the hole, taking one sixteenth over two inches as a maximum. At that size, the size to take the average ammeter, there is only one sixteenth of an inch clearance behind the dashboard where the steering column bracket is fitted.

Extra insulation from a builder's merchant is acceptable particularly around the gearbox tunnel and exhaust, and it is a popular modification in hot countries such as America, and Australia. Old Buick wheels are confined to America alone because they are plentiful and have the right offset, and Americans generally have not been following the rest of the world's trend in swopping disc wheels for wires to improve appearance.

Lots of 'goodies' are available from firms such as A-H Spares, John Chatham Cars, Southern Carburetters, and Thelma Segal's Gearbox, including alloy works-pattern rocker covers which do wonders for appearance and combating oil leaks aluminium alloy works-pattern manifolds. The actual works manifolds were made from magnesium, and needless to say, such exotic parts are like gold-dust today.

XIV

The Concours Men

LIKE IT OR NOT, concours men are acquiring a reputation as fastidious fellows who persecute pigeons passing anywhere near their cars. This is because the original concept of the concours d'elegance has long since been lost. Competitors in events such as the Monte Carlo Rally used to line up their cars when the road tests were over, rather like troops regrouping after a battle. Even the hard-pressed BMC team found time to wash and polish their battered cars after events such as the Liège-Rome-Liège rally; they made their cars as smart as possible, although the result counted for little more than a spot of good publicity. The most important part of the old rallies was the road section, with driving tests to follow. The concours was simply an expression of pride in their mounts.

Not so today. Many of the concours cars hardly turn a wheel in inclement weather, let alone exert themselves in competition. The aim is to create a vehicle which is absolutely without blemish, totally original and looking better than the day it left the factory. The degree of competition, especially in America, is such that the vehicle is virtually unusable if the owner is to do the work himself, lead a reasonable social life, and still stand a chance of winning. One thunderstorm or a couple of miles on a muddy road can ruin a month's fanatical cleaning.

So concours winners are a breed apart, rather like men such as Dave Ramstad, who have kept their cars as good as new, from new. However, they are to be admired and the also-rans could learn a lot from their experiences. Concours contestant or not, there is no way to rush a rebuild, if the job is to be done properly. For a start, the car should be parked where the restoration is to be done. Then remove the bumpers, hood, windscreen, bonnet, luggage boot lid, doors, lights, door surrounds, interior, wheels (substituting axle stands), wings, all the chrome, and the shrouds. Then put the wheels back on and take out the engine and transmission. Then off with the wheels again, and next the suspension, back axle and steering. If the panels or chassis is rusty or damaged, the cancer must be cut out and new metal welded in. It is best to get skilled help here or the joins will show. Then get down to shot-blasting and cleaning everything. Dismantle everything, clean it and inspect it, and make up your mind what needs replacing or repair, and order it. Store everything carefully in labelled plastic bags. List everything that has to leave your garage for specialist attention and keep a progress chart, paying particular attention to those parts which you will need first on reassembly. By the time you have finished all this you should be receiving the spares you need. The suspension, steering and brakes should have priority, so that the frame is free to move around again as soon as the chassis has been rustproofed and primed.

The engine and transmission should be installed next, followed by wiring, body, electrical components, interior and all the little bits and pieces. Sounds easy, doesn't it? Don't be fooled. It takes the average skilled enthusiast three years and professionals at least nine months. Paul Skilleter had had most of the mechanical work done before he started his body rebuild at DS Engineering in London. The car, a Mark III owned by *Thoroughbred and Classic Cars*, needed virtually a new body. Paul and the proprietor of DS Engineering, Derek Spencer, began by taking off the Healey's exterior equipment and trim: lights, bumpers complete with their irons, boot lid and grille. At least one headlight nut had to be drilled out, which needed care to avoid damage to the expensive alloy shroud. 'The grille was a bit of a fiddle to remove,' said Paul. 'The three bolts top and bottom were awkward to get to; but at least they came undone. The doors followed, the alloy Phillips screws undoing quite easily—they usually corrode where they go into the tapped plates on the front side of the door shut face and have to be drilled.'

The wings were in such a bad state they were cut off, which saved the painstaking job of unbolting them. 'It was a bit like opening a rusty tin can,' said Paul. The inner wings were rusted, but repairable. The screen was removed next, before Paul and Derek tackled the sills, or what was left of them. 'Screen removal is straightforward,' said Paul. 'Remember that you have to bend the tabs which hold the top trim panel in place and then lift the panel up from the front to release it, and then lift it up and out from the rear, as the bolts key into the air vents; don't lose the distance pieces the other side, when you are undoing the side pillars.'

After stripping the floor area, the alloy kickfaces were removed and the outer sills chiselled and hacksawed off. The inner sills were removed by similar methods. 'Treat the centre section of the sills between the door shut faces as separate entities, and tackle either end after you have removed the middle,' said Paul. 'The bottom of the leading door shut face has to be cut and chiselled off along a line above the rot to remove the forward projecting piece of sill—this can be quite a tough job as the door shut face and the side of the bulkhead form a lamination of steel three plates thick. Watch for bits of jagged metal, the wearing of protective gloves is highly recommended. The rearward door shut face more or less fell to bits on removal of the aluminium facing.'

The bottom parts of the rear inner wings where the radius arms are mounted also need rebuilding. Then the petrol tank was removed to reveal hardly any boot floor! The rear shroud was removed to reach this. Then came the turning point. Paul and Derek started to fit new parts instead of ripping off old ones. 'At first it was a slow patching process as rot was cut back to good areas of metal in the inner rear wings,' said Paul. 'A most important point to bear in mind at this stage is that the car must be standing on its own wheels, or axle stands. If the car is jacked up or supported elsewhere, for instance on the chassis, it will flex and render proper fitting of new parts impossible, and you won't get the doors to close afterwards.'

Paul and Derek found the new inner sills easy to fit and braze. They came in two halves and were mated together first with non-continuous brazing, although subsequent experience has proved that this process is not so good as originally thought. The door shut faces were fitted next after extensive refurbishing of the inner wings. The shut faces were quite flexible and not given their bracing stays until the doors and rear outer wings could be aligned properly. At the front of the car, minor holes were filled with new metal where the footwells join the front bulkhead. The brazed seams must be checked carefully for pinholes which will only show up when the rebuilt car is taken out on a wet road for the first time. The boot floor was replaced in similar fashion and the interior mountings had been repaired. Then the flanges on the shrouds were repaired and the shrouds refitted before new front wings were offered up. This was done to see that all the flanges met up properly, before bolting on the new wings, using Spire bolts and spring clips. 'If you are doing this job with the doors in place—we were not—you have to bend the wing's tabs at the door end back at about 45 degrees to clear the door,' said Paul. 'With the wing in place, you bend them back and pop-rivet them to the hinge plate. When securing the bottom part of the wing to the inner sill, you can either use pop-rivets or self-tapping screws because they look neater. Before any permanent fixing is done, you should ensure that the new wing matches up with the door line, which in turn must be carried through on to the rear wing when this is installed. You have to trim a little bit from the front wing at the door end, and the sidelight hole is not cut until last when the wing has been bolted firmly in position.

'The stainless steel beading isn't put in at this stage—the wing is bolted up and left like that until the car is painted. Then the wing bolts are slackened off, the beading pushed down between the wing and the shroud with sealing either side, and the bolts finally tightened.

'The rear wings gave a lot of trouble. Three pairs were rejected before we got hold of some original factory ones like those now made by Fred Draper. Incidentally, if the shroud has been damaged you should fit the front wings from the front to match with the shroud. At the door end of the wings, you have to take the inner edge of the wing up about $\frac{1}{4}$ in to clear the screen pillar. One point to watch is that the wings don't end up bulging outwards from the bottom mountings. Even then, don't bolt up the wing tightly until new outer sills and rear wings are fitted. The reverse applies for rear-end damage. With our front wings in place, the new outer sill was pushed into place. The door should be on the car when this is done, to make sure that the new panel seats properly. You will find that if you are fitting a new rear door shut face panel, that it probably has not got a cut-out to take the new sill, so you will have to hacksaw and clip it away. When you have one end fitting nicely, pop-rivet it in place while you tackle the other. You should end up with the front wing, outer sill and rear wing all together, but not irretrievably welded up as you might still have to make adjustments for the door to close properly. Don't forget the swage line—it should form a smooth sweep from beginning to end without any mismatching in the middle. It needs a lot of patience, you rarely get an exact fit even with factory parts.'

Healey's old service manager, Geoff Price, confirmed this. He said 'I can remember fitters trying four or five wings before they could get one to fit when the cars were being built. All the rejects used to end up in our shop, which made service repairs even more difficult.' One prominent enthusiast, who wished to remain anonymous, is in a quandry over his beautifully-restored, totally original 100. It has an early-style front wing one side and a late-style the other; exactly as it left the factory. 'I suppose I'll fit a matching wing one side or the other one day,' he said ruefully, 'but it won't be as original then!'

While all his work was being done, Paul was dutifully rust-proofing the Mark III before starting the hours of work replacing the interior and chrome trim. Some of the old interior parts were worth keeping, and Paul remembers one of the trickiest problems as matching up new vinyl covering with old. In all, the car's body took a year to rebuild, surviving changed premises as DS Engineering moved from one home to another, and then had to return for more treatment. The rear shroud had to be partially stripped back to deal with what happened to be a reaction caused by flux in the aluminium. The shroud was welded when off the car, but using ordinary oxy-acetelene equipment, not argon arc; the result was that a row of bubbles appeared along the wing beading. It just goes to show that you never stop learning with a Big Healey.

Gavin Gullery from Wanganui, New Zealand, owns a wonderful concours 100. He caught the Healey bug in 1956 when a client who owned several cars including a couple of M G T Fs, let him drive his new 100-Six. 'The risk of bending it scared me, so I kept myself in check,' said Gavin. 'In fact, I had to keep myself in check until my family of four began to leave the nest as money seemed to last only from one large income tax payment to another, with little opportunity for expensive hobbies. I had owned Jaguars as family and business transport, and a couple of restored motor cycles which led to Vintage Car Club membership . . . and then the seed sown by the 100-Six began to take root.

'There was only one thing to do; find one. So I went to see a chap called Dave Young, who has worked on most of the better cars in New Zealand—Alfas, Astons and so on and had served his apprenticeship on TDs, TFs, TR 3s and Healeys.

'I travelled around everywhere, following up clues in my Mark II Jaguar. Dave and I closely inspected various Healeys, including an abominable 100. All of them seemed too rough, until one night on my way home I spotted a 100 badly parked outside a pie shop. A quick U-turn blocked its escape and gave rise to the conversation: "Not a bad Healey! Do you think you may sell it some time?" This elicited the fact that the university student who owned it and his girlfriend were about to sell. A meeting was arranged with Dave for an inspection and a drive in it.

'"It's all there!"' he said. "Amazing—I haven't seen one all there for twenty years. Well, the speedo doesn't work, one rear shock absorber is missing, low and reverse are clonking, its rusty down below, the exhaust is held on by wire, but it still does 100 mph."

'I'll have it,' I said. 'How much? Agreed.'

Dave and I drove it home, but it was rather sad, hood and curtains were old and ill-fitting, the hard top and upholstery were disintegrating, the paint was faded, cracked and lifeless. But it drove well, despite its missing shock absorber.

'Unable to stand the sight of a sick car, we agreed to work on it in Dave's double

Top: Start of the concours trail: Gavin Gullery's 100 stripped to the bare bones.

Centre: Gavin Gullery's rolling chassis showing incredible standards of restoration.

Bottom: At last we're winning! Gavin Gullery (left) and Dave Young start to put the body back on.

Proud as punch they stand to admire
the finished example.

garage. How far should we go? I wanted to go all the way, but I'm still not sure how
far Dave wanted to go. However, after the first three months of 1973, a pattern began
to emerge. Dave did most of the taking apart, and I began to seek all the difficult
parts, organizing the supply of services and adding to my list of sympathetic friends.

'I suggest to anybody contemplating a complete restoration involving sandblasting that they finish the entire panel work before taking the car to pieces, and
then go easy with sandblasting. It is worthwhile, but it can hammer dishes into
panels and leave small craters in aluminium.

'The car was completely stripped to every nut, parts inspected, replaced if
necessary, and rebuilt systematically. A weekly night was put aside for the garage
work and a lot of searching went on in between. Delays occurred including a hernia
operation on the owner resulting from lifting and propping the chassis unaided while
sandblasting. Everything was stripped, rust-proofed and electrozinced. Nuts, bolts,
small fittings and new parts were zinced, bearings showing the slightest wear were
replaced, hoses, brakes, seals and so on renewed. Every moving part on the car,
which had done about 70,000 miles, seemed to be worn out.

'A new colour-coded wiring harness was obtained from California, and a windscreen located in New Zealand. Differential, gearbox, overdrive, steering box, braking and clutch systems were overhauled and renewed. Motor, generator, starter
motor, instruments, switch and electric gear were overhauled and new parts obtained
if required. Some parts were hard to find. Some Ferguson tractor suspension bushes
were used and new parts made in Wanganui included a steering box peg and door
shut wedge castings. The man who made them was very skilful . . . after careful filing
and chroming the castings look and work like new. Aluminium parts were buffed and
polished, including the fan and steering box. The carburetters were rebuilt and
polished, and stainless steel rod was used for trim between the wings and shroud.
The floor, boot, sills, wings, and doors were rebuilt with new metal. Painting,

Left: What a Healey 100 cockpit should look like.

Below: Healeys line up for the big concours.

The 3000 Mark I cockpit should look like this.

finishing and assembly took place steadily until the car emerged a deep shining lacquered red on Christmas Eve, 1976. Then it was a question of hanging the doors, boot lid, bonnet, fitting the lights, catches, shut face trims and upholstery. The upholsterer, who is a vintage car specialist, completed his work with red carpet, red boot lining, black seats and tonneau by May 1977. We still had not had time to make a hood frame or side curtains.

'A short shake down, and Dave and I took our BN1 to the annual Austin-Healey club rally at Rotorua, 240 miles and three and a half hours away. It was mid-winter in New Zealand, and we were away in the dark with no hood against the rain, but what a wonderful weekend we had. Only our elbows and the carpets got wet although driving rain made it difficult to see forwards at 70 mph, although visibility was good in any other direction. We were placed second in the concours, missing out by one point to a low-mileage BJ8. As twenty points were allocated for hood and side-screens, we are looking forward to the next time.

'The car is being reserved for a long, new life, and it is driven as it enjoys being driven by its owner and mechanic. It's kept polished and covered between whiles, never lent or parked side on to others, and it feels and acts like new. It will be used mainly on rallies and trips, but kept off gravel roads and other damage-causing environments. The New Zealand roads are free of salt and corrosion, but dairy farmers shifting cows on back roads leave a lot of dung—good for gardens when old and dry, but awfully sloppy and corrosion-making for cars when wet. I'm never tired of looking at, listening to, driving and enjoying Healeys—and I am proud to have a good one at last.'

A modern-day love story.

XV

The Healey Specials

IN THEIR capacity as design consultants, the Healey family became inveterate special builders over the years. In fact the first Big Healey special, code-named X11, was the left-hand-drive 100 prototype registered KWD947. Its headlamps were too low—a little less than the 26 inch minimum height brought in as it was designed. Originally it had 16 inch Austin disc wheels and 10 inch brakes—which were later changed to 11 ins for better operation, which also, happily, better filled the hole in the middle of its new 15 inch wire wheels! Chassis designer Barry Bilbie remembers two such prototypes, and so does service manager Geoff Price. Thompsons of Wolverhampton also made two prototype chassis—one of which was used for KWD947—but nothing more has been heard of the other Healey 100.

It is possible that it became one of the infamous Special Test cars. These included NOJ391, which eventually became a 100S development car after bearing a close resemblance to a 100M at one time. As it was, the first few 100S models made in 1954 were regarded as prototypes, but the car presented to the public at the 1954 Motor Show was considered to be a production car, priced at $5,000. At about that time, two four-cylinder fixed-head coupés were made, one of which was registered ONX113 and used by Donald Healey for many years. It was a BN1, but eventually acquired 100S engine and brakes, which must have made it a most desirable machine. Its sister was OAC1, fitted with an early six-cylinder engine and opening rear window. These BN1 coupés were serious production contenders, but got no further because it was considered essential to keep to open cars as the demand for these exceeded supply in any case. Ralph Boothe, an American, also built a four-cylinder coupé from the car he bought new in Los Angeles in 1956—and made a very good job of it.

'Boothe first completely disassembled the car and restored the chassis and lower body, even to the extent of completely re-wiring it,' said *Road and Track*. 'He then proceeded to design the hardtop, using a Healey 3000 convertible windshield, an inverted Renault Caravelle rear window and 18-gauge sheet steel, and had it built by California Metal Shaping, who made the panels for the Scarabs and Cobra Daytona coupé. This sturdy top extends rearward to the bottom tuck-under and makes the Healey a far more rigid car than it was originally.' Boothe modified the bumpers and interior and the very smart car is still attending Healey meetings in the United States.

Left: The original one-eighth scale model of the Healey 100 as the design was adopted.

Centre: The same model showing the rejected eyelid and fin on the rear wing.

Right: Side view of the prototype KWD947 outside Tickfords coach-builders at Newport Pagnell before having its body fitted. The unusual bulkhead was only used on that prototype.

Further early Austin-Healey specials included X3, a weird four-seater using a much modified Morris Minor bodyshell. 'Like every other 100, it was handicapped by having to use flat glass,' said Bilbie. In fact, it seemed as though nobody liked this attempt to produce a sports car using a cheap saloon body as a basis and it was promptly scrapped. A couple of years later a much more advanced project, the X201, was started using a multitube space frame and de Dion rear axle. Standard front suspension was used with an old racing engine and gearbox. 'The back axle used the Austin Gipsey differential,' said Bilbie. 'Unfortunately the splines were not up to the torque and there was no other similar commercial unit to be found, so it had to be scrapped. It's a pity we couldn't afford to engineer it properly as Jaguars were doing with a similar rear end at about that time.' The car, like many other prototypes, was sold for scrap, but later turned up as a hill-climb car!

At about the same time, another full four-seater prototype, the X170 was produced with de Dion rear axle and bodywork based on extended 100 panels, but it would have been too large and expensive and so it was scrapped. X224 was one of the most famous Healey projects: the single-seater Ferrari-Healey. It was based on a $2\frac{1}{2}$-litre Grand Prix car bought from the Marquis de Portago shortly before his death in the Mille Miglia. The engine was rebuilt to run on petrol and give around 200 bhp. It was mounted in a much-modified 100-Six competition chassis with the Ferrari de Dion transaxle unit grafted onto the rear. Ferrari-style radius arms which were later to find their way onto the Mark III series two were fitted with 100S brakes and hubs. An MGA rack and pinion completed the goodies. The ageing engine was down on power, however, and the car had to be fitted with a 100-Six competition engine before it was capable of a respectable speed. Roy Salvadori and Peter Collins drove it at Nassau, but could extract nothing worthwhile from it, so the Ferrari was rebuilt and sold and the prototype scrapped.

Throughout the 1950s and early 1960s, the Healeys persevered with de Dion rear axles, even fitting one to another six-cylinder car used as a four-headlamp styling exercise. This car, known as X230, also featured rack and pinion steering, which, like previous Healey installations proved rather heavy.

Parts of this car were used on a car which was sold and has survived, as have two later coupés, X312 and X313. These were based on the 3000 chassis and closely resembled the company's Le Mans Sprites. 'The first was made at Warwick and the second was built by Tickford,' said Bilbie. 'They made a beautiful job of the car.'

Of these two cars, X312 and X313, the former was the more advanced from the engineering point of view. It had Girling disc brakes on all four wheels and series two Mark III rear suspension with torque arms. The engine had an alloy head, high lift camshaft and triple S U carburetters. It also had a restyled interior and larger fuel tank. The second car was an attempt at rationalizing the coupé body panels with those of the current convertible's to cut production costs. In the end, it was decided that the Healey fixed-head coupé would clash with the new M G C G T and the project was abandoned. 'They remind you of an Aston Martin,' says the current owner, Austin-Healey Club member Don Humphries. That's hardly surprising. Tickford was taken over by Aston Martin in the mid-1950s.

Those were the only coupés built by the factory, although an enthusiast called Douglas Wilson-Spratt built at least one beautiful Big Healey coupé called the WSM. It bore a close resemblance to an E type Jaguar, except that it had a longer tail ending in a Kamm effect. The basis for the conversion carried out at the Healey Centre in Leighton Buzzard, Bedfordshire, was a smashed up Mark II, with 75,000 miles on the clock. Its engine was bored out to 3.1 litres and fitted with triple S U carburetters. The only standard body panels retained were the doors. The rest of the body was handmade in aluminium. Improvements included a larger bonnet aperture and better cooling from its long nose; improved vision through deeper windows; and much more luggage space in the E type coupé style fastback. The roof incorporated a substantial roll-over bar. With non-standard wide-rimmed wheels and oversize tyres, it was capable of 100 mph at 3,800 rpm in overdrive top. The good streamlining reduced wind noise and helped boost the maximum speed to 130 mph. It was a far better looking coupé than anything Healey produced, although there was more likelihood of their versions going into production, because undoubtedly the WSM would have moved up into the price bracket occupied by the E type Jaguar.

Other prototype Big Healeys built at Warwick included the BN3, a six-cylinder version of the four-cylinder cars, and the BN5, a very spartan, basic BN4 that never went into production, plus the Rolls-Healeys, which were meant to replace the 3000.

'We laid down for seven Rolls-Healeys, but made only three,' said Bilbie. 'The first used the automatic gearbox which came as standard with the four-litre engine and the second and third had Jaguar overdrive gearboxes. They were basically wider versions of the current Mark III. The extra width had the good effect of giving more

Left: Rear view of the same prototype. The fuel tank position was used only for running in chassis form and was not intended for production.

Centre: Three-quarter front view of the prototype chassis showing the steering box and idler mounted at the extreme front. This was soon modified to a mounting on the suspension housing.

Right: Close-up of the cockpit area of the prototype. Note the Jaguar X K 120-style steering column rake. This was improved when the steering box and idler were moved to the suspension housing.

Top: Front view of the Ferrari-
Healey chassis showing its rack and
pinion steering. This is the way the
Healey family would have liked the
production cars to have developed.

Centre: General layout of the Ferrari-
Healey chassis.

Bottom: How the Ferrari engine was
fitted into the chassis. It's a good job
the driver did not have to sit over that
exhaust system!

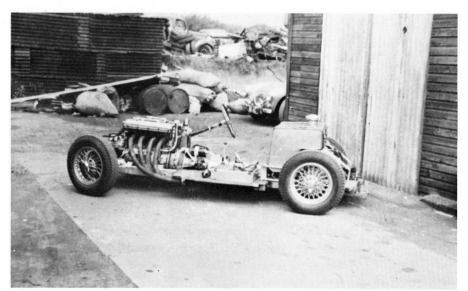

Top: Rear view of the Ferrari-Healey chassis showing the de Dion rear suspension with transverse leaf spring. The de Dion tube was located by a trunnion running in track on the differential housing and by parallel links—some features of which are apparent on DD 300 today. Again, this is the way the Healey family would have liked their production cars to have developed.

Centre: Side view of the Ferrari-Healey rear suspension showing the parallel links which led to the 3000 Mark III phase two development. The Ferrari-Healey's gearbox was integral with the rear axle, under the massive fuel tank.

Bottom: The ill-fated Healey coupés, X312 and X313.

Above: Dream car in production . . .
the 100S line at Warwick.

Right: Joe Cox's father Peter shows
off their Rolls-Healey before restoration was started.

Above: Yet another attempt at producing a Healey coupé, this time using a 100 as the basis.

elbow room than that of the rather cramped convertible. They also had built-in transmission tunnels to eliminate the troublesome scuttle shake.'

The power unit was the Rolls-Royce engine used in the current Austin Princess R saloon. Like the original four-cylinder Healey engine, it was designed for an Army Jeep. These six-cylinder engines, which produced around 175 bhp with twin 2 inch SU carburetters, had aluminium alloy cylinder blocks and heads with overhead inlet valves and side exhausts—a basic configuration that dated back to an old Bentley Motors' design of around 1930. 'But like the A90 unit, there was this pile of engines lying about . . .' said Geoff Price.

Despite its extra capacity, the Rolls engine was 7 kilograms lighter than the cast iron six, and despite the power loss resulting from its standard Borg Warner automatic transmission, gave the car an impressive performance. With standard 3000 front suspension, the car cornered with a minimum of roll and had good directional stability. The smooth, silent engine was also a good deal sweeter in operation than the old six.

Naturally, the BMC hierarchy were most interested in this Healey prototype, and Syd Enever was told to get on with it as quickly as possible.

The car received its Abingdon designation, ADO24, and work started immediately. Healeys were to look after the chassis side and Jensens the body. Austins, who were backing the project, ordered another six prototypes, two with automatic transmissions, two with Jaguar E type gearboxes, and two with overdrive, in February 1967. Rolls-Royce were responsible for modifying the engines to comply with American emission laws and producing engines with flywheels for the manual boxes. The interior was also redesigned in view of the looming American safety regulations which were to have such an effect on sports cars from 1968 onwards.

When prototypes two and three, one with the standard Jaguar gearbox and one with overdrive, were nearing completion in April 1967, Austin changed their minds about the other four, and soon after the whole project was killed. Geoffrey Healey speculates that the expense of a new model to follow the 3000 at the end of the year was too much, or that perhaps Jaguars spoke out against this 125 mph contender (the E type's former 150 mph performance had been whittled down to around 130 mph by the emission regulations). The most likely theory, of course, is that BMC hoped the MGC would fill the gap in the market vacated by the Big Healey.

'This was substantiated by the fact that gasket sets were marked by BLMC as MGC and Austin-Healey 3000 Mark IV,' said Fred Draper. 'We still have one in stock! The grape vine had it at the time that Donald Healey had flatly refused to have his name on it.'

The only complete pre-production prototype, the original automatic car, chassis number 1001, engine number 40 FB AH 4444, was registered TNX 65G in 1969 and sold to a schoolfriend of the Skipper's, a Mr Andrews, of Bristol, who was accustomed to buying modified or prototype Healeys from the Warwick factory when they had finished with them. Chassis 1001 had covered by far the highest mileage of the three, being sold with 28,000 miles on the speedometer. Andrews used the car for several years before leaving it, dusty and seemingly forgotten, in a garage in the city. The strange-looking '3000' was spotted by John Chatham's garage manager, Joe Cox, then an estate agent. 'My father and myself had enjoyed Healey motoring from Mark One Sprites through to the 3000 Mark III and dearly loved the cars,' said Joe Cox. 'The Healey fraternity knew of the existence of the Rolls-Healey, but few had seen one. I was, to say the least, excited at finding one "on the doorstep" and entered into the negotiations with Mr Andrews that resulted in my father, Peter Cox, buying the car. Actually, John Chatham was aware of the car's presence in Bristol, but did not rate it highly, as he says: "With all that space under the bonnet, it should have had an Aston Martin engine in there."'

Peter Cox ran the car for some three years before it was totally restored at John Chatham Cars. 'The automatic transmission, with even this small mileage behind it, had failed,' said Joe Cox. 'So the gearbox was rebuilt with heavy-duty clutches and bands. A special (and expensive) exhaust system has been substituted for the original 3000 system to cure the unpleasant "suck back" of exhaust fumes into the cockpit due to a change, we suppose, of turbulence characteristics of the wider body. We had a new screen made at incredible expense by Triplex as the old one was cracked. Apart from the interior trim, which was entirely different from that of a Mark III, a different bonnet and bootlid, made in aluminium, had been fitted. Chassis number 1001 runs on standard Healey hubs with MGC type sixty-spoke five-inch wheels. The other two cars were on Jaguar-type hubs.'

How the Rolls engine was installed in the Big Healey. Note the wider shroud.

Joe Cox's four-litre Healey under restoration. The extra width of the car is readily apparent.

'It's a magnificent car to drive,' says Peter Cox, 'and a great improvement over the 3000.' He particularly likes the automatic gearbox.

Joe Cox says: 'The actual car was built up using second-hand doors because piles of them were lying around, which had been taken off standard cars being fitted with alloy doors for racing. Its quite a game, guessing where the parts came from. There's an Austin Princess R rear axle, Morris 1000 rear lamps, Austin 1800 bumpers, TR 5 sidelamps, and so on . . .'

The other two cars were completed soon after the project was killed with one going to the very private collection of Mr Carter in Kings Lynn and the other finding its way to Australia, where it was bought by Stephen Pike. *Healey Highlights*' technical correspondent, Rich Loccasso, reported on it: 'Starting from the ground, the car is fitted with seventy-two-spoke Jaguar wheels with their large hubs. These are five-inch by fifteen-inch wheels with 185 radial tyres and triple ear type knock-on spinners. The suspension is similar to that of the 3000, with 3000 front disc brakes, but a different rear end with wider drum brakes (from an MGC). Braking is through a dual circuit and is power assisted.

'The chassis rails are the same as the Mark III except that they are twenty-three inches apart instead of the standard seventeen. The front cross member has been modified and substantially reinforced to secure the engine which mounts at the front. The footwells and sub-frame area around the firewall have been modified, the tunnel cover now being made of steel and permanently welded to the chassis, giving extra strength. The gearbox can still be checked from the top, but could not be lifted out through the small inspection cover . . .

'The gearbox is an all-synchro four-speed Jaguar unit with electric overdrive on top. The engine is cooled by two thermostatically-controlled fans and the fuel tank is six inches wider than standard.

'The body is the same as the Mark III lengthwise, but across the car the boot lid has been made from two panels cut to allow three inches extra in each and then welded in the centre. Similarly, the bonnet, shrouds and subframes show signs of the extra width. There are two reversing lights mounted on the shroud under the bumper, an MGB chrome vent mounted on the front shroud in front of the windscreen to allow ventilation into the cockpit. The windscreen and soft top are Mark III widened by six inches, and the seats and trim are Mark III. The dashboard has been modified, being finished in crinkle spray with Mark III instruments and rocker-type switches. The overall dash finish is disappointing compared to the woodgrain Mark III.

'The firewall has a Donald Healey Motor Company identification badge like that of a Sebring car with the type left blank, chassis number ADO/1002, engine number F41. There is an Austin-Healey badge on the boot lid, but no other badges are fitted to the car.'

What is it like to drive this 125 mph prototype? Pike says that 'after driving over 1,000 miles in the past two months, I am now beginning to enjoy and appreciate the car for what it is. The extra interior space is quite noticeable, not being cramped between the centre console and the door as a Mark III tends to make me feel. Leg room for the driver is excellent. The seat being positioned closer to the car's centre.

enables it to be pushed further back without hitting the trim on the right side of the seat. Performance is similar to the Mark III, the handling is excellent and the overdrive operates through a switch on the gear knob . . .

'My car was first registered in May 1968 and was used by Healeys until sold to Frank Allenby in 1970. I purchased the car from Frank in July 1974, and on arrival in Australia in November of that year the speedo showed 23,060 miles. The car is red, having been repainted after an accident in 1974. Originally all three cars were white. The overall weight of the car is 24 cwt.'

While the Healey family were responsible for most of the specials, there was a man in Canada called Harold Hunter who apparently produced an extraordinary twin overhead camshaft A90 engine that was thought to have helped inspire the MGA twin cam of the late 1950s. Arch Healey enthusiast Dave Remstad recounts that the chief people involved with the twin cam A90 engine were Harold Hunter and various employees of the Austin Motor Company of Canada, reporting to Mr C. F. Fowler, director of service for North America. Initial production consisted of four twin overhead cam conversions; the first was sent to Longbridge for test and development; the second installed in a 100S racer for competition evaluation; with the third and fourth being made for sale. 'It was claimed that delivery of either the conversion kit or a complete engine could be made in two weeks upon receipt of order in Waterloo, Ontario,' Dave reported in *Healey Highlights*. 'Terms, not surprisingly, were full cash with order.

'The price of the kit was $1,100 and for this, one received domed 9.5:1 racing pistons, pulley, cams, valves, springs, castings, studs, oil lines, distributor shaft, and, of course, the head itself. Valve timing listed was: intake opens 35 degrees before top dead centre, closes 65 degrees after bottom dead centre, exhaust opens 65 degrees before bottom dead centre and closes at 35 degrees above top dead centre. The conversion included a special intake system of Weslake design for $1\frac{3}{4}$-inch or 2-inch SU carburetters and lacked only the installation of a suitable throttle linkage and balanced exhaust system. For $1,600 you could buy either of two completely converted engines—one of stock 2,660 cc displacement—and the other of enlarged 2,994 cc capacity. The latter required 2-inch SU carburetters exclusively.

'The output of either conversion was little short of shattering. Dyno readings obtained by Austin technicians were an astonishing 215 bhp at 6,000 rpm and 206 lb ft or torque at 4,000 rpm for the 2.6-litre engine, while the virile three-litre four pumped out an incredible 240 bhp at 5,500 rpm, and some 227 lb ft of torque. Acceleration figures quoted for a converted Healey Hundred were: 0–60, 6.4 secs; 0–100, 14.8 secs; and a standing quarter mile covered in 14.6 secs.'

Apparently this head was used with some success in mid-1950s sports car racing but why no more were made is as great a mystery as why many more of the other Healey specials, were not made.

XVI

Comparisons with Contemporary Rivals

THE BIG HEALEY came in a blaze of glory and went out in just as big a way fifteen years later. When it was introduced it dealt a death blow to the top-selling MG T series great rival, the Triumph TR. The Healey occupied the middle area of popular sports cars between the cheap TR and the more expensive, if even faster, Jaguars. Big Healeys sold well throughout the 1950s, despite the introduction of a second serious rival, the MGA. People bought Big Healeys because of their rugged appeal, extraordinary strength, low price and high speed. Triumphs, Porsches, Alfas and MGs came and went, and the Chevrolet Corvette changed yearly, but the Big Healey was still selling well in substantially unaltered shape fifteen years after it first appeared. Then it was killed, by looming American regulations and British Motor Corporation rationalization which led to the MGC. This replacement for the Big Healey under-steered its way out of the market and Datsun took over with their cross between a Healey and an E type, the 240Z. To rub it in for BLMC, the price of second-hand Healeys soared as soon as people realized that they were gone for good.

Nineteen fifty-two was a good year for new cars after the austerity of the post-war period. John Bolster proved himself to have well-near prophetic powers with his *Autosport* reports on the London and Paris Motor Shows and his historic Healey 100 test. Bolster said: 'The sports car of the future, as Paris showed, is an aerodynamic two/three seater coupé with plenty of luggage space and delightful contours. The DB2 Aston Martin and the Lancia Gran Turismo were certainly to be seen at Earls Court, as were the superb Fiat 8V and, in a lower price bracket, the Simca 9 Sport. Panhard et Levassor, however, showed only their family saloon and Junior roadster, so the DB and Callista coupés were evidently considered too smart for us. It was most disappointing that the Singer coupé was not on view, for though the well-known roadster is a very worthy car, an attractive appearance is not one of its virtues.

'Nevertheless, Britain is leading in one new trend, and that is the development of the large-engined small car. It has been known, for many years, that this recipe could produce a vehicle of charming manners and delightfully easy performance. In the past, though, a satisfactory combination of comfort and roadholding has not been achieved, and the heavy car of long wheelbase has been preferred. Modern suspension technique has now rendered possible the design of short, light, chassis that are inherently stable and smooth-riding. In consequence, these sports cars of the new school may well have $2\frac{1}{2}$ litre engines and yet be of a size and weight that was formerly only associated with 1,100 cc power units.

'The star example of this trend is the new Healey 100, which dominates the sports car field just as surely as the Cooper-Bristol heads the racers. It is a neat, aerodynamic two-seater in which the comfort and protection of the occupants has been given first consideration. The lightly-stressed 2,660 cc Austin engine simply plays with its small load and a recent road test by this journal recorded that speeds of well over 100 mph are quickly and easily obtained. The appearance is attractive and at a basic price of £850 it represents astonishing value. Stop Press news is that it is to be produced in quantity by Austins themselves.

'A similar engine can be fitted to the Frazer Nash Targa Florio two-seater. This also has an all-enveloping body style, with a central air scoop in the top of the bonnet. One cannot applaud the designer for embracing a steering column gearlever at a time when nearly all sports car makers are going back to the short central control. Previous performances by this chassis, when fitted with two-litre Bristol-build engine, guarantee that the roadholding and steering will be of a very high order. Unfortunately, the price is £1,500, which entails a purchase tax of £834 16s 8d, and is scarcely competitive.'

Bolster was right about the Frazer Nash being uncompetitive for price and wrong about the roadholding. It was the one and only Frazer Nash to have really bad handling. 'The engine was too heavy and the car handled terribly,' said Michael Bowler, editor of *Thoroughbred and Classic Cars*, and one of the Isleworth marque's most ardent supporters. 'The Austin-engined Targa Florio was listed for a couple of years and was a good deal cheaper than the standard model, but there were no takers. The only one made ended up in the States.'

But back to Bolster and his class of 1952. 'Another new sports two-seater of generous engine capacity is the Triumph,' he reported. 'This has a Standard Vanguard engine linered down to 1,991 cc capacity, and fitted with two semi-down-draught carburetters. With a 7 ft 4 in wheelbase, and 3 ft 9 in track, the weight is only $15\frac{1}{2}$ cwt. The power unit develops some 75 bhp at 4,500 rpm, so the performance must be more than lively. The car shown has very deeply cut away body sides which narrowed considerably just ahead of the rear mudguards. This gave rather a wasp-waisted effect and looked as if it would be very draughty, so one hopes that the production models will be deeper sided. The price of £555 is most interesting, and with a 3.8 to 1 axle ratio, the claimed speed of 90 mph should certainly not be impossible.'

A Herculean development programme by former BRM engineer Ken Richardson and designers led by Harry Webster turned the floppy Triumph TR1 prototype into what was to become one of the Healey's toughest rivals over the next fifteen years: the TR2. So good was the work of Richardson, Webster and company that within a few months they had the TR2 going faster than the original Healey 100! With full-length metal undershield, a metal tonneau cover, aero screen, spats and overdrive it did 124 mph on the celebrated bit of motorway near Jabbeke, and 114 mph in near-standard trim. From the class of 1952, two winners had emerged already, although the Healey had a head start over the Triumph because it was practically fully developed when shown at Earls Court. It is interesting to note that part of

Above: Carroll Shelby's version of the Big Healey: the AC Cobra 289, pictured near the factory at Thames Ditton.

Right: The Big Healey's Abingdon stablemate: the MGA 1600.

Above: One of the Big Healey's greatest rivals, the Triumph TR 3, fitted here with an optional hardtop.

Left: Brute power, in the form of the Corvette on the left, and sophistication—in the form of the Lotus Elite behind it at Snetterton—rivalled the Big Healey.

Right: The cheap and cheerful Morgan.

Below: The magic wooden ship called Marcos.

Standard chief, Sir John Black's, reasons for instigating the TR2 was a strong desire for revenge over the Morgan family. They had resisted his attempt to take over their firm and produce a car to fill the gap in the American market between the cheap little MG and the bigger, more expensive Jaguar XK120.

Bolster slotted the current Morgan into his big-engined small car class in his historic report. 'Although it is not new, the Morgan Plus 4, with its 2,088 cc Vanguard engine'—basically the same engine as used in the TR—'follows the same idea. Light and compact, this machine is a joy to drive, and no changes are apparent since *Autosport*'s road test of this model. All the familiar chassis features are retained, including the well-known vertical pillar front suspension, and no attempt has yet been made to reduce the wind resistance of the body. This is very much a traditional sports car, and by today's standards, it is cheap at £565 basic.'

The Morgan Plus 4 was a good example of the old-fashioned sports cars that had been overtaken by the Healey and the TR. Its engine, from the Standard Vanguard saloon, was basically the same as that in the TR and similar to that in the Healey, from the Austin A90 saloon. As fitted to the Morgan in its basic form, the overhead push rod four-cylinder engine produced 64 bhp at 4,300 rpm. This was 26 bhp less than the more highly tuned, although smaller, unit used in the TR2, but enough to give the Morgan 87 mph and 27 mpg despite its square-rigged body, because the car weighed only 16 cwt. But Morgans could produce only about five vehicles a week in that period and were hardly a threat to the Healey or Triumph, even when the Plus 4 eventually got the TR2 unit in 1954 and promptly laid claim to the Healey's title of the cheapest 100 mph car. Morgan could never get hold of enough TR engines and had to use the 1,172 cc Ford engine in many cars to keep up production. This smaller Morgan was, of course, no match for a Healey.

So far as basic price went, the TR was the clear class leader in the under £600 stakes in 1952 from the Dellow, produced in tiny quantities, the MG TD produced in vast quantities, the Morgan and the Austin A40 Sports. The MG was already looking rather ponderous and dated even if full of nostalgic appeal, and the Austin A40 was not a proper sports car, more of a pretty little thing for the ladies to play with. It could just about ruffle your hair . . . there was simply nothing to compare with the Healey. Allard produced an £800 Palm Beach powered by a Ford Consul engine, which looked promising until Bolster and Richardson had their burn-ups in Belgium. The performance figures of the Healey and the Triumph did no good at all to the Palm Beach and several prospective sales came to nothing when the would-be owners realized that nothing similar was coming from Allard. 'In most people's minds, the Allard name signified a car with sports performance, and the unfortunate Palm Beach, considered by the company to be just a pleasant touring vehicle, always suffered by reason of its limited performance when compared with the contemporary sports cars in the same price bracket,' said Tom Lush in *Allard—the Inside Story* (MRP). HRG could do an 1100 relic for £820 in Morgan quantity and Jowett's were making the Jupiter for £825 up in Bradford. The Jupiter was a fine sports car, but much slower than the Healey, and rather softer. It almost had a foot in each camp, the sporting and the family fields.

If you had more than £850 or the dollar equivalent, plus purchase tax if you lived in Britain, the best buy was a Jaguar XK120. It was even faster than the Healey, being capable of nearly 130 mpg, but it cost half as much again and a lot more to run. The Jaguar really dominated the higher price class and single-handed spelled the end of many sports cars such as the big Allard J2 and the Lea-Francis. Only Aston Martin could match its performance but, like all things Aston, it was at an enormous price. So that was the scene in the year that the Healey was born. It was the great in-between car, with the cheap MG dominating the class below and Jaguar the class above. Until the TR got into its stride, there was nothing to compare with the Healey.

Ninety per cent of the 10,688 BN1s that left Longbridge and Warwick went to eighteen different countries, with the United States taking three quarters of the total production and paying fourteen million dollars for the privilege. This was despite the introduction of a prettier version of the MG, the TF, in 1953 and the brilliant new AC Ace, based on the highly-successful Tojeiro and Cooper racing sports cars. The Ace was beautiful to behold and capable of 100 mph despite an antique engine producing only 90 bhp. But like Morgan, the Thames Ditton firm was not big enough to make many cars and was no threat to the Healey. The expensive Ace had much better roadholding than the Healey, or the TR for that matter, but could not leave them on the straight, and that was what mattered when it came to selling the cars. The Healey was always one up on everything else in those years because of its fantastic acceleration. In 1953, for instance, of the couple of dozen new cars tested by *The Motor*, whose evaluations were rightly held to be the best, the fastest car was the Bentley Continental at 116.5 mph; the most economical, the Renault 750 saloon which averaged 43.2 mph, and the quickest off the mark was the Big Healey which reached 50 mph from rest in only 8.5 secs. Roadholding did not count for a lot in the early 1950s. Top speed, acceleration and price were the public's yardsticks for a sports car, departments in which the Healey was tops.

In America, General Motors and Ford had been watching the soaring sales of imported cars with interest. Chevrolet had also been experimenting with the new-fangled glassfibre developed during the Korean war. They decided to use it for the new low-price sports car they had had in mind since 1951, when it had become evident that British imports were on the increase.

Sales of European sports cars, including the Austin-Healey, were soaring in 1953 when they rushed out their two-seater plastic-bodied Corvette. They had decided to use glassfibre because it was easy to work and cheap for low-volume products, such as sports cars. This all-new American sports car used the same basic layout as the Healey, Jaguar, MG and Triumph, although it looked like nothing else on earth.

American enthusiasts were eager to buy a two-seater made by Uncle Sam, but the first Corvettes were disappointing and sales failed to take off. The cars leaked, their instruments were styled virtually out of sight and you couldn't have a sporty manual gearbox. You had to have a GM slushbox auto instead of four-on-the-floor. It would be twenty years before the public went for automatic sports cars in a big way. The first Corvette was not all that bad, though. *Road and Track* quite liked their test car, powered by a four-litre engine that bore a close resemblance to that used in

Right: Beautiful, but expensive, the Aston Martin DB2-4 Mark II.

Below: The abbreviated tail of a TVR 1800.

a pre-war Chevvy truck and was good enough to take it up to 60 mph in 11 secs and 106 mph flat out. Still, the cockpit leaked and the Healey could burn it off at the lights, so only two-thirds of the 4,000 Corvettes made by 1955 had been sold in the first two years. By American standards, it was a flop.

Meanwhile, Ford had been experimenting with what they called the 'personal car' concept. While this concept was somewhat vague, it was generally taken to mean that they were fiddling about with sports cars. Ford's first post-war effort in this direction produced the two-seater Thunderbird in 1954. Demand was not high, however, in the face of the European onslaught, and only 53,000 two-seaters were made before the model was discontinued in 1958 and the name transferred to a ponderous drop-head.

Sales figures were to prove that there was room for more than two cheap 100 mph sports cars when MG launched their much-delayed MGA in 1955. They had wanted to replace the TD with it back in 1952, but had been thwarted by the Big Healey. They updated the TD, bring out the TF in 1953, but it was little more than a facelift and received only a mixed reception, although the TF was to go on to become what is considered one of the most beautiful traditional sports cars. In the early 1950s, though, the public's appetite for good, cheap, sports cars had been whetted by the Austin-Healey and the TR2, and MG saloon car sales overtook those of the TF in 1955. Result: the TF had to go and the MGA made its debut in prototype form that year at Le Mans and in production form at the autumn motor shows.

The new car from Abingdon really was a winner and a strong competitor for the Austin-Healey and the Triumph, although its push-rod overhead valve engine was a good deal smaller at 1,489 cc. Nevertheless, it produced 68 bhp and with a properly streamlined body and a dry weight of only $17\frac{1}{2}$ cwt was capable of nearly 100 mph.

Its acceleration—0–60 in 15 sec—was reasonable, and its fuel consumption more than competitive at 30 mpg. As if that was not enough, the basic price was only £595 (£844 in Britain with purchase tax), the same as the current Morgan Plus 4. This made the MGA by far and away the cheapest volume-produced sports car in the world. Only Morgan with the small Ford-engined model and Dellow could undercut MGs, and they could produce only a handful of cars.

The MGA, directly descended from George Phillip's Le Mans TD special, was an immediate success. It sold in huge quantities, especially in America. MGAs were churned out initially at the rate of 13,000 a year; roughly three times as fast as Austin-Healeys. But the Austin-Healey and the Triumph TR were faster, even if their handling was considerably inferior to that of the rack-and-pinion steered MGA, and they continued to sell well. On the American scene, some of the 700 Corvettes made in 1955 had V8 engines and were good for more than 100 mph, with a 0–60 time of 9 secs. The Thunderbird took 11 secs to complete this test.

By 1956, the magic ton had become the essential qualification for a high-performance car. New sporting cars which met this standard included AC's lovely fixed-head version of the Ace, the Aceca; Allard's J2R racer; Alfa Romeo's 1,290 cc Giulietta Spring Spider; Aston Martin's DB2/4; BMW's 507 roadster; Bristol's 405; Frazer Nash's Sebring; Jaguar's XK140 and brilliant new 2.4 litre saloon;

Jensen's 541; Lancia's Spider GT2500; Mercedes-Benz's fabulous 300SL; Porsche's cabriolet, Speedster and Carrera and the odd Ferrari bought by a millionaire.

The class leaders were indisputably the MGA with its mixture of performance, roadholding, economy and low price; the TR2 with its speed, economy and low price; the Big Healey with its sheer performance at a reasonable price; the XK140 with its tremendous speed and sophisticated performance in a higher price bracket and the exotics like Aston-Martin.

Apart from the Suez fuel crisis, the most significant changes in the sports car world were the introduction of the 100-Six, the 'new' TR3 and the start of Zora Arkus-Duntov's involvement with the Corvette. This European-born development engineer immediately set about improving the Corvette's handling and standardizing the V8 to combat a pepped-up T-bird and all those foreign sports cars. He raised the Corvette's power to 210 bhp, and a manual gearbox was offered for the first time. The car promptly did 120 mph, 0–60 in 7.5 secs and sales never looked back. Suddenly it was up to Healey standards of performance.

The 'new' Triumph acquired a slightly more powerful engine at 95 bhp, an egg-box grille, tiny rear seats and wonderful new disc brakes. Like most sports cars of the early 1950s, including the Austin-Healey, the TR2 had inadequate brakes. The old drums were being buried further and further inside disc wheels and new all-enveloping bodywork gave extra speed at the expense of brake cooling. Obviously the disc brakes which had helped Jaguars to a hat trick of wins at Le Mans, were the answer. Triumph used discs on the front only to save money and to ensure that their handbrake worked properly. Few handbrakes operating on rear discs have been really efficient. The TR3 became the first mass-produced car to offer disc braking. Most others followed suit fairly quickly, including the Austin-Healey, although it was to be another eight years before the massive Corvette got real anchors.

Sadly, however, the TR3's uprated engine used more petrol and gave the heavier new model no extra performance, and the skittish handling, shared with the Austin-Healey, was unchanged. It was a legacy of the old axle-over-chassis design that remained until 1965 with the 'Mark IIIA' in the case of the Healey and the TR4A with the Triumph.

A string of rallying successes boosted TR sales from around 9,000 for 1954 and 1955 to nearly 10,000 for 1956 alone. Sales continued to rise to more than 20,000 in 1959, leaving the Big Healey far behind. There was a good reason for this, however. When the Healey was transferred to Abingdon in 1957 it had to share the factory with the popular MGs, of course, and later the new small sports car, the Austin-Healey Sprite. Although production rose to 8,000 cars over roughly the same period as 6,000 had been produced at Longbridge, it could go no higher, such was the success of the MGs and Sprites. There was never any problem selling a Big Healey, though. They went like hot cakes, particularly when the BMC team started winning rallies with them. On other fronts, AC started to have some success racing with the first installation of a 125 bhp, 1,971 cc Bristol engine similar to that used in the Frazer Nashes.

Nineteen-fifty-seven saw the introduction of the sleek new Jaguar XK150.

Like the Jensen 541 introduced soon after the TR3, it had four-wheel disc brakes and outperformed the Healey, but in a considerably higher price bracket. That year was also significant for the debut of the brilliant new disc-braked Lotus Elite, which showed the way to an entirely new concept in sports cars, as had the Healey 100 in 1952. The sensational Lotus's body and chassis were made mostly from fibreglass and with its aerodynamic lines and highly-tuned 1,216 cc Coventry Climax engine was capable of astonishing speeds and economy. But there was a penalty: production problems which took more than a year to sort out and an almost total lack of reliability in average hands.

Contemporary road tests show just how good the design of this car was. 'Its roadholding reached a pitch of perfection which was outside the experience of the vast majority of people, in many respects like that of a racing car, but much more forgiving and providing adequate warning that the limits of adhesion and safety were being approached,' said Martyn Watkins, founder editor of *Cars and Car Conversions*, in his book, *British Sports Cars* (Batsford). 'The steering was light and direct and fast curves were negotiated by little more than wrist movement, a rapport being established between driver and car that was difficult to put into mere words. Performance was exciting, with a top speed of an incredible—for a car of only 1.2 litres—109 mph, with easy 100 mph cruising. More than 80 mph was possible in third gear, with 54 mph coming up in second gear of the delightfully close-ratio gearbox. Acceleration from rest to 60 mph required less than 10 secs, full-throttle acceleration being possible on almost any surface without a trace of wheelspin, so effective was the rear suspension.

'This performance was what could be achieved with the engine in a relatively low state of tune and racing versions of the Elite, their engines developing up to 98 bhp at 7,200 rpm and with their total weight possibly even a little below the standard car's 11 cwt, were timed at 6.6 secs from 0–60, just over 17 secs from rest to 100 and with maximum speeds of over 130 mph.'

The Elite fixed-head coupé was a great contrast to the Big Healey in everything except speed; but it cost more and while there were people who wanted the wind in their hair, Healeys kept selling. And when the Elite eventually went into production it quickly became apparent that they were as fragile as they were fast; a total contrast to the tank-like Healey.

Yet another update of the TR3 was launched in 1957, the TR3A. The first 3A was produced in August, 1957, and was immediately shipped to America in large quantities, but it was not until January, 1958, that it was introduced in Britain.

'The latest car had a full-width grille (callously called a "dollar grin" by its detractors), with external handles to the doors and boot lid. The headlamps were made a little less "pop-eyed" by pushing them back slightly into the front panel, and there were slight changes to the facia and trim; the basic price in Britain was raised from £680 to £699,' said Graham Robson in *The Story of the Triumph Sports Cars* (MRP). The power was also increased to 100 bhp to match a rise in weight which meant that performance was unchanged. Only the fuel consumption suffered at around 27 mpg, as opposed to well over 30.

In America, Arkus-Duntov was still hotting up the Corvette, following the example of the Mercedes-Benz 300 SL in fitting fuel injection, and a four-speed gearbox. This yielded 270 bhp and gave the Covette 122 mph and a 0–60 time of 6.8 secs. Repeated styling changes and some racing successes boosted sales to 6,000 in the year. Chevrolet needed an exciting sports car to improve their boring churn-it-out image.

There was a good selection of new sports cars for 1958, the year that Fords ended their brief flirtation with a two-seater. Aston Martin introduced their DB Mark III with a race-bred 2,993 cc twin-cam engine turning out 160 bhp, giving it a phenomenal performance at their usual price; Mercedes moved into a slightly cheaper market with their 190 SL; Lancia had their Aurelia GT coupé and Porsche their 356; all were out of the Healey man's income bracket. He could have afforded an Elva Courier if he could have got one, but he would have had to have waited a while for delivery of the bright new car from Hastings. However, had he the patience, he could have had a pretty little car with a ladder-style tubular frame, wishbone independent front suspension and a rigid rear axle mounted on coil springs with trailing arms and Panhard rod. It had a fibreglass body and MGA engine and gear-box and in many ways represented a compromise between the advanced Lotus Elite and the good old Healey. Elva sold as many as they could make of this rapid little car, but unfortunately they were only a small manufacturer and did not have a Leonard Lord to take them over.

TVR were just getting under way with the first of their modern fixed-head sports cars in basically the same shape as they use today, with the help of an MGA power train for the top model; they won quite a few orders from America but were beset with financial trouble. Much the same story applied to Peerless with the TR-engined projectile. Another small firm, Fairthorpe, founded by war-time air ace Pathfinder Bennett, produced a car called the Zeta which was even faster than a Big Healey with its Ford Zephyr engine of the same capacity. But it was produced only in small quantities and had well-near lethal roadholding. It also looked awful.

Then MGs launched an assault on the Healey empire with the MGA Twin Cam. It had centre-lock disc wheels like a Le Mans racer, disc brakes all round and a 1,589 cc engine giving 108 bhp and a top speed of 110 mph despite its 19 cwt, all at a Healey-style price! It was introduced with an eye on the American market and to counter production racing successes by some of the expensive Continental makes. Unfortunately it gobbled oil like a well-worn Healey and was generally unreliable and temperamental; with development it could have been an even bigger threat to the Big Healey than the standard MGA and the TRs.

The staid old Daimler company certainly caused a stir when they introduced their extraordinary new Dart sports car in 1958. It was a sort of mini-Corvette with a Citroen fish-like nose for good air penetration and a huge luggage boot in its glass-fibre body, plus a brand new 2,530 cc V8 engine based on the mighty Triumph twin motor cycle unit. It churned out 140 bhp and the 19 cwt car was good for 120 mph and 24 mpg and could stop quicker than a Corvette thanks to its four-wheel disc brakes. Its handling, however, was dubious and its doors flew open when you drove over bumps. It was not a great success.

Corvettes were beginning to get bigger and heavier in 1958 as the stylists made them even tartier. The top engine was a 290 bhp V8 but it was not enough to impress the enthusiasts shocked at the car's poor seats and styling. Some of the Corvette's designers really had no idea what sports car people wanted and sales failed to soar that year.

There were two all-new sports cars for 1959, Aston Martin's DB4 and the Sunbeam Alpine from Rootes. The Aston was a real indicator of how the exotics were going in the 1960s: it had a completely new twin overhead cam 3.7-litre six-cylinder 'square' alloy block engine producing 263 bhp with a four-speed gearbox and platform chassis. The whole lot was clothed in a luxurious alloy body and capable of 140 mph and 0–60 in 9.3 secs.

It had everything the wealthy enthusiast wanted, providing he could wait for delivery at £4,000 including tax. There were quite a few who could afford that, but opted for an instant Healey at less than a third of the price. Sadly, the early DB4s were most unreliable, too, with clutches and tyres lasting little more than 10,000 miles and the gearbox suffering mightily from the powerful new engine.

The Alpine was much more of a competitor for the Healey. It was a two-seater with a distinctive finned tail, low bonnet line and wire wheels. The mechanical specification was similar to its sister Rapier saloon, with a 1,494 cc 84 bhp four-cylinder engine, independent front suspension and integral chassis. The body was quite luxurious, unlike that of the Big Healey and the whole car turned out rather heavy at 19 cwt. This affected performance, but the Alpine could still do 97 mph with 0–60 in 14 secs and as much as 35 mpg in overdrive. It appealed to a slightly different class of sports car driver to Healey people—especially women. Elizabeth Taylor did a lot for the cause of the Alpine by using one in her Butterfield film, even if she did drive the car over a cliff in the end. The Alpine was the car for the cosseted with its wind-up windows and nice interior; it was introduced three years before Healeys tried to get into the same market.

MGs uprated their push-rod A to 1,588 cc at the same time as the Healey 3000 was introduced. The new engine produced 80 bhp, and disc brakes were fitted at the front for only £940 in open form and £1,026 for the fixed-head coupé; this was against £1,168 for the cheapest 3000. *Motor Sport* and *Autosport* combined to test the cars and the gastronomic delights of France. The great drive to the South of France started with *Motor Sport* in the MGA 1600 and *Autosport* in an overdrive 3000. Both cars had been supplied by BMC's Paris distributor and were not fully run-in. Nevertheless the little MGA had no difficulty keeping sight of the Big Healey. Once in the mountains, bounding from one restaurant to another, the testers swopped cars and the *Motor Sport* men immediately commented on the heaviness of the Healey compared with the MGA. They found the overdrive useful in the mountains, though, and observed that the engine had an easier time. Top speed of the MGA was 100 mph with 0–60 in 14 secs.

In America, Arkus-Duntov got the upper hand over GM's stylists and rid the Corvette of some of their excesses, to *Road and Track*'s approval. He also modified the suspension to the benefit of roadholding and set the Corvette on course as a sales success again. All-in it cost $5,000 in its best form and $4,000 in its cheapest guise— against $3,300 for a Big Healey.

Nineteen-sixty saw the first Marcos, designed by the renowned aerodynamicist, Frank Costin, with, initially, small BMC and Ford engines, a wooden chassis and gull-wing doors. Produced by Jem Marsh, it was the forerunner of one of the most spectacular sports cars of the 1960s.

TVR struggled on, trying to meet great orders from the United States and running out of capital time and again. The Blackpool firm could have been a great threat to the Healey had they been able to organize themselves properly at the time.

Meanwhile Arkus-Duntov was organizing things beautifully at General Motors. He steadily improved the Corvette, with even more power and an alloy head engine. Demand continued to rise with more than 10,000 Corvettes being sold in a year for the first time. About 6,000 Big Healeys were produced in the same period, with around 5,000 of them going to America.

So there was not much new in 1960, just cars pouring off the production lines and rumours of great things to come. The greatest of them all hit the sports car world in March 1961: the sensational new Jaguar E type. It turned the sports cars of the 1950s into museum pieces overnight and Healey had only their magnificent rally record and incredibly low price to sustain them. The Big Healey was still extremely fast, of course, but nobody who could have scraped together the price of an E type would have thought of buying a Healey had the Jaguar been readily available. The people who bought new Healey 3000s were the ones on tight budgets and the ones who couldn't wait for an E type, plus, of course, the owners loyal to the Healey cult. It is a well-known part of sports car history that the 3.8-litre E type cleared 150 mph with 0–60 in a fraction over six seconds.

With such competition, Triumphs had to have a new model, too, bringing out the TR4, re-styled by the brilliant Italian Giovanni Michelotti. Mechanically, it was similar to earlier TRs except for a 2,138 cc version of the engine with all-synchro-mesh gears—one up on other sports cars, including the Austin-Healey. The basic price was a little cheaper than the Big Healey at £1,032 including British tax, and the performance was similar to all TRs, 102 mph maximum with 0–60 in 10.5 secs. It was much better looking than earlier TRs, though, and its handling had been improved by a wider track.

AC ran into problems with the Ace in 1961 when Bristol stopped producing the engine now that their latest saloon, the 407, was using a Chrysler V8. Ken Rudd, who had produced such a good Healey conversion, saved the day by fitting a readily-available 2.6-litre Ford Zephyr Six engine tuned to exceed the Bristol's output. Apart from odd Aces fitted with Jaguar engines by American racing men, the Ford-powered Ace became the fastest of the sadly-limited line.

Big things were happening to the Corvette in 1962. The car changed dramati-cally for the better with the introduction of the Sting Ray design. This was based on a 1959 racing version of the Corvette built for GM stylist Bill Mitchell. As it happened the first Sting Ray was not too successful in American racing because its slippery shape and light weight took it out of the realms of its braking power. But the irrepressible Arkus-Duntov turned it into a super road car with 128 mph and 0–60 in 5.5 secs in its hottest form. Sales, predictably, continued to rise, and reached 11,000 that year.

Left: The wind-up windows and generally high level of comfort of the Sunbeam Alpine made Donald Healey think . . .

Below: After the Big Healey, the Little Healey: a Frogeye Sprite.

AC took off in a big way that year, not in terms of the number of cars produced, but in the way the AC went when Texan Carroll Shelby decided to make his version of a Big Healey. Remembering his record run of 1954, Shelby set to work on building himself an American-style sports car using all that was good from Europe. 'What I had lurking in the back of my mind was something to compete against, say, the Austin-Healey that bought around $3,500 and sold as many as 7,000 or 8,000 cars a year in this country,' Shelby wrote in *The Cobra Story*, 'and still used an engine that surely must have been descended directly from a 1918-model London bus. It would have been so easy to get an American Chevrolet V8 or something like that and come up with the same thing at the same price but with a vastly different performance: a car that would have been 50 mph faster with almost double the acceleration.

'This was the type of thinking that was going on in my mind. I wasn't particularly interested in the idea of building some kind of a "special" or an out-and-out racing car. In fact, despite the present General Motors policy which pretends to condemn racing as useless in improving the breed, and "dangerous" to boot, the only reason why I'm racing today is because from an advertizing standpoint it's cheaper for me to race than to take ads in *Time* and *Life* or anything of that sort. Racing, aside from the fact that I enjoy it, costs far less—an awful lot less—than a two-page spread in a big national magazine, say. And I get more mileage out of racing, or in other words more advertizing and sales rub-off for a given outlay.

'Looking back now, it's a strange thing how an idea can stare people right in the face and they don't even see it. Besides GM, I went to other companies, trying to peddle this idea. I went to Jensen in England (and what do they have today but a whopping big Chrysler V8 mill that makes this car, heavy as it is, one of the fastest production machines in the world, at any price!). I talked with John Wyer of Aston Martin; I talked to Maserati and to de Tomaso; I argued the point with people in all walks of life and at all levels of the automobile industry—in fact with anyone who would listen—and they all thought it was a pipe dream. Everybody seemed to think I was smoking marijuana! Finally, this thing became a standing joke. "Ha, Ha! Shelby's gonna build a car. He's gonna build a car to end them all. Only thing is, he doesn't have any money! Ever heard of that before?"

'No, my faster, easily-serviced, cheap-to-buy automobile, one which would combine the virtues I have already mentioned—the ability to go to market or race at weekends—this, people said, was not "practical." Let's stick with Austin-Healey and Triumph and the others, but let's not take any chances.

'I will say this for General Motors, they did have some cause to feel sensitive because of the big egg that the Corvette had laid. This project at about that time was so groggy that they were uncertain whether to go on with it or write it off.'

Fortunately General Motors did not write off their Corvette and Shelby shoe-horned a Ford V8 into an AC chassis, producing the wildest sports car seen for years: the Cobra. Development work took the car out of the Austin-Healey price range, and production did not exceed more than a couple of dozen a week, but the Cobra was a shatteringly fast car. Even the 4.2-litre versions could hit 145 mph with a 0–60 time of only five seconds! The power continued to rise until it reached seven litres by the end of the Healey's time. Lots of Cobras were unleashed on the streets, although many were confined to the race tracks. If only the Healey could have had the same power in less than a ton. . . .

Corvette power continued to keep pace with 360 bhp from the best versions, and sales climbed in proportion, to 14,500 in 1962. Americans still wanted European-style sports cars and the more European the Corvette became, the more it sold.

Among the more mundane sports cars, MG kissed the A goodbye and brought out the B, which was to become one of the most successful of all time, selling even better than its predecessor. It was a car of its time with unitary body and chassis of timeless appearance but it was not so efficient aerodynamically and despite a new 95 bhp, 1,798 cc four-cylinder engine, top speed in overdrive form was only 108 mph with 0–60 in 12 secs; it was no match for the Big Healey, which was getting progressively faster. But the B was an immensely controllable, safe, brisk and comfortable car, lacking the fire of a Big Healey, but winning thousands of friends. It is interesting to consider the drag co-efficients of the 3000 and the B, virtually the same at 0.448, against a much lower figure for the likes of the E type (.367) and Porsche 365 (.333). The MGA was somewhere in between, and that made all the difference with the B.

Britain's famous three-wheeler maker, Reliant had been experimenting with a four-wheeled sports car. This was the Sabre, using a 1.7-litre Ford Consul engine in a tubular chassis that had roadholding little better than its parent saloon. But despite that and only 61 bhp, its glassfibre body kept the weight sufficiently low for the car to do around 100 mph. Development continued to include a six-cylinder engine, but it was not until after the Big Healey's time that Reliants became a force to be reckoned with. It was a car that interested the Healey family, though, and after Donald Healey had finished his association with Jensen, there were moves for a tie-up with Reliant.

Nineteen-sixty-three saw the end of DB4 production with around 1,000 cars made, including GT, Zagato and Vantage versions. The replacement was the DB5, considered by many Aston enthusiasts to be the best of the lot. The DB5 looked like the DB4 Vantage, with faired-in headlights, but mechanically it was updated. The engine capacity was enlarged to 3,995 cc, giving much more torque and a five-speed ZF gearbox was fitted as standard, with a Borg Warner automatic as an option. The Corvette was beginning to sting the sports car world; who would have thought of an automatic Aston otherwise? Among the exotics, only Ferrari and Maserati held out much longer. Even Healeys tried a Rolls-powered automatic prototype.

Meanwhile, over at Lotus, Colin Chapman was finding that the cost of the Elite's classic body/chassis unit was leaping. After making 988 of his wonderful, if fragile, little cars, he was forced to replace them with a separate chassis model. So he brought out the Elan in 1963, which, co-incidentally, enabled him to get back into the open car market so favoured abroad. As with everything Chapman, the Elan was an extra-ordinary performer with its twin-cam Ford engine, which was capable of 115 mph with 0–60 in 8.7 secs, astonishingly good roadholding, and a fuel consumption of 28 mpg. The price was nearer that of an E type than a Big Healey, though, and the car was never anything near like so tough as the 3000—but it represented a technology that Healey could not aspire to until the 3000 was gone.

Morgan also flirted with modern ideas by producing fifty full-width glassfibre fixed-head coupés, which, weighing in at only 16 cwt, were good for 110 mph and 0–60 in 12 secs with their TR4 engines. The coupé, called the Plus 4 Plus, turned out to be the most expensive Morgan yet at £1,275, and after getting right into the Big Healey price bracket, the little company shied away from 'expensive' cars for a time.

Over in America the Corvette's rear axle was still hopping and chattering under acceleration despite radius rods, so transverse leaf independent rear suspension was fitted. With its new shape the spectacular-looking car sold 20,000. Arkus-Duntov heaved a sigh of relief and said: 'For the first time I now have a Corvette I can be proud to drive in Europe.' British magazines tested it and liked the acceleration, although they were critical of other aspects, notably its European price tag which put it in the Aston class. Nevertheless, the performance was similar in its hottest form, although achieved with a good deal less finesse. In American racing, the Corvette found it could not compete with the Cobra, and the Cobra found that it could not compete with the Corvette in the market place. The Big Healey sold somewhere in between and was rapidly becoming a cult car. It was an axiom of the soaring sporting American sixties that in their automobile business, no matter how good your car was one year, you had to change it for the next year, even if you made it worse. The other Americans kept buying the Big Healey because they didn't want anything to change.

In 1964, Jaguar smoothed out braking and gear changing difficulties on the E type and gave it a softer 4.2-litre engine, and like the Big Healey, had customers queueing for every one they could make. Marcos introduced the first of their futuristic large engined cars: the Volvo 1,800 cc model that was capable of 130 mph providing you could slither into its extremely low reclining seats. Once you were in there you felt just like Jim Clark, stretched out in his Lotus grand prix car. Nineteen-sixty-four was a good year for Sting Rays. The styling was simplified and the engine boosted to 375 bhp in its top form. Ford came back on to the scene with a veritable bang; their four-seater Mustang sports convertible and fixed-head coupé sold nearly half a million in its first year. This was because it was a four-seater, though, not a real sports car. Wisely, Ford had wasted little serious thought on two-seater configurations after their Thunderbird of the Fifties. The Corvette and imported two-seaters like the Big Healey filled that gap adequately, and nobody could seriously claim that a Big Healey with back seats was a four-seater!

In 1965 the Corvette was at last fitted with disc brakes like other sports cars. These units were based on the popular Girling brake, and, as if to celebrate, the engine was uprated yet again, to 375 bhp in its best form. Sales promptly went up from 22,229 in 1964 to 23,562 in 1965. The Corvette stylist managed one quirk, though. It acquired side exhausts rather like a Healey rally car.

Aston Martin also replaced the DB5 with the DB6, on which the roofline was altered to provide increased headroom at the back and the tail got a spoiler, which was a sign of things to come. Production also went up to twenty cars a week; mass production by Aston standards. MG brought out yet another successful sports car, the MGB GT, which shared the specification of the open two-seater but with a steel roof and estate car style rear door, plus Healey-size rear seats. Designers obviously thought they were practical for some person, although they would have to be legless, of stunted growth or canine.

Triumph were no doubt inspired by the example of the 'Mark IIIA' Healey when they revised their rear suspension on the TR4A. But the Triumph men went one better with independent rear suspension, obtained with an ingenious set-up of semi-trailing arms, swing axles and coil springs. Needless to say the maximum speed remained at 108 mph with 0–60 in 10.5 secs—but the car handled a lot better. In basic form it cost £958 in Britain and did about 25 mpg. The Big Healey of the day cost £1,166 and did 122 mph with between 18 and 24 mpg, and 0–60 in 9.5 secs; the Daimler Dart cost £1,355 and was similar to a Healey in speed; the MGB cost only £834 in open form, but did only 108 mph with a 12 sec 0–60 and 26 mpg; the Alpine which had had its engine upped to 1,600 cc in 1961, cost £904 and did 97 mph with 0–60 in around 14 secs. There was still nothing quite like a Big Healey because the Daimler was a totally different car in appearance and construction.

Porsche introduced the 911 series and Ferraris and Maseratis came and went, but you could have bought four Big Healeys for the price of one of these exotics. By the next year, 1966, Corvettes had lost their expensive fuel injection option now that a gigantic seven-litre engine could churn out 450 bhp on carburetters. This made the top model really go, with 152 mph and 0–60 in 4.8 secs. Sales soared with the performance, to 27,720 in 1966.

In the same year the Alpine's engine was uprated to 1,725 cc in keeping with its parent Hillman saloons and with 92 bhp its top speed nearly touched 100 and the 0–60 time was cut to 11 secs. But for real power the Sunbeam enthusiast could now buy a Tiger. This car took a leaf out of the Shelby book with a 4.2-litre Ford V8 in an almost standard Alpine chassis. The result was 121 mph and 0–60 in less than 10 secs. The Tiger was everything that Shelby had dreamed of, but it was to be killed by politics in 1967. Rootes had by then become a Chrysler subsidiary and could not carry on using a Ford engine—and Chrysler had nothing which would fit. If the Tiger had been produced when Shelby was campaigning for such a car it would have changed sports car sales patterns throughout the 1960s. As it was, Corvette sales hiccupped down to 21,000 in 1967 because it became known that a spectacular new model was on its way. The Mako Shark was born in the year of the Big Healey's demise. But that is another story.

XVII

Your Healey Log Book

ONE of the most taxing problems when restoring, repairing, respraying or rebuilding a Big Healey is to find out exactly what it was like when it left the factory. Apart from the aesthetic pleasure of returning the car to virtually mint condition, originality is becoming of prime importance at concours competitions. With the Big Healey being made so many years ago, considerable confusion has arisen over the original colours, and there is some confusion about the colour of later models. So how do you go about finding the original colour of your much-resprayed car? Look at the insides of the doors and wings and see what colour that paint is, and if you are certain they are original components—not second-hand ones fitted at some later date—then take that as a good guide. Otherwise it probably means lifting the gearbox and cleaning off the grime under the rear mounting points and seeing if that paint matches everything else. Hardly anybody took off that paint before respraying, and the frames were usually sprayed in the car's original colour because it was done at the factory at the same time as the body. In the case of duo-tone cars, the secondary colour (which was of the same specification as a main colour), was added afterwards, over a coat of primer on top of the car's main colour. The result was often that the secondary colour was slightly different to the matching basic colour. The exception to the rule about the colour of the frame would appear to be the Florida Green and Golden Metallic Beige cars, which seem to have had white frames.

These are the basic colour schemes: 1 Healey Blue; 2 Old English White; 3 Healey Blue/Old English White; 4 Healey Blue/Ivory White; 5 Old English White/Healey Blue; 6 Ivory; 7 Ivory White/Healey Blue; 8 British Racing Green; 9 British Racing Green/Old English White; 10 British Racing Green/Ivory White; 11 Old English White/British Racing Green; 12 Ivory White/British Racing Green; 13 Reno Red; 14 Reno Red/Old English White; 15 Old English White/Reno Red; 16 Black; 17 Black/Reno Red; 18 Reno Red/Black; 19 Old English White/Black; 20 Black/Old English White; 21 Ivory White/Black; 22 Black/Ivory White; 23 Colorado Red; 24 Colorado Red/Ivory; 25 Ivory/Colorado Red; 26 Colorado Red/Black; 27 Black/Colorado Red; 28 Florida Green; 29 Florida Green/Ivory; 30 Ivory/Florida Green; 31 Primrose; 32 Primrose/Black; 33 Black/Primrose; 34 Pink/Black; 35 Black/Pink; 36 Pacific Green; 37 Pacific Green/Black; 38 Black/Pacific Green; 39 Aluminium; 40 Black/Aluminium; 41 Aluminium/Black; 42 Metallic Golden Beige.

Trim: Black, Grey, Blue, Dark Red, Dark Green, Tan (after the BN2); contrasting piping except Black with Black piping on BN1 and BN2; the piping usually matched the subsidiary colour on a duo-tone car. Basically, Black cars had red trim with black or red piping and red carpets; Healey Blue cars always had blue trim with blue lining and blue carpets, plus a blue hood; Florida Green cars had grey trim with green or grey piping and green carpets; Pacific Green cars had the same interior as Florida Green; Colorado Red cars had red, grey or black trim with contrasting red or black piping and red or black carpets; Ivory White cars had red or black trim with contrasting black, white or red piping and red or black carpets; primrose cars had black trim with yellow piping, primrose and black cars had yellow trim with black piping and black carpets; Aluminium cars had black or red trim with contrasting black or red piping and black carpets; Metallic golden beige cars had black or red trim with contrasting black or red piping and black or red carpets; British Racing Green cars had an all-black interior; Black BN1 or BN2 cars had an all-black interior; later black cars had black, red or white trim with contrasting red or black piping and red or black carpets; Black and Colorado Red cars had black, red or grey trim with contrasting black, red or grey piping and black or red carpets; Colorado Red and black cars had red trim with black or red piping and red carpets; Ivory and Healey Blue cars had blue trim with blue or white piping and blue carpets; Ivory and Florida Green cars had grey trim with green or grey piping and green carpets. To make this seem even more complicated, it was possible to order special finishes or combinations of colours! But the basic mechanical specifications were straightforward, with the paint available according to model:

Austin-Healey 100, series BN1

10,688 built between January 1953 and June 1955, chassis numbers 133134 to 228046.

ENGINE

Four cylinders, **cubic capacity** 2,660 cc; **bore and stroke** 87.3 mm × 111.1 mm; **max. power** 90 bhp (gross) at 4,000 rpm; **max torque** 150 lb ft at 2,000 rpm; **compression ratio** 7.5:1; **carburetters** twin SU $1\frac{1}{2}$ in H4; **clutch** Borg and Beck 9 in dry single plate.

CHASSIS

Weight (dry) with alloy body, about 2,016 lb; with steel body 2,148 lb; **wheelbase** 7 ft 6 in; **front track** 4 ft 1 in; **rear track** 4 ft 2 in; **length** 12 ft 7 in; **width** 5 ft $\frac{1}{2}$ in; **height** 4 ft $1\frac{1}{2}$ in (with hood erect); **turning circle** 30 ft; **front suspension** independent wishbone and coil springs, anti-roll bar; **rear suspension** semi-elliptic leaf springs, early cars: seven-leaf 5-inch camber, later cars: seven-leaf $5\frac{3}{4}$-inch camber, latest cars: eight-leaf $3\frac{3}{4}$-inch camber, Panhard rod; **brakes** 11-inch drum all round, Girling hydraulic; **gearbox** three forward, one reverse; (ratios) 1st-2.25, 2nd-1.42, 3rd direct, reverse-4.981, with overdrive reduction in engine speed 32.4 per cent from number WN1260/1-WN1260/763, 28.6 per cent from WN1292/1 on; **overall gear ratios** with standard 4.125:1 rear axle: 1st-9.22, 2nd-5.82, 2nd overdrive (32.4 per cent) 4.43, 2nd overdrive (28.6) 4.56, 3rd direct; 3rd overdrive (32.4) 3.12, 3rd overdrive (28.6) 3.28, reverse 20.5; **rear axle** type: spiral bevel; **steering** Burman cam and lever, ratio 12.6:1, steering wheel diameter, $16\frac{1}{2}$ in; **front wheel alignment** toe-in   th-$\frac{1}{8}$th in; **tyres and wheels** Dunlop 5.90 × 15 wire; **colours** schemes 1, 2, 8, 13, 16; **wheel arch** shape changed to match latest (raised) rear spring models.

Austin-Healey 100, series BN2

*3, 924 built between August 1955 and August 1965.
Chassis numbers 228047 to 233455, includes 100M*

ENGINE
As BN1.

CHASSIS
As last steel BN1 with 28.6 per cent overdrive until number BN221535 when hypoid bevel axle fitted giving 4 ft 2¾ in rear track; **gearbox** (all BN2s) four forward, one reverse (ratios) 1st-12.6, 2nd-7.85, 3rd-5.46, 3rd overdrive 5.46, 4th direct, 4th overdrive 3.18, reverse 17.1.

Austin-Healey 100, series 100M

1,159 produced between 1955 and 1956, plus conversions marketed 1953 to 1956. No separate record of chassis numbers, integral with BN1 and BN2.

ENGINE

As BN1 or BN2 except: **compression ratio** 8.1:1, high-lift camshaft; **carburetters** twin 1¾-in SU H6, special inlet manifolds, special distributor, steel-faced head gasket; 110 bhp at 4,500 rpm, 144 lb ft torque at 2,000 rpm, single SU fuel pump.

CHASSIS

As BN1 or BN2 except: **weight** 2,168 lb; optional 3.667:1 **rear axle** and 28.6 per cent overdrive only. **Colour schemes** 1, 2, 3, 5, 8, 9, 11, 13, 14, 15, 16, 17, 18, 19, 20, 34, 35. Option of louvred bonnet and strap.

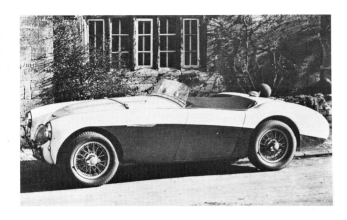

Austin-Healey 100S

55 built between January 1954 and July 1955. This number included five prototypes built from early 1954. The fifty production cars were built between February 1955 and July 1955. Chassis numbers for last fifty: 3501–3910.

ENGINE
Four cylinders; **cubic capacity** 2,660 cc; **bore and stroke** 87.3 mm × 111.1 mm; **max power** 132 bhp (gross) at 4,700 rpm; **max torque** 168 lb ft at 2,500 rpm; **compression ratio** 8.3:1; **carburetters** twin SU 1¾-inch H6; **clutch** Borg and Beck dry single 10-inch plate; twin SU fuel pumps.

CHASSIS
Weight (dry) 1,960 lb; dimensions as BN2 except height (over windscreen) 3 ft 6 in and length (without bumpers) 11 ft 9 in; **rear suspension** eight-leaf springs; **brakes** Dunlop 11 in disc all round; **gearbox** four forward, one reverse, no overdrive (ratios with standard 2.92 axle), 1st-8.98, 2nd-5.57, 3rd-3.88, 4th direct, reverse 12.2; **rear axle** as BN2 with optional ratios 2.69, 3.66, 4.125; **racing tyres and wheels** 5.50 × 15 wire; **body finish** as BN2 100M with option of BN1 and BN2 single colour finishes.

Austin-Healey 100-Six, series BN4

10,286 built between August 1956 and about November 1957. Chassis numbers 50759 to 77766.

ENGINE

Six cylinders; **cubic capacity** 2,639 cc; **bore and stroke** 79.4 mm × 89 mm; **max power** 102 bhp at 4,600 rpm; **max torque** 142 lb ft at 2,400 rpm; **compression ratio** 8.25:1; **carburetters** twin SU $1\frac{1}{2}$-inch H4; **clutch** Borg and Beck dry single 9-inch plate, single SU fuel pump.

CHASSIS

Weight (dry) with overdrive and wire wheels, 2,334 lb; **wheelbase** 7 ft 8 in; **front track** 4 ft 1 in; **rear track** 4 ft $2\frac{3}{4}$ in; **length** 13 ft $1\frac{1}{2}$ in; **width** 5 ft $\frac{1}{2}$ in; **height** 4 ft $1\frac{1}{2}$ in (with hood erect); **front suspension** independent wishbone, coil springs, anti-roll bar; **rear suspension** semi-elliptic leaf springs, seven leaves, Panhard rod; **brakes** 11-inch drums all round, Girling hydraulic, two leading shoes front; **gearbox** four forward, one reverse, overdrive optional: **ratios** (with overdrive) 1st-12.6, 2nd-7.84, 3rd-5.47, 3rd overdrive 4.24, 4th direct, 4th overdrive 3.19, reverse 16.4; **rear axle type** hypoid bevel (ratio with overdrive 4.125, without overdrive 3.91); **steering** Burman cam and lever, ratio 14:1 until car number 68959, 15:1 after that, steering wheel, $16\frac{1}{2}$ ins diameter, turning circle 3 ft 7 in, front wheel alignment, toe-in $\frac{1}{16}$th-$\frac{1}{8}$th in; **tyres and wheels** Dunlop 15 × 4J ventilated steel disc, 15 × 4J wire optional; Modified hood after chassis number 68960. Door lock after chassis number 48386. **Colour** schemes 1, 4, 6, 7, 8, 16, 21, 22, 23, 24, 25, 26, 27, 28, 29, 30, 31, 32, 33, 36, 37, 38.

Austin-Healey 100-Six, series BN6

4,150 built between about November 1957 and June 1959. Chassis numbers 501 to 4650.

ENGINE
Six cylinders; **cubic capacity** 2,639 cc; **bore and stroke** 79.4 mm × 89 mm; **max power** 117 bhp at 5,000 rpm; **max torque** 150 lb ft at 3,000 rpm; **compression ratio** 8.7:1; **carburetters** twin SU 1¾ in HD6; **clutch** Borg and Beck single dry 9-inch plate, single SU fuel pump.

CHASSIS
As BN4, except: **weight** 2,354 lb; **steering ratio** changed from car number 1995.

Austin-Healey 3000, series BN7 and BT7 (mark one)

2,825 BN7 built between July 1959 and April 1961; 10,825 BT7 built in same period. Chassis numbers 101 to 13750.

ENGINE

Six cylinders; **cubic capacity** 2,912 cc; **bore and stroke** 83.36 mm × 89 mm; **max power** 124 bhp at 4,600 rpm; **max torque** 175 lb ft at 3,000 rpm; **compression ratio** 9.03:1; **carburetters** twin SU 1¾-inch HD6; **clutch** Borg and Beck single dry 10-inch plate, single SU fuel pump.

CHASSIS

Weight (dry) with overdrive and wire wheels, 2,358 lb approximately; **dimensions** as BN6 and BT7; **brakes** Girling 11-inch discs front, 11-inch drums rear; **gearbox** before engine number 10897 with overdrive and before engine number 11342 without overdrive; **overall gear ratios** (with overdrive and standard 3.909 rear axle): 1st-11.453, 2nd-8.025, 3rd-5.116, 3rd overdrive-4.195, 4th-direct, 4th overdrive-3.205, reverse 14.776; (without overdrive and with standard 3.545 axle), 1st-10.386, 2nd-7.877, 3rd-4.640, 4th-direct, reverse-13.4. From engine number 10897 with overdrive and from engine 11342 without overdrive: overall gear ratios (with overdrive and standard 3.909 axle): 1st-11.257, 2nd-8.052, 3rd-5.120, 3rd overdrive-4.198, 4th-direct, 4th overdrive-3.205, reverse 14.541; (without overdrive and with standard 3.545 axle), 1st-10.209, 2nd-7.302, 3rd-4.743, 4th-direct, reverse-13.127; **rear axle** type hypoid bevel (alternative ratio 4.125). Disc brake back covers fitted from chassis BN7 9450 (disc wheels), BT7 9088 (disc wheels), BN7 9453 (wire wheels), BT7 9090 (wire wheels). Stiffer front springs from chassis numbers BN7 10329, BT7 10303. Hand choke from chassis numbers BN5234, BT5310. Reverse helix gears from engine number 11344. **Colour** schemes 1, 4, 6, 7, 8, 16, 21, 22, 23, 24, 25, 26, 27, 28, 29, 30, 31, 32, 33, 36, 37, 38, 39, 40, 41.

Austin-Healey 3000, Mark II, series BN7 and BT7

355 BN7 built between April 1961 and March 1962; 5,095 BT7 built in the same period. Chassis numbers 13751 to 19853.

ENGINE

Six cylinders; **cubic capacity** 2,639 cc; **bore and stroke** 79.4 mm × 89 mm; **max power** 131 bhp at 4,750 rpm; **max torque** 165 lb ft at 3,000 rpm; **compression ratio** 9.03:1; **carburetters** triple SU $1\frac{1}{2}$ in HS4; **clutch** Borg and Beck dry single plate 10-inch, single SU fuel pump.

CHASSIS

As late BN6, except: **weight** 2,375 lb; Revised gearchange from BN7 16039, BT7 15881. Fuel pump relocated on right from BN7 17547 and BT7 17352.

Austin-Healey 3000, Mark II, series BJ7

6,113 built between April 1962 and February 1964. Chassis numbers 17551 to 25314.

ENGINE

As BN7 and BT7 except: **max power** 129 bhp at 4,750 rpm; **carburetters** twin SU 1¾-inch HS6; **clutch** Borg and Beck dry single 9-inch plate after engine number 4898.

CHASSIS

As late BN6. Sixty-spoke wheels after chassis number 24367.

Austin-Healey 3000, Mark III, series BJ8 (phase one)

390 built in February and March 1964. Chassis numbers 25315 to 25705.

ENGINE
As BJ7 except: **max power** 148 bhp at 5,200 rpm; **carburetters** twin SU 2-inch HD8.

CHASSIS
As B57 except: **weight** 2,390 lb; **gearbox** four forward, one reverse, overdrive optional; **overall ratios** (with overdrive and standard 3.909 axle) 1st-10.308, 2nd-8.0095, 3rd-5.105, 3rd overdrive-4.188, 4th-direct, 4th overdrive-3.207; (without overdrive and with standard 3.545 axle) 1st-9.348, 2nd-7.341, 3rd-4.629, 4th-direct, reverse-12.021; **rear axle** type hypoid bevel (alternative ratios 4.125, 4.3, 4.875).
Colour schemes 1, 4, 6, 7, 8, 16, 21, 22, 23, 24, 25, 26, 27, 28, 29, 30, 31, 32, 33, 36, 37, 38, 39, 40, 41, 42.

Austin-Healey 3000, Mark III, series BJ8 (phase two)

16,322 built between March 1964 and March 1968. Chassis numbers 25706 to 43026.

ENGINE
As BJ8 phase one.

CHASSIS
As BJ8 phase one except rear suspension, semi-elliptic leaf springs, six leaves, radius arms.

XVIII

The Austin Healey Clubs

HEALEY people are unlike most other motoring enthusiasts. They have not banded together into one big club, like the MG Car Club or the Jaguar Drivers' Club, with offshoots such as The New England T Register and EJAG (North America). Austin-Healey owners are individualistic and grouped into numerous separate organizations which remain on good terms with one another, but do their own thing, meeting only for such events as National Healey Day in Britain and Austin-Healey West in California. To all intents though, the Pacific Centre is America's national organization, although the other centres remain strong.

The British clubs were not always as fragmented as they are today. A Healey Drivers' Club was formed in 1955 with a mixture of Big Healey and Riley-Healey owners. When production was moved to Abingdon in 1957, John Thornley, who had helped form the MG Car Club in 1930, suggested that the Healey Drivers' Club should be organized in a similar way. Healey owners were given a lot of space in the MG Car Club's *Safety Fast* magazine and shared the MG Car Club's offices at Abingdon. With the inspiration of Thornley and the help of men such as Peter Browning and Les Needham, the club thrived despite bickering between opposing factions of Big Healey and Sprite owners. They have always tended to squabble.

As interest in the early Riley-powered Healeys declined, the Austin-Healey Club was formed in 1961 by combining the well-established Healey Drivers' Club and the Southern Counties Sprite Club. Peter Browning became the first general secretary and did much to unify the Big Healey and Sprite factions, organizing numerous meetings, film shows, forums and so on with works drivers and personalities in frequent attendance. Club racing was also very popular. The founder centres were soon joined by the Northern Sprite Group and the Eastern Sprite Group. Attempts were made to persuade the Scottish Sprite Club to join the rapidly growing Austin-Healey Club of Great Britain but they remained aloof and eventually disbanded. The Healey Drivers' Club membership then became the Midlands Centre, and the Sprite clubs the Southern, Northern and Eastern Centres. In late 1961 and early 1962 a South Western Centre was formed by Frank and Edna Walker, who also set up a Devon and Cornwall Centre between 1962 and 1964. In early 1965, Frank and Edna left Bristol and the South Western Centre was taken over by Gordon Prowse. In these four years, the first of the centre newsletters were published: *Ten*

Big Healeys dominate this historic line-up at Silverstone in August 1968. On the first row are two 100Ss and a Le Mans Nash Healey, strangely bearing the same registration number as the Healey 100 prototype!

Tenths, by the Southern Counties and *Top Gear* by the Devon and Cornwall Centre.

Frank and Edna Walker then formed the Bucks and Berks group near their new home in Middlesex and in November 1967 the New Forest group was formed by Gordon Pearce. The president was a former Brooklands driver, Wally Porter, who continued racing until he was more than seventy years old! Wally is still going strong today, although he confines his driving to the road. The New Forest group, as all other groups, was an offshoot of an already established centre. These groups were set up in areas where it was difficult for members to get to the main centre, and were controlled by an officially-recognized centre until they could prove a membership of at least fifty, and could support themselves financially. They were then given a proportion of the subscriptions by the parent club to enable themselves to become established.

In April 1968, the Bucks and Berks group became the Thames Valley Centre and soon after produced a newsletter called *Opposite Lock*. Until November 1968, the Austin-Healey club scene was developing in a conventional unified manner, and then the new Leyland chief, Donald Stokes axed *Safety Fast*. The affairs of the national club were handed over to Donald Healey and his family. After a few meetings at Leamington Spa, Brian Healey became general secretary briefly, before handing over to a general executive committee. 'The organization of the clubs through one central organization created a vast amount of paperwork and consumed a lot of money,' his brother, Geoffrey Healey, said later in *Austin Healey: The Story of the Big Healeys*. 'We realized that this was not the way to continue and so the various local clubs were given greater autonomy in a form of devolution. The somewhat rigid club organization has now disappeared and the separate clubs continue under their own volition.'

Not all British Healey club members agree, however, particularly Joyce Pearce, one of the leading lights behind the New Forest group, which became a centre in April 1971. 'This original executive committee was chaired by Doug Worgan of the Southern Counties,' said Joyce, 'and the body of the committee was made up of two representatives from each centre's committee. They met bi-monthly to iron out problems and to discuss policy and events. The representatives then reported back to their committees, and in 1976, after a great deal of discussion, two executive committee members were admitted on to the board of directors with the Healey family and others. This ensured the future of the club to some degree.

'Attempts to unify the club over the previous four years failed. First there was the adoption of the New Forest Centre's magazine title, *Rev Counter*, for a national magazine. This was a good production but floundered in 1973 because of financial, editorial and printing problems. For the second time in five years a gap in communications opened up and morale and enthusiasm seemed to deteriorate. Then a sudden jump in the cars' value revived the flagging spirits.

'Various centre newsletters took over including *Ten Tenths* and the New Forest's *Piston Broke*. Meanwhile centres such as the Midland and New Forest tried to establish groups elsewhere, of which two, the South West and the Northern, survived to become centres. *Rev Counter* was revived in 1974 as a bi-monthly produced on a rota basis by each centre. Quality, naturally, has fluctuated as a result.' Joyce goes on to advocate a central organization producing a single magazine, a set-up favoured by many other clubs; and vigorously opposed by many Healey club members. The majority view is that a local committee is best able to look after its members and that a national basis is used only for major events such as National Healey Day—organized at Dodington Park, near Bath in 1977 with John Smith of the South West Centre as chairman, and responsible for the venue and stalls; Robin Church of the Midlands Centre in charge of the concours; Roger Byford of the Eastern Centre organizing the gymkhana, and Carolyn Waters of the Midlands Centre co-ordinating it all—no mean task.

Parallel events are run in America in the East and West by the Austin-Healey Club's Pacific Centre. It was formed in 1969 by an ex-patriot New Yorker called Hank Leach who did much to consolidate membership by launching the excellent magazine, *Healey Highlights*, at the same time. The present editor, Kevin Faughnan said: 'Initially the club membership consisted of about 100 members who lived within a reasonable distance of San Jose; however, the club opened its doors to the nation in 1970. The enthusiastic response pointed out the definite need for such an organi-

Healey folk tend to stick together . . . this picture was taken at the British National Thoroughbred and Classic Cars concours at Weston Park in 1977.

zation. Membership has grown steadily since to its present level of 1,600.

'Our club caters only for Big Healey owners. The owners of earlier Healeys are welcome, as are owners of the new Jensen-Healey, but only until they have clubs of their own. The Healeys in the centre range from concours to basket cases, but most owners express an interest in restoring or at least preserving their cars.

'Besides *Healey Headlights*, the club offers regalia items and used parts at very reasonable prices. We are occasionally able to offer new original parts as we buy out discontinued stocks from dealers. We are also organizing events now on regional lines so that members throughout the United States and Canada can participate closer to home.'

Other enthusiastic centres include the Austin-Healey Club of America formed in 1960 from the old Mid-Western Centre and the Austin-Healey Owners' Association of Southern California. Various chapters of these clubs are scattered throughout the United States. The Austin-Healey Owners' Association of British Columbia is run on an independent basis, although it keeps close links with the Pacific Centre and is one of the prime movers behind the annual Austin-Healey West meeting.

There are five organizations for the Healey enthusiast in Australia: the Austin-Healey Owners' Clubs of New South Wales, Victoria, South Australia, Queensland and Western Australia. Jim McConville, secretary of the Victoria club, says: 'Our club was the first to be formed when Dave Rapley and Iain McPherson realized that the Big Healey was in trouble in 1967. Tirelessly, Iain and David looked up Healey owners through a friend in the Motor Registration Branch in Melbourne and then personally contacted each owner. I was one of the owners contacted in this way because I have had my BN2 since 1959.

'It wasn't long before the other Australian clubs were formed on a State-wide basis having as their major aim the preservation of the marque. Some of these clubs incorporated the Sprite owners—Western Australia and Queensland. Queensland eventually became a big club and is so today.

'We all meet socially every Easter and in competition in the spring. The National

Rally at Easter draws all the keen members from each club and is held in various states with the emphasis in the past being on Victoria and New South Wales. It lasts for the four days and usually involves much travelling. For instance, some of the Western Australian members would have done 7,000 miles for the round trip to Queensland and back this year. It is expected that New Zealand could become the venue for a rally in the mid-1980s, although that is still a long way off.

'Each club has a delegate to the National Rally who is instructed by his own committee on how to vote on matters of national interest. In this way duplication of effort is minimized. The New South Wales and Queensland clubs meet at Coffs Harbour once during the year and Victoria and South Australian clubs meet at some halfway point in the same way on a social level.

'Our club in Victoria is properly constituted with by-laws. We meet once a month and usually have a guest speaker, films, auctions, armchair rally or technical discussion. A committee run the club and arrange future events.'

Healey enthusiasm has been high in New Zealand since their own club was started in 1971. Since then the Austin-Healey Car Club of New Zealand has gone from strength to strength with president Mark Donaldson who also edits their magazine *Healey Torque* and his wife Cathy as the leading lights. Apart from the usual officers, the club boasts a parts manager, historian and representatives in Waikato, Manawatu, Gisborne, Wellington, Canterbury and Otago—and organizes all manner of events almost every other week. Small wonder it is so well supported and that its really emotive poster 'Bring Back the Big Healey' by David Kerr sold thousands worldwide.

The Austin-Healey Club of Southern Africa is based in Johannesburg, where the parent centre was formed in 1974 by a group led by Ron Field. Two years later another centre was opened in Cape Town, 1,000 miles away, and a year later the club expanded further to Natal Province with a third centre. Future plans include expanding into Rhodesia where Austin-Healey owners are accommodated by the Salisbury Centre of the MG Car Club. The South African Healey club runs a full social and competitive programme despite the handicap of being only three years old. All motoring activities in South Africa are strictly controlled and only clubs which have been affiliated to the Automobile Association for years have any chance of getting onto the approved calendar of sixty-one events per year. 'This puts a severe damper on our activities,' says Bruce Caw, editor of their excellent newsletter, 'but we are working on ways and means to overcome this problem.'

The Austin-Healey Club of Sweden is also a flourishing organization with around equal numbers of Big Healey and Sprites among its several hundred members attending meetings at five centres, in Stockholm, Goteberg, Malmo and the remote middle and northern territories. Rather like the South Africans, they are expanding into Norway. They produce an excellent newsletter, the *Healey Enthusiast*, printed in Swedish.

There are also active Austin-Healey clubs in West Germany, Switzerland, Austria and Holland, which combined last year to stage an international Continental Healey Day. These clubs, with the Danish Club, were all formed in the mid-1970s when the Big Healey became universally accepted as a classic sports car. One of the latest clubs to be formed was in Hawaii in 1975. They held their first meeting after Pearl Harbour policeman Rod Hudik spent months writing letters to Healey owners throughout the island. Thirty-eight members turned up for that meeting and the club is still growing, with rallies, club regalia and a spares service.

As the Big Healeys increase in value, the clubs are continuing to grow. A list of contacts at the clubs is as follows:

United Kingdom

The Austin-Healey Club of Great Britain: *Midlands Centre:* Keith Boyer (chairman), 410 Allesley Old Road, Coventry, Warwicks; *Eastern Centre:* David Hicks (Secretary/Editor), 102 Fairfax Drive, Westcliff-on-Sea, Essex; *Thames Valley Centre:* Nigel Unsworth (Editor), 44 Galsworthy Drive, Caversham Park, Reading, Berks; *Northern Centre:* Mike Goodrich (Chairman), 32 Noel Gate, Aughton, Ormskirk, Lancs; *Southern Counties:* Phil Wakefield (Secretary), 99 Bourneside Road, Addlestone, Surrey; *South Western Centre:* Carol Marks (Secretary), 171 Coldharbour Road, Bristol, Avon; *New Forest Centre:* Mrs Pat Martin (Secretary), 104 Winchester Road, Shirley, Southampton, Hants.

U.S.A.

Austin-Healey Club, Pacific Centre: Kevin Faughnan (Editor), PO Box 6267, San Jose, California, 95150, USA. *Austin-Healey Club of America:* Mrs Edie Anderson (Secretary), 603 East Euclid Avenue, Arlington Heights, Illinois 60004, USA; *Chicago area:* Ray Osmus, 205 S. Lorraine, Wheaton, Il 60187; *Indianapolis area:* Jim Alderson, 4124 Shelby Street, Indianapolis, In 46227; *Detroit area:* Kay Jublet, 1413 N. Blair, Royal Oak, Mi 48057; *Carolina area:* Gerald Thomas, 108 N. Westover Drive, Monroe, NC 28110; *Columbus area:* Dave Daniels, 2076 A Bridlington, Columbus, Oh 43229; *Fort Wayne area:* Tom Busch, 6010 Vance Ave, Fort Wayne, In 46805; *Ontaria area:* Lyn Chrysler, 506-2609 King St East, Hamilton, Ont, Canada L8K 1Y4. *Austin-Healey Owners' Association of Southern California:* Jim Mayfield (President), PO Box 4082, Riverside, California, USA. *Austin-Healey Club of Oregon:* 3102 SE 7th Portland, Pregon 97202, USA.

Canada

Austin-Healey Owners' Association of British Columbia: Dave Birchall (Editor), PO Box 80274, South Burnaby, British Columbia, Canada V5H 3X5. *Ontario Centre:* John Trobait, 749 Brimley Road, Scarboro, Ontario, Canada.

Pacific

Austin-Healey Owners' Club of New South Wales: Pat Quinn (Secretary), PO Box A471, Sydney South, NSW 2000, Australia; *Austin-Healey Owners' Club of Victoria:* Jim McConville (Secretary), c/o Thermal Heat Treatment Pty Ltd, 32 First Avenue, Sunshine 3020, Victoria, Australia; *Austin-Healey Owners' Club of Southern Australia:* John Read (President), 24 Monalta Drive, Belair, South Australia 5052. *Austin-Healey Owners' Club of Western Australia:* 25 Bedwell Crescent Booragoon, Western Australia 6156; *Austin-Healey Owners' Club of Queensland:* Carl Stecher (President), 17 Morehead Avenue, Norman Park, Queensland 4170, Australia; *Austin-Healey Car Club of New Zealand:* Mark Donaldson (President), PO Box 25-016, St Heliers, Auckland 5, New Zealand.

Africa

Austin-Healey Club of Southern Africa: Bruce Caw (Editor), 3 First Avenue, Edenvale, Johannesburg 1610, South Africa.

Europe

Austin-Healey Club of Sweden: Ken Andren (Chairman), Loviselundsvagen 34, 162 35 Valingby, Sweden; *Austin-Healey Club Germany:* Peter Kuprianoff, Leopoldstr. 24a, 7500 Karlsruhe 1, West Germany; *Austin-Healey Club Austria:* Franz Aigner (Chairman) A-1220 Wien, Plankenmaisstrasse 20, Austria; *Austin-Healey Club of Switzerland:* Felix Gugolz, Uberlandstr. 199a, 8600 Dubendorf, Switzerland; *Austin-Healey Club of Holland:* Hans Broers, Van Kinsbergen, Laan, 35 Baarn, Netherlands; *Austin-Healey Club of Denmark:* Morgans Rosenkilde (Secretary), Rørmosevej 20, Copenhagen N.V.

Hawaii

Austin-Healey Club of Hawaii: Rodney Hudik (President), PO Box 22531, Honolulu, Hawaii 96822.

XIX

Farewell Big Healey

THERE are two Big Healeys in Tokyo, and they were both first registered in the name of the Nissan Motor Company. There is no doubt that they were the inspiration behind the Datsun 240Z, the fastest-selling sports car of recent years. Throughout its life, the Big Healey suffered from a lack of capital investment. That is why nothing was done about the shocking problems with the exhaust system for so long; it is why nothing effective was ever done about the dispersal of engine heat; it is why the built-in rust traps remained and it is why the scuttle shake so evident in later models was tolerated (remember that Donald Healey was one of its most vigorous opponents in the early days). Conversely, however, lack of capital investment was also the reason why the Healey remained so cheap and such a bargain. Only Sir William Lyons at Jaguars could work miracles and produce a really fast, beautiful sports car at a price that many people could afford; and all his cars cost much more than a Healey, although they were a good deal faster. Triumphs and MGs cost less, but after the early TRs, they were always that little bit slower; and they never had the brute appeal and sheer power of the Big Healey.

So what were British Leyland to do when looming Federal regulations made a redesign imperative just when the Big Healey was achieving the status in its major market, California, of a brand-new vintage car? To invest more money in the Big Healey would have taken it into the same class as the Jaguar E type, and nobody could conceive a better design than that. So they compromised: they tried to drop the Healey's magnificent engine into the MGB. The result, like so many compromises, was a dismal failure. Hundreds of thousands of pounds that could have been spent on a new shape for the Big Healey that would have met the US laws were wasted on a car that had two important faults: its engine was far too heavy and it looked like the MGB, which was known to be much slower. Given a lightweight engine and consequently better handling it could have been a winner in the late 1960s, and perhaps Donald Healey would have put his name to it to make sure that it sold. As it was, when British Leyland at last took notice of a South London garage that was producing a wonderful conversion with a light alloy engine that made the MGB into a modern Healey, it was too late: the petrol crisis was upon them. With a little bit of styling I think that Donald Healey would have taken a cut of the MGB V8. But not out of the MGC. He was an individualist and the MGC was not. Instead he pro-

The Big Healey lives on in the form
of the Datsun 240Z and its derivatives.

duced the Jensen-Healey, but ran into problems where he had had none before. 'There was this line of new Jensen-Healeys waiting for Vauxhall engines,' said Geoff Price, 'and none were forthcoming. So the Skipper had to go to Lotus and take what he could. Colin Chapman was delighted.'

So, when it was obvious that the MGC could never succeed, it was left to the Japanese to fill the gap that was left by the Big Healey and to produce the Datsun 240Z. The Japanese were quick to spot the problem of lack of capital and to correct it. They spent as much as was needed and produced a winner, a Big Healey that looked like an E type coupé. It was a car that was as fast and dependable as the Big Healey with a lot of the allure of the Jaguar in its basic market: the United States. It deserved to be such a success, despite a rust problem reported to be even worse than that of its British ancestors. 'The Nissan Motor Company have always said that Austin taught

Halfway to a Big Healey coupé or a 240Z: the Le Mans Sprite.

them to build cars,' says their respected public relations officer, Maxwell Boyd. 'No doubt they would have liked to have got hold of one of the Healey prototype coupés. They were very much like the 240Z. Since then it has become the most successful sports car of recent years; bored out to the 260 for Britain and the 280 with fuel injection for America, where the emission regulations are that much tougher. Yes, Nissan have always been willing to give credit where it is due, particularly to Austin.'

So the Big Healey goes marching on in a Japanese cloak. Is there no place for such patriots as the Healey family? There was no need for their mighty car to die and for James Ewing to have written this moving farewell in *Safety Fast* in 1968: 'This is going to be sentimental. For years they've been telling me that the Big Healey is out of date. "You're running a vintage job, there old boy," they'd say, and when I bought my third in a line they wrote me off as bonkers.

'Well that's all right with me. The Healey has always had a vintage feel about it and that's why I bought another. I like the ruddy things, and now they are out of production my affection is all the greater. They are a link with the heroic days of motor cars. The 3000 looks what I have always considered a sports car should look like. And they have got better and better. My first, 2838 UE, took to the road in 1960, and compared with later models, was a comparatively sedate method of transport. This still had the odd gear change coming out of the side of the tunnel and I made some quite appalling changes at first. But we soon came to terms and I would not have parted with it had some nit in a garage not squirted brake fluid all over the bonnet. I managed to make a satisfactory exchange for a Mark II, 838 ENX, which, as it happens lives nearby and is kept in splendid trim. This car was a snorter. It was tweaked a little and had competition rear suspension with works exhaust system. It was very fast indeed and when the rumours hardened about the end of the Healey, I thought long and painfully about the whole business. To carry on with the Mark II or go out with flying colours with a brand new Mark III—the last of the line.

'I bought a new one, Colorado Red it is and this is the best of the lot, LNX 628 E. Better torque, better balance from the new rear axle location, and vastly better trim. And a deal more poke even than the Mark II.

'Whether there is going to be any point in really fast cars in the future remains to be seen. This may be my last, and I will have no regrets if I end my sports car career with a Healey. They have served me well and faithfully. I will never forget the feeling of exhilaration when I first sat behind that huge wheel and looked away down the long sleek bonnet; nor the nose lifting under power, the rev counter swinging up, the roar of the wind and the scream of the tyres. There seemed to be such a hell of a lot going on.

'All my cars have been bought from and admirably maintained by that nice bunch of blokes at the Donald Healey outfit at Warwick where their knowledge and enthusiasm has added greatly to the pleasures of Healey motoring.

'So it's hail and farewell to a great sports car. The competition records and statistics are there for posterity. Soon the Healey will be a collector's piece. But no one who has sat behind the wheel of a Big Healey will forget the enduring excitement of it all—the huge surge of power, the tumultuous exhaust, and the rest of the pack shrinking into the mirror. Great days . . .'

Index

Index of Illustrations

Acknowledgements

The publishers are grateful to the following for permission to reproduce illustration material:

AC Cars, 190 top
Associated Press, 68 top, 130
Austin-Healey Car Club of New Zealand, 143
Austin Motor Company, plates 5, 6, 7, 8, 9, 10, 11, 2, 10, 11 bottom, 19 top, 20 top, 22 bottom, 28, 70, 78 bottom, 144, 145 right, 154 top, 210, 211, 212, 217
Autocar, 7, 8, 10, 11 top, 34, 142 top, 213, 219
Bilbie (Barrie) Collection, 178, 179
Birchall (Dave) Collection, 139
Bixter, Alice, 88, 133
British Leyland, 29 bottom, 230
British Leyland Historic Vehicles Division, 125 bottom, 150, 157 top, 163 bottom, 176, 182 top, 213, 216, 218

British Motor Corporation, 89, 91, 98 bottom, 99 top, 149, 190 bottom, 203 bottom, 222
Brown (David) Corporation, 195 bottom, 196 top
Camera Press, 145 left
Chatham (John) Collection, 63 bottom
Foster and Skeffington, plate 18, 98 top
Gullery (Gavin) Collection, 140, 173, 174, 175 top
Healey, Geoffrey page 180 top, middle, bottom, page 181 top, middle
Holder, Tim, plate 19, 232
Masefield, John, 2, 185 top
Motor, 33, 57, 58, 60, 61, 62 bottom, 64, 67, 68 bottom, 72, 73, 74, 78 top, 92, 154 bottom left, 164 bottom, 229
Motor Trader, back cover
Packer, Bob, 128
Rootes Motor Company, 203 top
Segal, Thelma, 99 bottom

Skilleter, Paul, cover, inside cover, plates 1, 2, 3, 4, 12, 13, 14, 15, 16, 20, 6, 16 bottom, 23 top and right, 25 bottom, 27, 62 top, 63 top, 97 top left, 104, 105, 106, 107, 125 top, 160 top, 163 top, 164 top, 168, 175 bottom, 185 bottom, 215, 220, 224
Temple Press, 16 top, 19 bottom, 20 bottom, 22 top, 23 bottom, 25 top, 29 top, 43, 45, 48, 50, 51, 53, 55, 75, 77, 79, 81 bottom, 82, 84, 85, 86, 87, 93, 94, 142 bottom, 153, 154 bottom right, 155, 156, 159, 192 top, 216
Tolomeo, Guiseppe, 97 top right
TVR Cars, 196 bottom
Woods, Jess, 13
Worswick (Ted) Collection, plate 17, 91, 97 bottom right